IMAGES
of America

FOUNTAIN INN

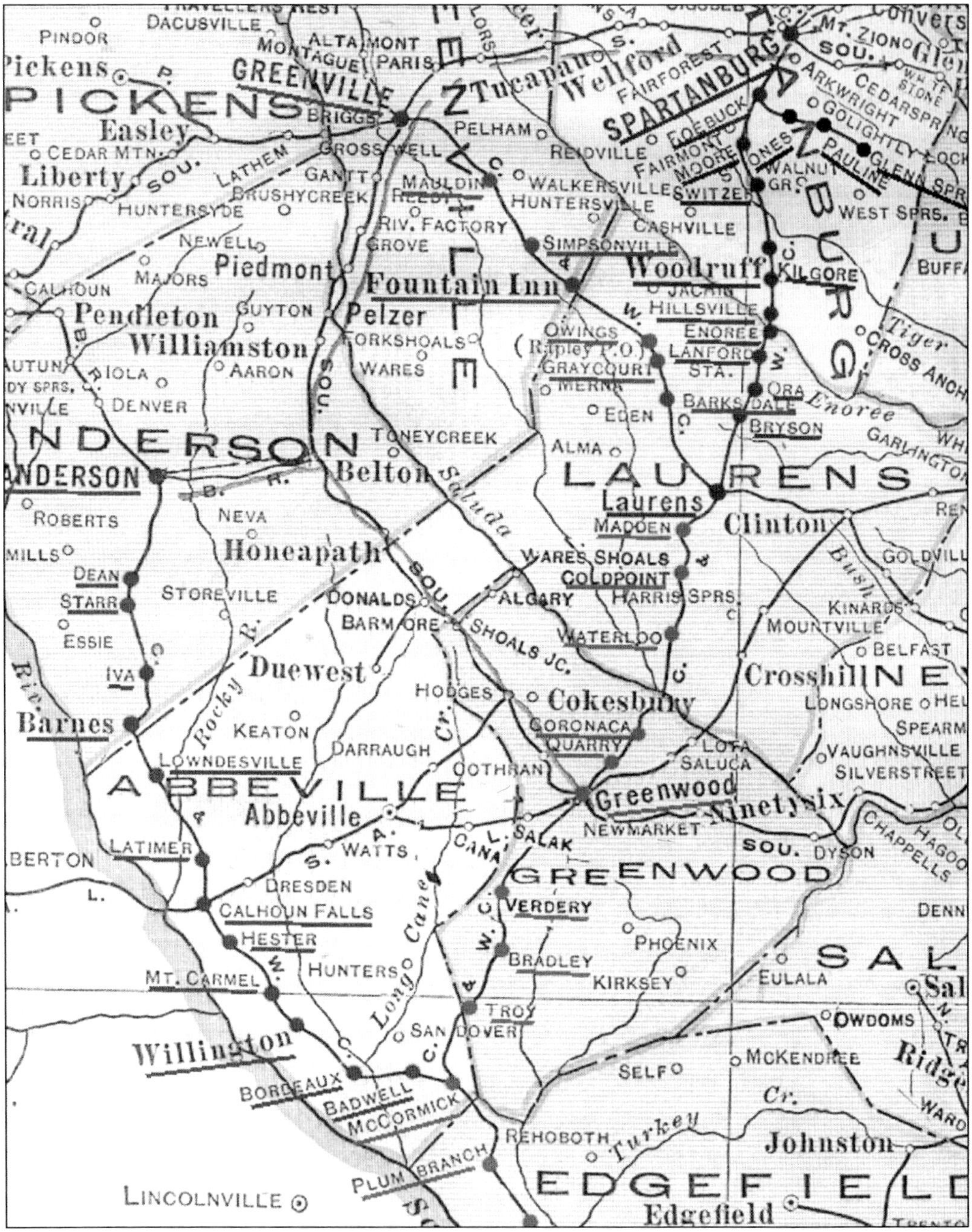

A copy of this old map of western South Carolina is located in the Fountain Inn Museum. It is believed to be between the years of 1895 and 1914.

On the Cover: Fred Holland is seated on the right in this photograph from May 11, 1929. Fred was a substitute mail carrier and worked with the acting postmaster, Mrs. J.A. Adams. The gentleman to the far left has been identified as Judge J.A. Barry. Others have not been identified, nor has the exact location of this building, though it is possibly on Trade Street. (Courtesy of Elinor Holland Mowbray.)

IMAGES
of America

FOUNTAIN INN

Caroline Smith Sherman
and Dianne Gault Bailey

ARCADIA
PUBLISHING

ISBN 978-1-4671-2509-3

Published by Arcadia Publishing
Charleston, South Carolina

Printed in the United States of America

Library of Congress Control Number: 2017932971

For all general information, please contact Arcadia Publishing:
Telephone 843-853-2070
Fax 843-853-0044
E-mail sales@arcadiapublishing.com
For customer service and orders:
Toll-Free 1-888-313-2665

Visit us on the Internet at www.arcadiapublishing.com

This book is dedicated to the Fountain Inn Museum, keeper of our history. To paraphrase a quote, "If you don't know where you've been, how can you know where you are going?"

Contents

ACKNOWLEDGMENTS

Thank you, Fountain Inn folks and those of our surrounding communities. As always, you have come through for us. Without you, we could not have compiled this book. A big thank you goes to museum board members Steve Cox for the many hours of work that he put in scanning the photographs and Ron Urso for taking pictures that were needed. Museum member Peggy White Nickson found information from the old *Fountain Inn Tribunes* for us. Thank you to all who went through your attics for old photographs; answered our questions time and again as we wrote captions; and in many instances wrote captions for us. You are listed with your photographs and we do appreciate the hard work. Being limited in the amount of pages, photographs, and verbiage we could include, we had to eliminate more than we wanted to, but the scanned copies of all will be kept by the museum. We also want to apologize to any families who may have been left out. It was not intentional.

We found information in the old *Fountain Inn Tribunes*, *History of Fountain Inn* by Caroline S. Coleman and B.C. Givens; *History of Fairview Presbyterian Church* by Mary Lou Garrett; *The Pedens of America* by Jessie Peden, Lizzie Peden, and Lila Peden Sprouse; *A Little Bit about a Lotta Things* by Blake Garrett Sr.; *Oh Lordy* by Elinor H. Mowbray; *Greenville* by Archie Vernon Huff Jr.; *Scotch-Irish Life in the South Carolina Piedmont* by Millie Huff Coleman and Caroline Smith Sherman; the *1999 Historical Survey of Fountain Inn*; and many websites. The Fountain Inn Museum provided pictures from those who donated them previously. Unfortunately, we do not have names to give individual credit. Pictures with no courtesy line are credited to the Fountain Inn Museum. This book is not a complete history of our town and countryside. We just scratched the surface. It must be continued. We urge you to read the previous books mentioned here and search websites and write your own family history before it is lost.

INTRODUCTION

It has been said that when newcomers move to Fountain Inn, they must be warned not to talk about just anybody. They may be kin! This book will help newcomers and old residents alike to understand the intricacies of the old families and how the farming communities influenced the town. It will show how the small village evolved into the Fountain Inn of today.

In the early 1700s, Scotch-Irish settlers came down the Great Wagon Trail and upland from Charleston to populate the Chester, Spartanburg, Laurens, and Newberry Districts. The Revolutionary War was not a great concern to many in the Upcountry until Tories and marauding Indians attacked. Patriots built blockhouses and palisade forts, places of safety. One such place was built by local frontiersman Joseph Kellett and his neighbors in 1778. This blockhouse was located on what is now Knickerbocker Road, about 300 yards east of South Rabon Creek, in the Greenpond area. There is a marker commemorating this fort at the bridge. Three armed combat actions were fought against the British and Tories not too far away. Four actions were against the Indians.

It was not until after the Revolutionary War that lower Greenville district was settled because of the previous treaty with the Cherokee. When they sided with the British, the treaty was voided and their land was confiscated. That new territory was granted by the new state of South Carolina as payment to the Patriot soldiers who fought for the new country and their families. Many small farming settlements, such as Fairview, were established with churches and schools. Country stores such as Toney's, on what is now Highway 418, were few and far between. Peddlers made their way, as did visiting preachers who spent the nights in "prophet's rooms" of the farm houses. Many churches, such as Hillside, started in homes or as brush arbor. Families were self-sufficient. In the early 1800s, a stage line was established, and an inn served weary travelers.

In 1861, conflict with the Northern states came home to South Carolina when President Lincoln sought to bring reinforcements to Fort Sumter off the coast of Charleston. It was fired upon by South Carolinians. Recruits joined the Confederate army from all communities. Greenville County provided 2,000 soldiers. Many of the families who disagreed with the war had already moved away. War touched the Upcountry through poverty, hunger, and death. A portion of Stoneman's Raiders were sent to the Greenville area, looting and destroying property. A white man and former slave were killed. The late owner Susie Huff told Caroline Coleman of the damage to their plantation outside of Simpsonville. After the war ended, black families left the churches of their former owners to establish their own. One was Bethlehem Baptist Church. It was organized as a brush arbor church by Reverend David M. Morton on land given to him by his former owner, Mr. Morton of Fairview. Today, it is one of the most successful churches in lower Greenville County. Soon a few stores and a post office grew up south of the inn. J.I. West and J.A. Cannon bought land in today's Fountain Inn and became the first realtors.

The railroad brought progress; Fountain Inn was chartered in 1886 and began to grow. Some country folks moved into the village and opened general merchandise stores. Churches and civic organizations were established. Paul Patton said that the Knight's Masonic Lodge No. 192 was chartered in 1875 by the Grand Lodge of South Carolina, before the town. The name changed in 1888 to Fountain Inn Masonic Lodge. The Fountain Inn Boosters Club was organized about 1918, having as early presidents Drummond, Kellett, and S.A. Karelitz, the first Jewish merchant and family in town. In 1955, under the leadership of outgoing president Blake Garrett Sr. and incoming president Max Karelitz, the name changed to the Fountain Inn Chamber of Commerce. In Blake Garrett's humorous book *A Little Bit about a Lotta Things*, he says that he contacted Duke Power in Charlotte for a speaker for the annual banquet and was told that they did not provide speakers for athletic events, only civic.

In the late 1890s, the Graham family opened the first cotton mill. The *Fountain Inn Tribune* reported 42 businesses in 1911. The census that year reported 979 persons in the whole town. Simpsonville had 521. The board of trade instructed the town to investigate electric lights to replace the three gas lights. Presidential candidate William Jennings Bryan made a stop. In 1928, the *Tribune* reported on the opening of Baty's Theatre for vaudeville and pictures; three cotton gins produced 250 bales a day; and a crowd in Durbin listened to John Givens's radio, a first for many. In 1930, the census reported that the town had increased to 1,284 residents. The chief occupation of the area was still farming, even if residents had another job. Caroline Coleman reports that the average family lived comfortably on a salary of $100 to $150 a month.

The first library opened in 1905, organized by the Ladies Improvement Society. It was in a store on Main and Fairview Streets operated by Tom McGee next to his father John's hotel. There is a drugstore there now. In 1920, the buildings burned, but some young boys saved many of the books, and the library reopened on Main Street.

Again war broke out—World Wars I and II, Korea, and Vietnam—and the Fountain Inn area sent its boys to fight. Many did not return. Those who did and are still living thrill residents with their tales of heroism and what they considered was their duty for their country. Many have told their stories at museum programs.

Fountain Inn has produced many educators, legislators, ministers, missionaries, doctors, and two college presidents: John Barry of Coker College and the College of Charleston and Robert Edwards of Clemson College. It has also been represented in the Miss American Pageant by two Miss South Carolinas: Peggy White and Wendy Willis. Famous athletes include Chris Patton (golf), Robert Kellett (walking horses), and Travelle Wharton (football). Fountain Inn has had excellent leadership with city hall and all that it entails. There are so many wonderful people that they are too numerous to list.

As this small city grows, it should remember where it has been and work to retain the history and the small-town friendliness that has made Fountain Inn known as a place where people want to live and work and raise their families.

One

Early Days

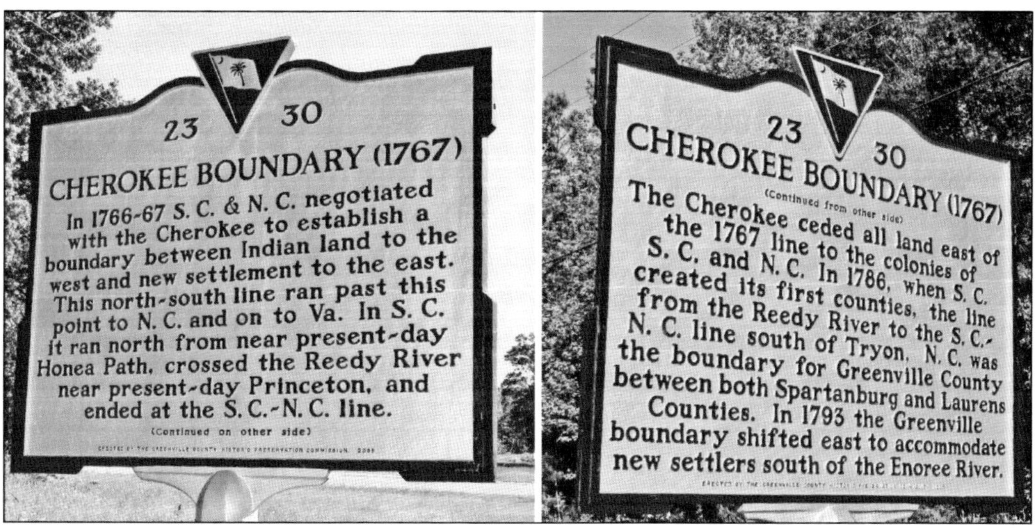

At one time, all of Greenville County was Indian territory. An early surveyor was James Abercrombie of the Babb and Abercrombie families. The Indian Boundary Line bisected what is now the town of Fountain Inn. No doubt settlers and Indians hunted on each other's land. The historical marker is located on Highway 418 and Interstate 385 at the Charles G. Garrett Interchange in Fountain Inn. (Courtesy of Ron Urso.)

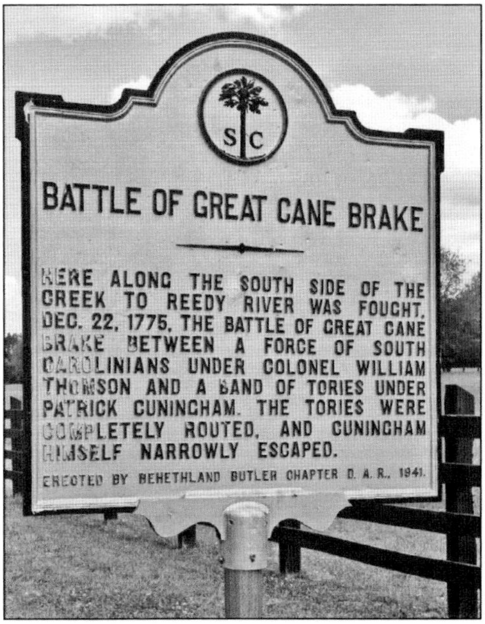

In the area of Fork Shoals Road, historical markers on the historic John Hopkins farm tell the story of the Snow Campaign, in which the Patriots were victorious and strengthened the cause of freedom in the Upcountry during the Revolutionary War. (Courtesy of Ron Urso and the John Hopkins family.)

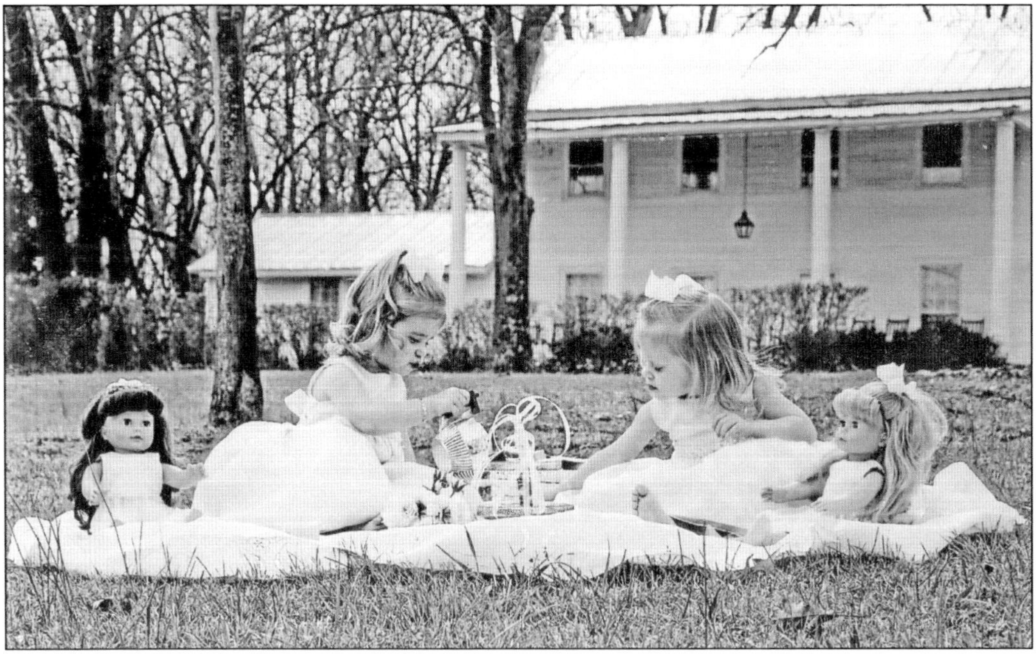

Madison Ricard (left) and Mollie Ann Causey (right), granddaughters of Elaine Jones Carver, have a tea party on the lawn of the Con-Lilla plantation east of town. The old Dev Garrett home was renovated by the late Conway and Lilla Jones. This land paralleled the Indian Boundary Line. A trail crossed the original 593 acres. It is reported that there was a fort. A trapdoor and lookout station for Indians were included in the plans of the home. A cave was used for hiding. The home was fashioned with 14-inch wooden pegs and large, square, hand-forged nails. A large rock with a hollow depression used by Indian women for pounding corn into meal has disappeared from the property. The home is owned now by the Charles Alberson family. (Courtesy of Elaine Jones Carver.)

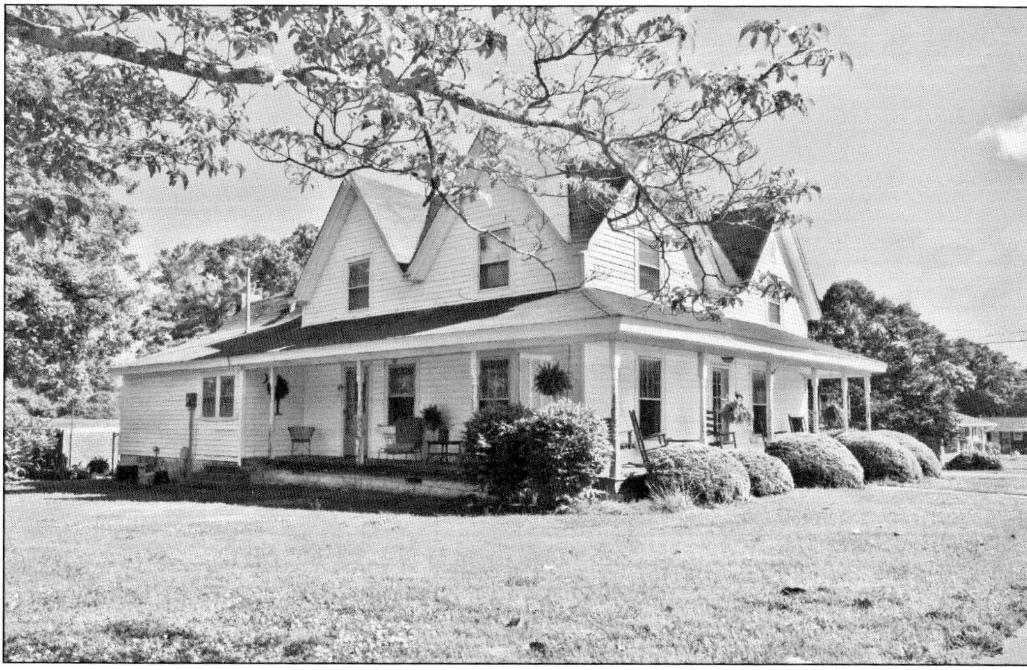

One of the first settlers brave enough to go near Indian territory, Edward Howard fought in the Revolutionary War. On his way home, he fell from his horse and died with a broken back. He was buried at this site. Not much is known about Howard. Edward Thackston, grandson of W. Shell Thackston, tells that there was a grave at this site when the house was built on Hellams Street. The underpinning stones were brought from the field at Cherry Lane. Wood for the window sills came from the wooden First Baptist Church. (Courtesy of Ron Urso and Edward Thackston.)

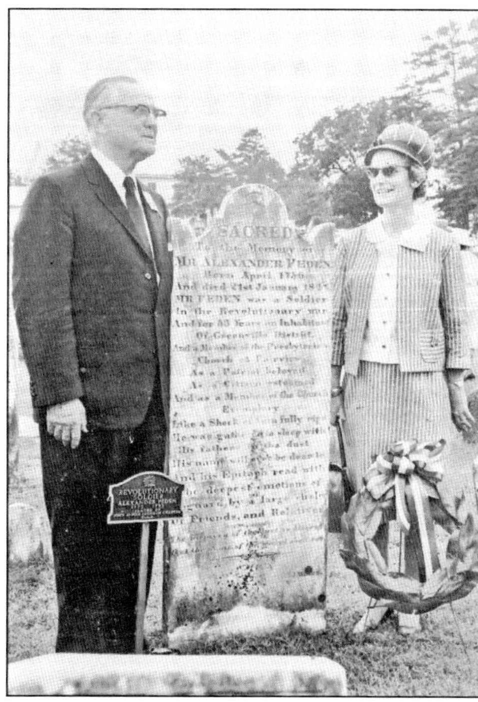

The late Mary Lou Stewart Garrett, president of the local chapter of the Daughters of American Revolution, introduced her cousin, longtime Mississippi Democratic senator John C. Stennis. In 1965, Stennis made dedicatory remarks at the unveiling of the marker for their ancestor Alexander Peden. Alexander was buried at historic Fairview Presbyterian Church with other Revolutionary War soldiers. The son of John and Peggy Peden, Alexander Peden was born in County Antrim, Ireland. He was 17 when he arrived in South Carolina in 1772. The Pedens were among the first in lower Greenville County after the Revolutionary War. (Courtesy of the Caroline S. Coleman family.)

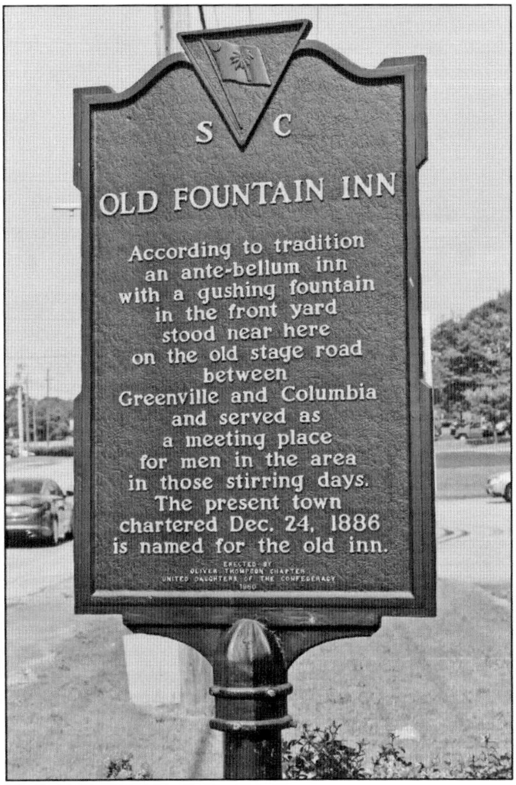

This marker, erected in 1960 by the Oliver Thompson Chapter of the United Daughters of the Confederacy, is on the corner of North Main Street, Highway 14, and Howard Drive. It tells the story of the beginning of Fountain Inn. Fountain Inn received its name from the old inn and the spring of water that gushed two feet into the air. In 2016, the remnants of the spring were located on private land nearby. (Courtesy of Ron Urso.)

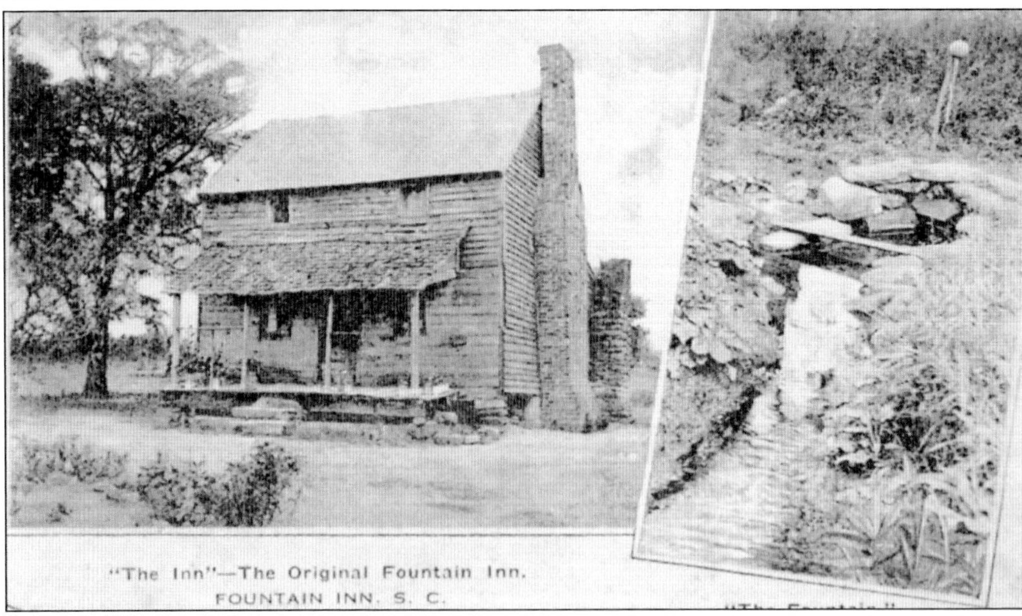

The 1830 stagecoach stop was located about halfway between the town of Greenville and Laurensville on the route from Asheville, North Carolina, to Charleston, South Carolina. The painting by famous Fountain Inn artist Art Frahm depicts the old inn, pretty Polly Massey, daughter of the innkeeper, and stagecoach driver William Darnell, who claimed her for his bride. A copy of the original is in the Fountain Inn Museum. (Courtesy of the Caroline S. Coleman family.)

Two

Farming Communities

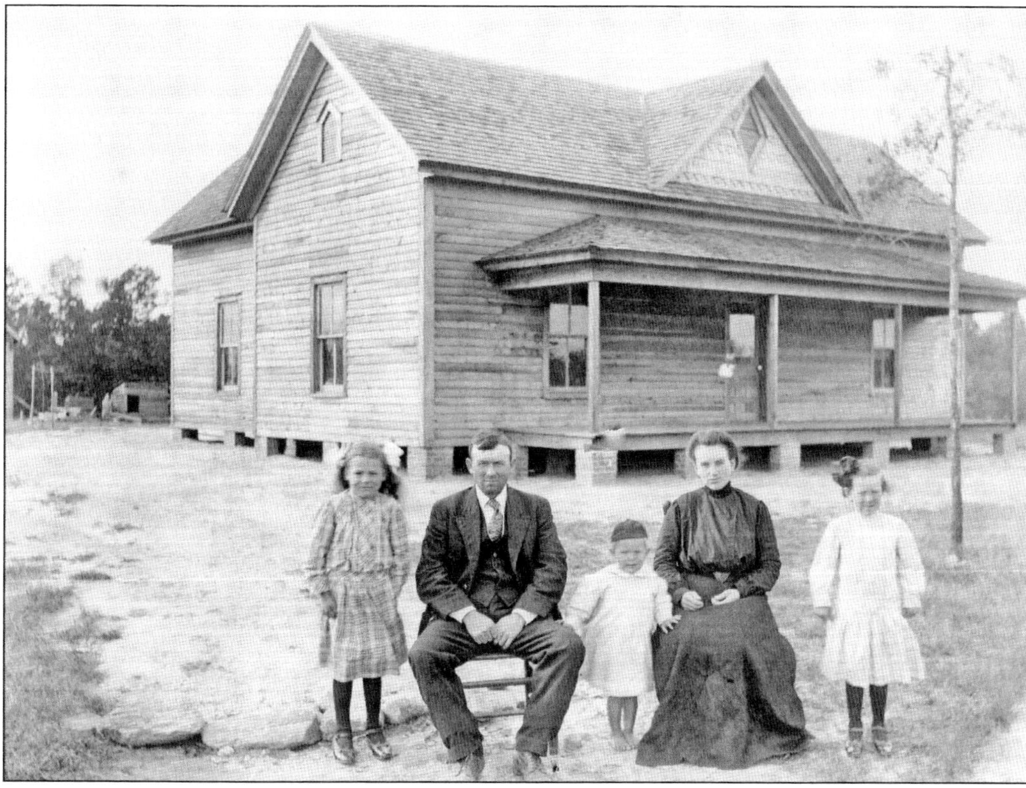

The William Pinkney Patton home was located on Highway 418 East in the Bethany community and is still occupied. From left to right are Betty Patton, William Pinkney Patton, William Avery Patton, Lidie Cooper Patton, and Goldie Patton. The community before was known as Huntersville. According to church history, it began in 1791 as a land grant to the George Marshbanks family. About 1890, a post office and school were opened, followed in 1910 by Bethany Baptist Church. (Courtesy of the Avery Patton family.)

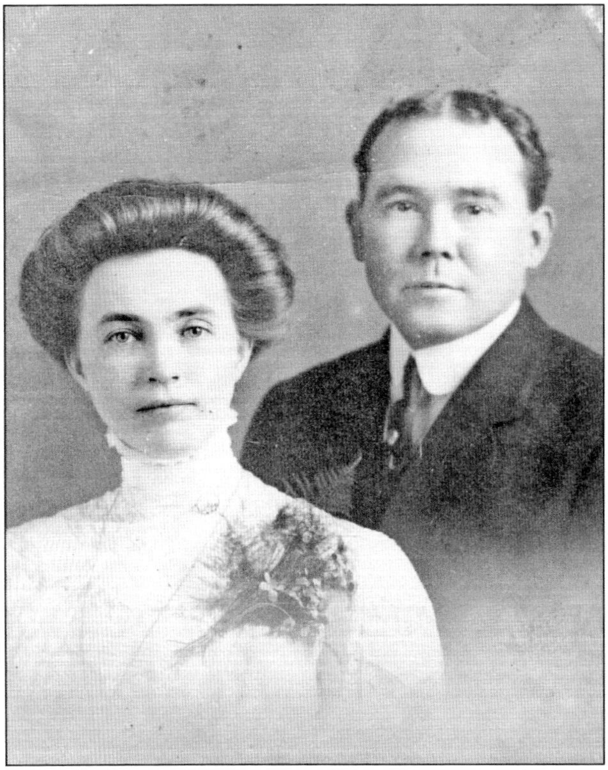

Tobe Hunter Garrett (1879–1932) grew up in the old home that overlooked the lake on Highway 418 East. His parents were John Irvin Garrett and Mary Jane Thackston. After brother Wade Hampton Garrett died, they moved to Pelzer, where Tobe attended Augusta Business School, working as a bookkeeper in Greenville. He attended Clear Springs Baptist Church, then Bethany. May Eliza Peden (1879–1946), daughter of John McVey Peden and Nancy Smith, grew up near Fork Shoals, attending Pisgah Methodist Church. She and Tobe were married in her home. About 1915, they moved to Simpsonville, where David Hunter and Preston Tobe were born. Back on the family farm, they built the house David and Mary Lou Stewart Garrett later occupied. It was ordered through a Sears catalog and delivered by train. (Courtesy of the D.H. Garrett family.)

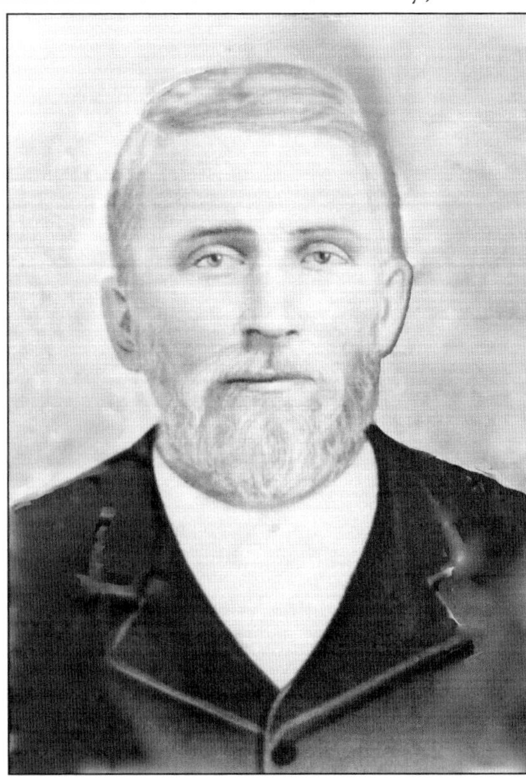

Absalom, born in 1836, was one of six sons of Solomon King White. Solomon married Elizabeth Jones in 1823 at Centerville (between Fountain Inn and Durbin). All their sons served with Company I, 16th South Carolina Volunteer Infantry, Greenville Regiment. Only Absalom and John survived the war. Absalom and four generations of descendants lived on farms on Cook's Bridge Road in the Durbin area; the home he built for wife Amanda Walker White still stands. He purchased his parcel from his father, who had owned the larger farm since the early 1800s. Absalom ran a cotton gin and raised sheep. (Courtesy of Peggy White Nickson.)

The 1952 wedding of Bobbie Davis and Bonnie Wilson was performed in the old Durbin Baptist Church that burned down in the 1970s. Bobbie was valedictorian of her Fountain Inn High School class. She was a probate judge of Laurens County. Her father was Harvey Davis, supervisor at Woodside Mill. Bonnie served in the Navy during World War II. He was from Gray Court and Warrior Creek Church. Note the old stone steps of the church. Started by Jacob Roberts in 1781, it was one of the earliest Baptist churches in the area and belonged to the strictest of five sects of Baptists in South Carolina. (Courtesy of Bobbie Davis Wilson and Peggy White Nickson.)

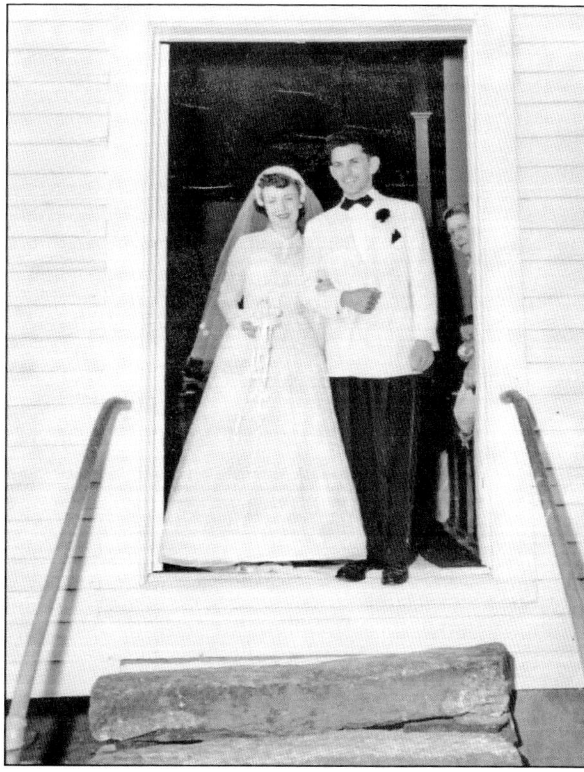

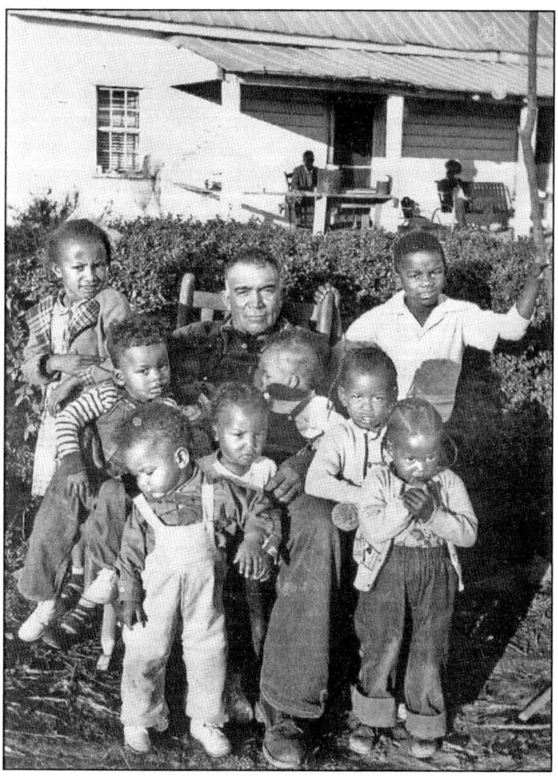

Henry Bryson was a successful farmer in Durbin. He is shown here with his grandchildren. Henry and his wife, Maggie Fowler Bryson, had 16 children. Pat Jones was one of the grandchildren and remembers playing with all her cousins there. The Brysons lived near the Ralph Hughes family before the Hugheses moved to town. All the children played together. (Courtesy of Pat Jones.)

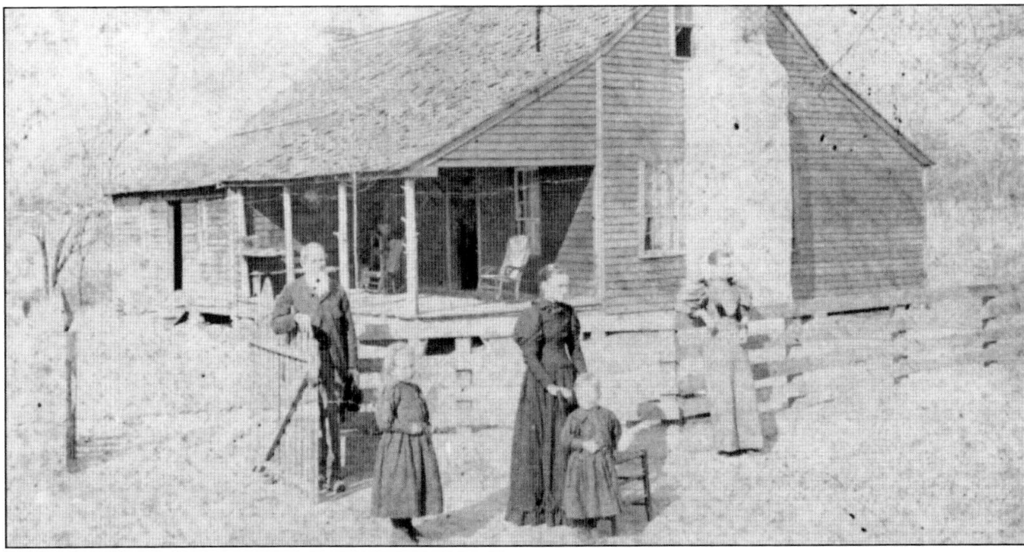

Robert Stewart and older sons built this log home on 400 acres purchased in 1843 in the Durbin Creek community. This earlier residence served as a temporary home when the family moved in 1844 from Bethany Presbyterian community near Clinton. Emmie Belle Stewart and her siblings were born to Samuel Turner and Louisa Holcombe Stewart in this house. Samuel's sister passed away in 1901, and he moved his family into the more commodious Robert Stewart home place. From left to right are Samuel Turner Stewart, Willie Mae Stewart, Louisa Ann Holcombe (Samuel's wife), Frank Stewart, and Annie Stewart. (Courtesy of Henry Fulmer.)

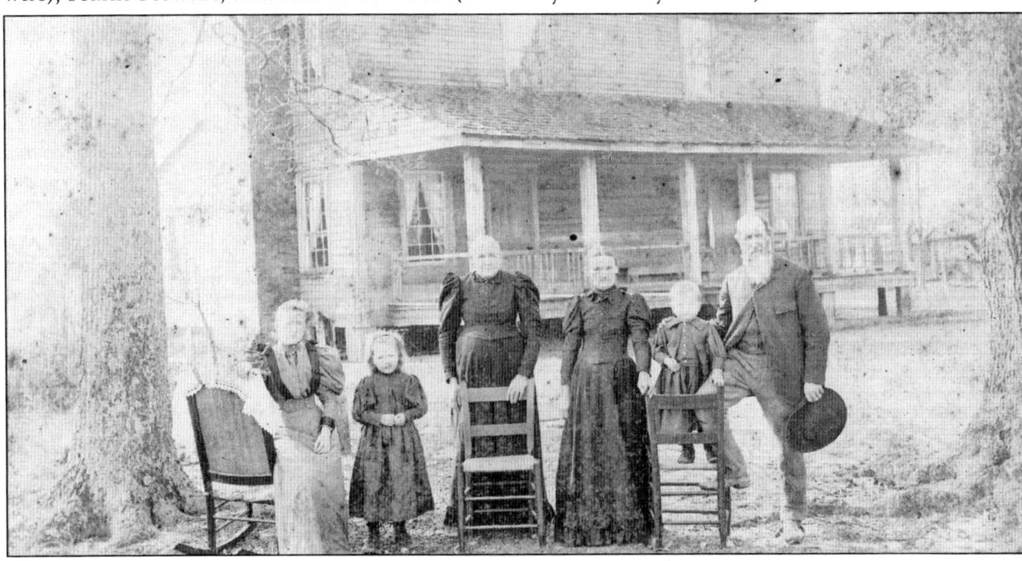

This home was built by Robert Stewart as a permanent dwelling for his family. Robert died in March 1845, just months after the birth of his youngest child, Samuel Turner, in November 1844. Robert's widow, Rachel, completed the construction of the house and raised their 13 children there. After the Civil War and death of Rachel in 1867, the homestead became the home of Isabella Ann Stewart and Martha Jane Stewart. The Wade Cox family later occupied this house. Pictured from left to right are Annie Rebecca Stewart, Willie Mae Stewart, Martha Jane Stewart (sister of Samuel Turner), Louisa Ann Holcombe Stewart, Samuel Frank Stewart, and Samuel Turner Stewart. (Courtesy of Henry Fulmer.)

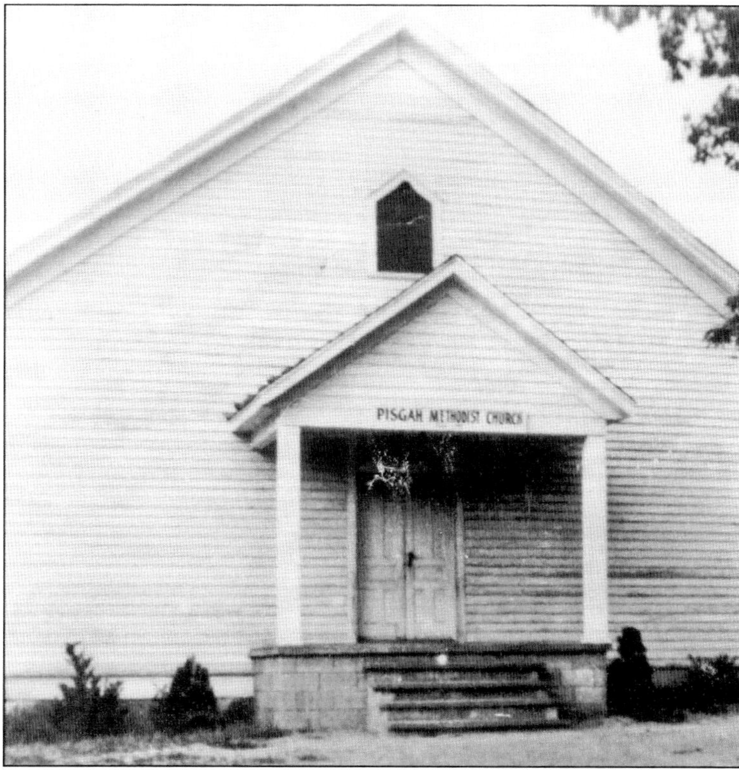

Pisgah United Methodist Church was established by Thomas Terry in 1791 as Terry's Chapel. The original chapel was made of hewn logs. The cracks were filled with mud, and windows were oiled paper. In 1801, Francis Asbury, one of the founders of Methodism in the United States, visited this chapel. In 1843, children of Thomas gave four acres and erected a new church close by. In 1904, a third building was erected, as shown at right. It is located on McKelvey Road on the west side of Fountain Inn. (Courtesy of Edwin Terry.)

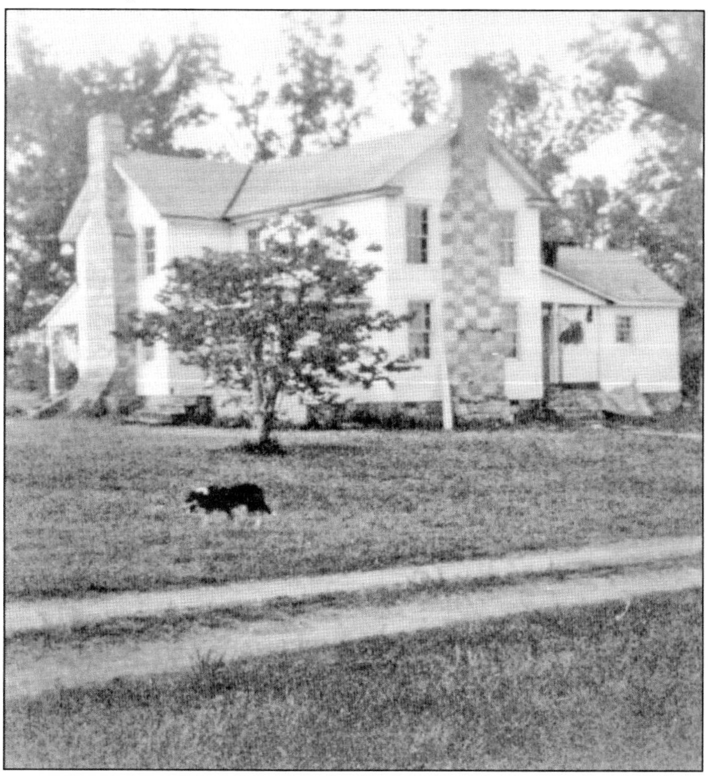

In 1790, Thomas Terry, a native of England, came to America seeking a home. After several months in South Carolina, he found a place near Fork Shoals. This became known as the Old Terry Place. Traveling by wagon from Charleston to the Upcountry with her brother John Harrison, Mrs. Terry became ill and died. Harrison had to bear the unfortunate news. Thomas later married Rebecca McDowell, a wealthy merchant's daughter from Charleston, in 1791. John Harrison married Susan McDowell. This 1826 home on Terry Road was built by Gaston Terry, son of Thomas. He was the great-great-grandfather of Edwin Terry. (Courtesy of Edwin Terry.)

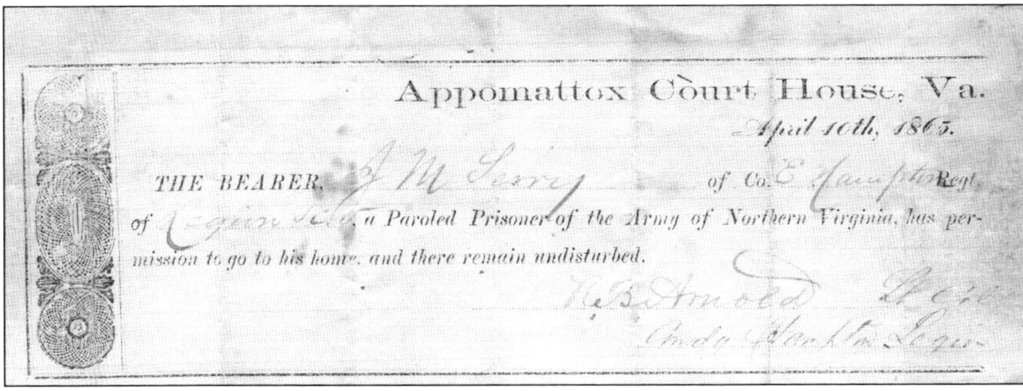

Appomattox Court House, Va.

April 10th, 1865.

THE BEARER, J M Terry of Co. E Hampton Regt, of Legion, a Paroled Prisoner of the Army of Northern Virginia, has permission to go to his home, and there remain undisturbed.

R. B. Arnold Lt. Col.
Cmdg Hampton Legion

On April 10, 1865 John Macklin Terry, son of Gaston Terry, was serving in Company E, Hampton's Legion. He was issued a pardon at Appomattox Court House, Virginia, and allowed to return to his home in South Carolina. John was a cotton farmer and in 1899 patented a cotton planter. (Courtesy of Edwin Terry.)

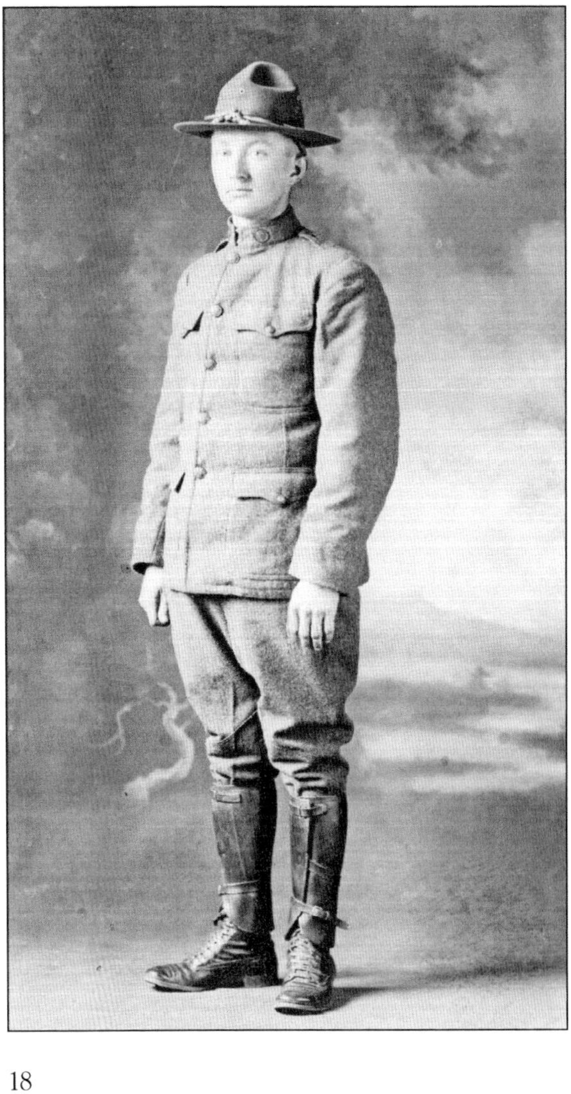

James Lewis Sprouse, pictured in his World War I uniform, was the grandson of Henry Hill Sprouse (1826–1865) and Mary Caroline Hopkins (1830–1869). Henry Hill Sprouse served in Company A, 6th South Carolina Regiment, Hampton's Cavalry, and was captured at Stony Creek, Virginia, during the Civil War. He was sent to the Federal prison at Point Lookout, Maryland, where he died just before Lee's surrender and was buried in a mass grave. His name is engraved on a monument there. When Mary Caroline died, the five children were parceled out to various members of the family to be raised. One son, Warren Hill Sprouse, married Martha Jane McKittrick. They had three children, Mary Caroline, Lucinda Hopkins, and William Warren Sprouse. (Courtesy of Edwin Terry.)

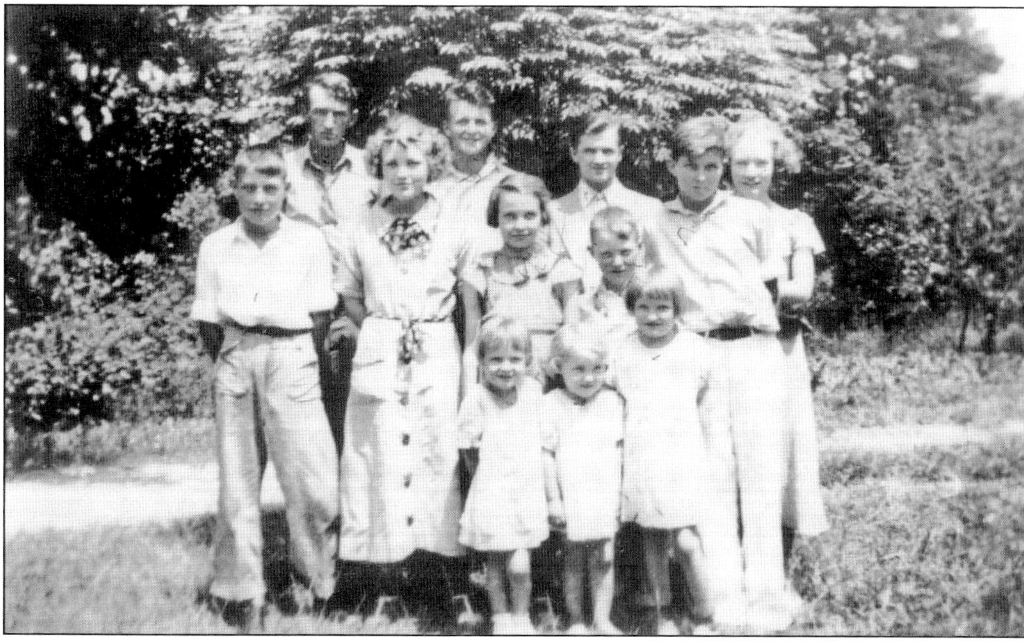

Grandchildren of John and Mettie Thackston Sprouse are pictured in 1935. From left to right are (first row) Caroline Terry, Betty Sprouse, and Lucy Terry; (second row) Warren Sprouse, Hazel Sprouse, Frances Terry, Jim Sprouse, and Ansel Terry; (third row) Lewis Terry, John R. "Bill" Terry, J.W. Terry, and Margaret Sprouse. This home on Sprouse Lane has since been demolished. (Courtesy of Edwin Terry.)

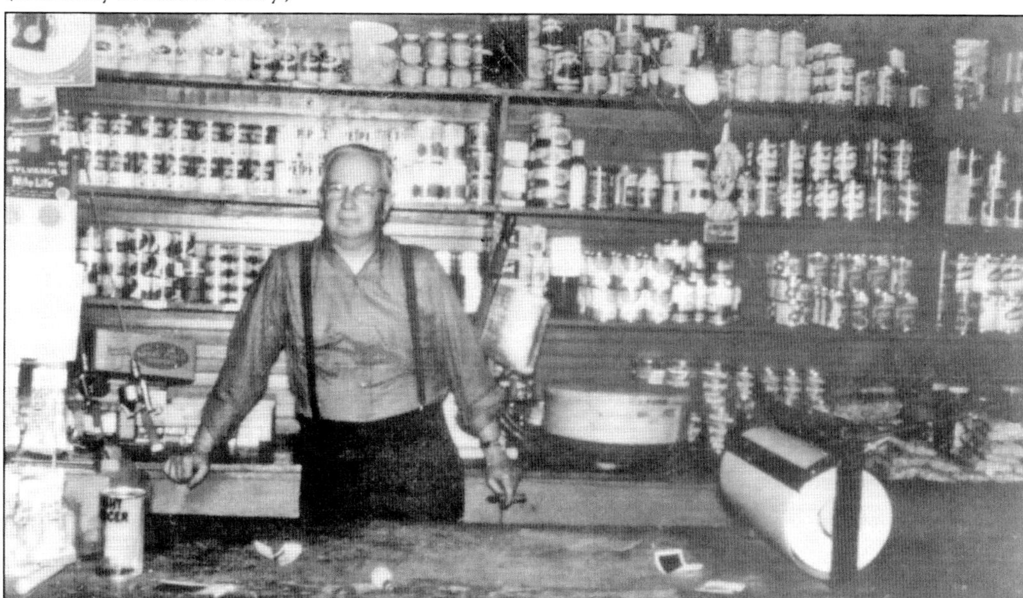

Clyde Sprouse's country store was located on Fairview Road not too far from McKelvey Road. Remnants of the store are still standing. John Clyde married Eliza Meares "Lila" Peden, twin sister to Elizabeth Stenhouse "Lizzie" Peden. Clyde and Lila's home was located on Sprouse Lane. Lila and Lizzie were sisters of Henry Peden. Along with Jessie Peden, they produced *The Pedens of America*, a 650-page edition of Peden history and genealogy. (Courtesy of Edwin Terry.)

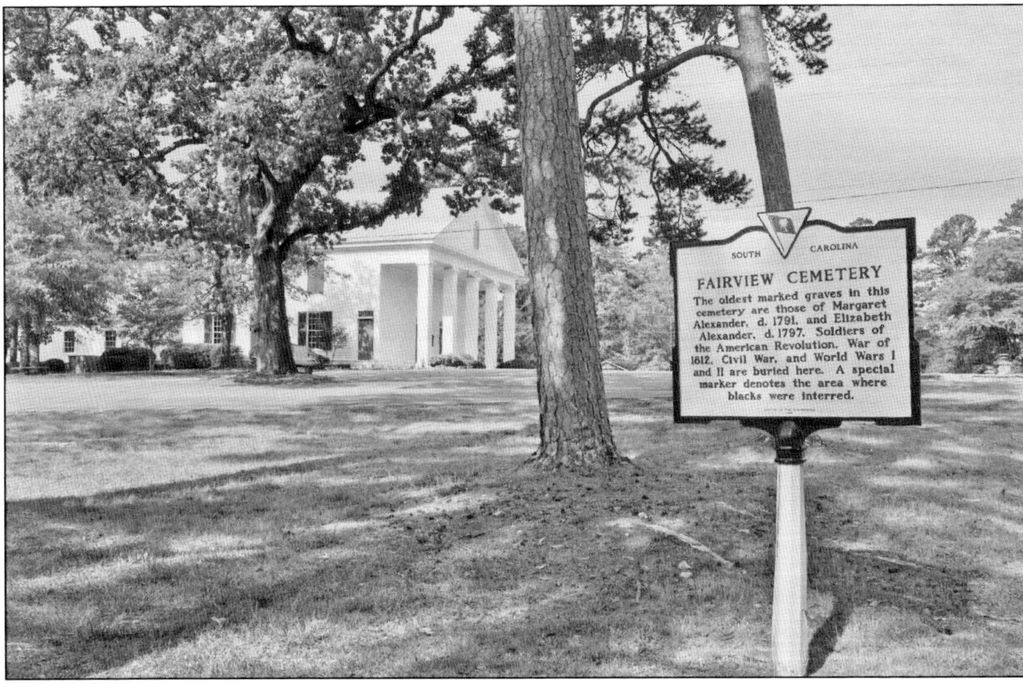

The above photograph is of the Fairview Cemetery historical marker, which states that the oldest marked graves date to 1791 and 1796. The Fairview Presbyterian Church marker below dates the founding of the church in 1786. (Both, courtesy of Ron Urso.)

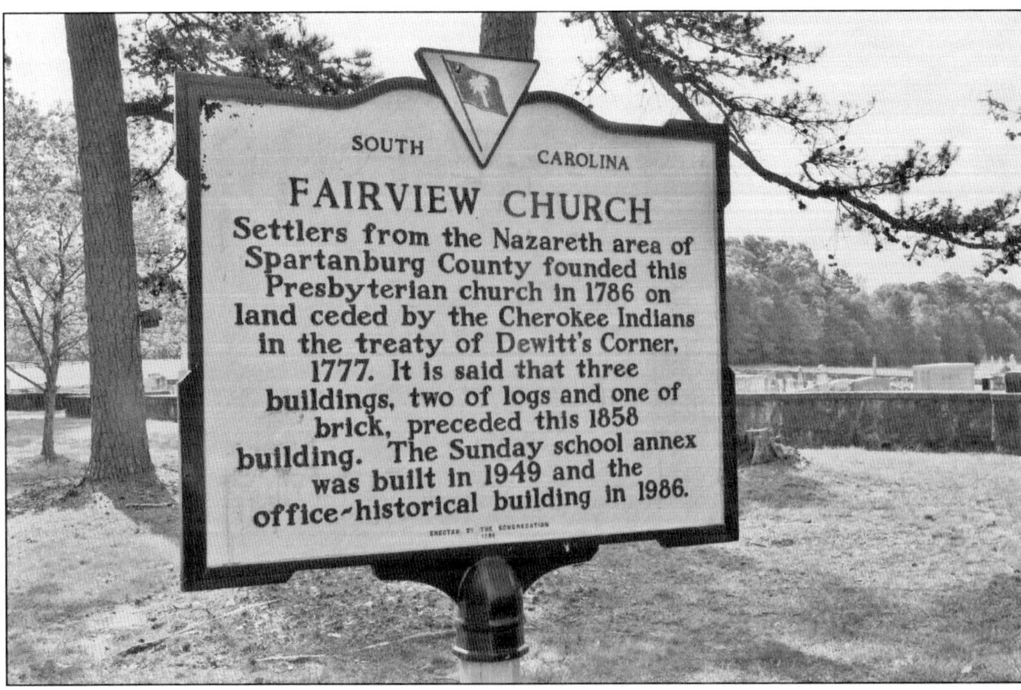

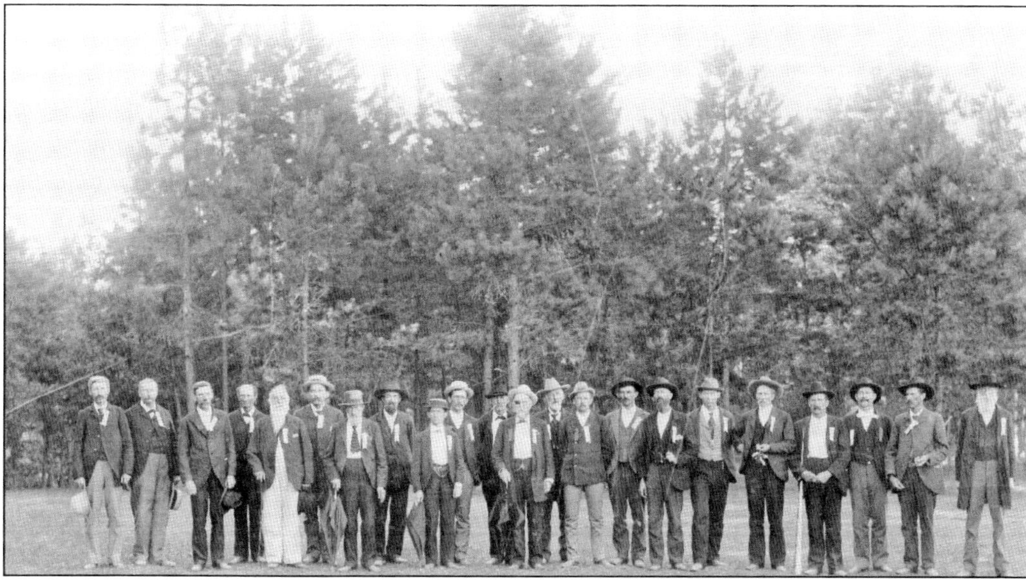

Above is a photograph taken at the Peden Reunion in 1899 at the Fairview Presbyterian Church. At right is a poster advertising another Peden reunion in 1909 that encouraged all descendants to attend.

Peden-Alexander-Morton-Morrow

RE-UNION

The Second Re-union of the Descendants of John and Peggy Peden

Will be held at FAIRVIEW CHURCH, Greenville County, South Carolina, on the **25th** and **26th** of August, 1909. All descendants, as well as those who are connected by marriage or otherwise, are cordially invited to meet again on the historic grounds of old Fairview Church, where ten years ago (1899) a monument was erected to these venerated ancestors. An interesting program is being arranged, and prominent speakers are expected, most of whom are descendants of John and Peggy Peden. As at the first re-union, you are urgently requested to advise all other Pedens, Alexanders, Mortons, Morrows of your acquaintance of this re-union, and invite them to attend; also, kindly ask your local papers to publish notices of this re-union. Those who hear of the re-union and attend it will be just as welcome as those known to us and to whom these circulars are sent. Fairview is five (5) miles from Fountain Inn on the C. & W. C. R. R. Write A. S. Peden as early as possible what time you will reach Fountain Inn so the Arrangement Committee may provide conveyance to Fairview, as well as entertainment for you.

Respectfully your kinsmen,

A. S. PEDEN, Fountain Inn, S. C.

J. R. HARRISON, Fountain Inn, S. C.

W. P. ANDERSON, Westminster, S. C.

D. D. PEDEN, Houston, Texas.

J. F. PEDEN, Simpsonville, S. C.

DR. H. B. STEWART, Fountain Inn, S. C., R. F. D. No. 1

J. T. PEDEN, Gray Court, S. C.

W. S. PEDEN, Fountain Inn, S. C., R. F. D. No. 1

R. W. GASTON, Woodruff, S. C.

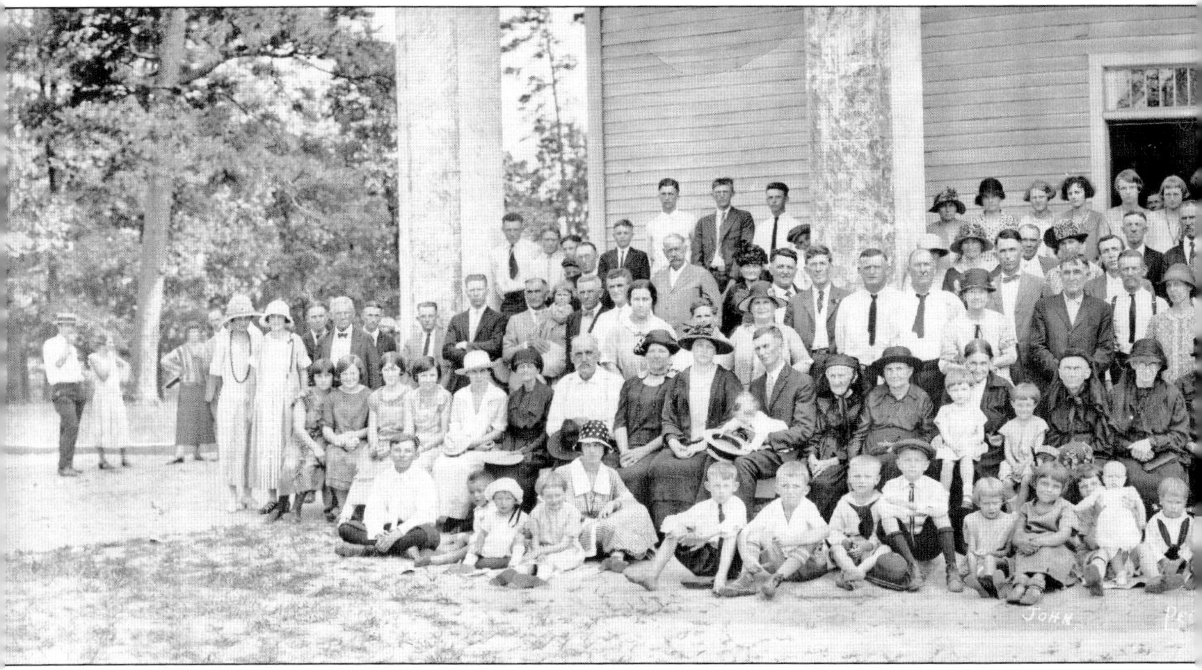

The 1909 Peden, Alexander, Morton, and Morrow reunion was the second held since 1899. Relatives came from many different states, camping in tents around Fairview Church. They were summoned to meetings by a long tin horn. The church was decorated with the colors of Scotland,

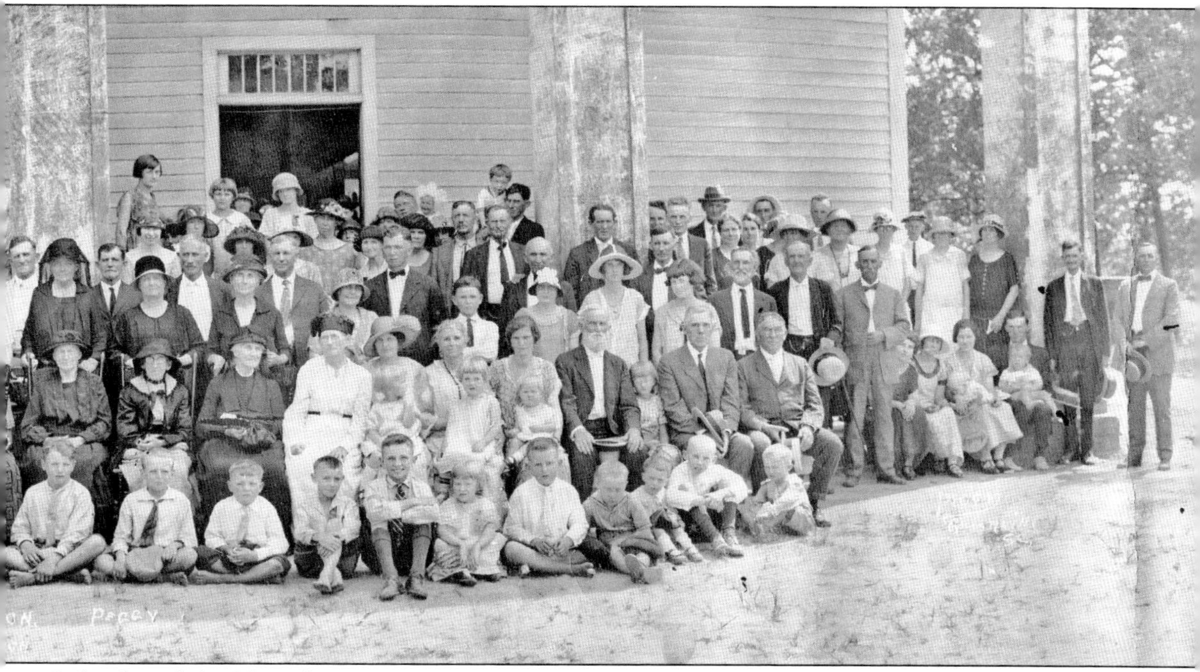

Ireland, and the United States. Fairview was established in 1786 by Scotch-Irish families. Now the Peden reunion is held every year on the third weekend in July. All families who are related to the first settlers of Fairview are welcome to attend.

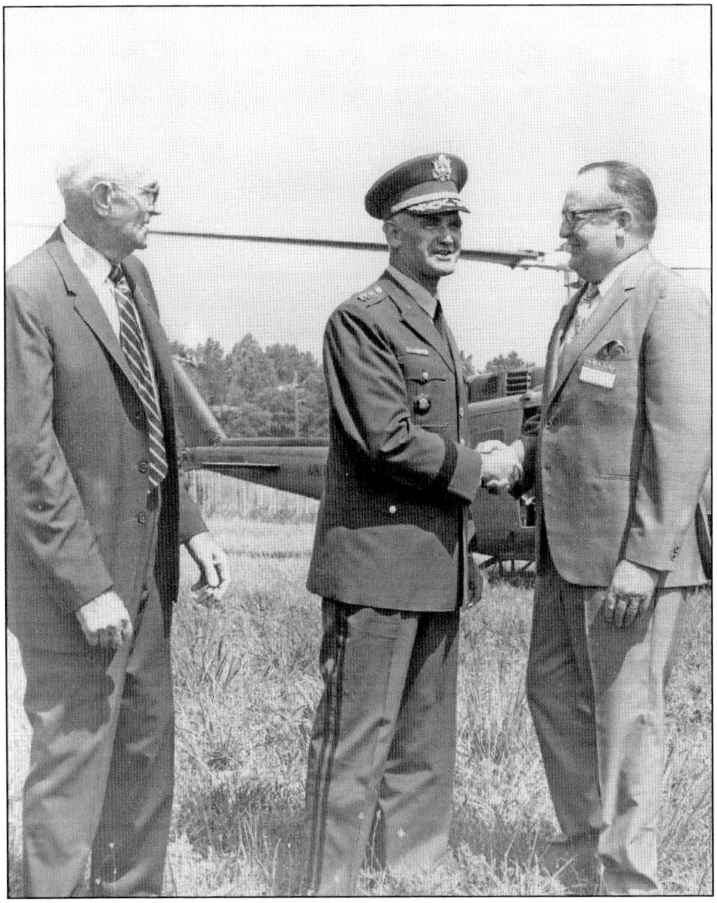

It was an exciting day when Maj. Gen. William Westmoreland (1914–2005) came to speak at the 1971 Peden reunion. He was brought by a helicopter that landed on the grounds of Fairview Church. His grandmother was Rebecca Esque Peden (1827–1895), who married James Riley Westmoreland and lived in Woodruff; Rebecca was descended from Thomas Peden, son of John, founder of the Peden clan. Thomas lived in the Spartanburg area and attended old Nazareth Presbyterian Church. From left to right are clan president Henry B. Peden, Westmoreland, and chief John Calvin Peden. (Courtesy of the D.H. Garrett family.)

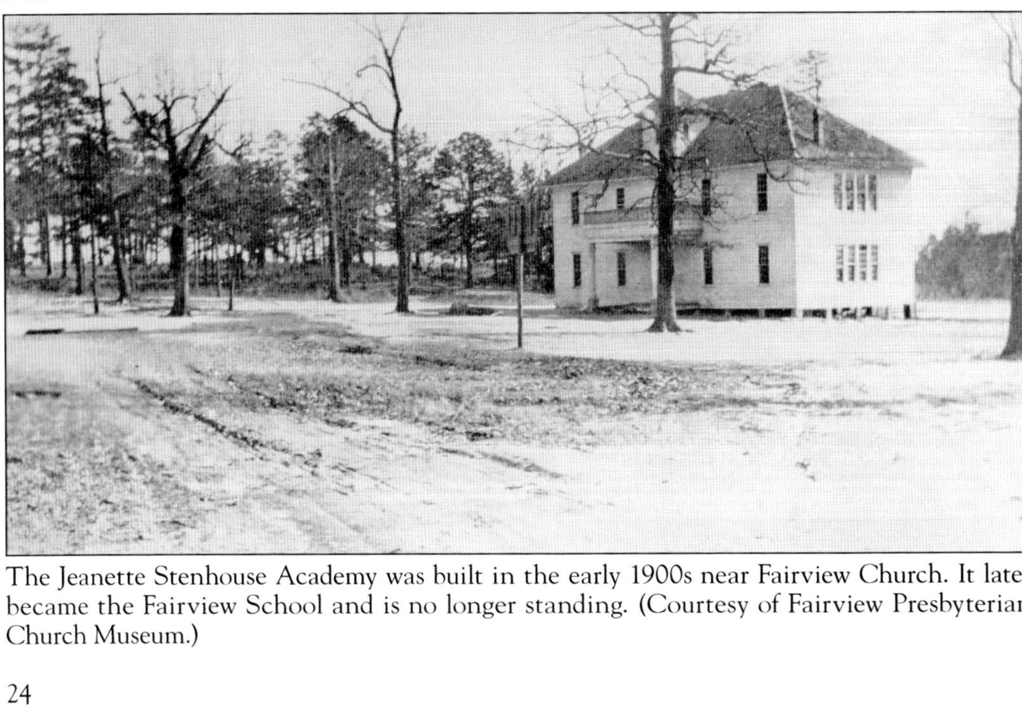

The Jeanette Stenhouse Academy was built in the early 1900s near Fairview Church. It later became the Fairview School and is no longer standing. (Courtesy of Fairview Presbyterian Church Museum.)

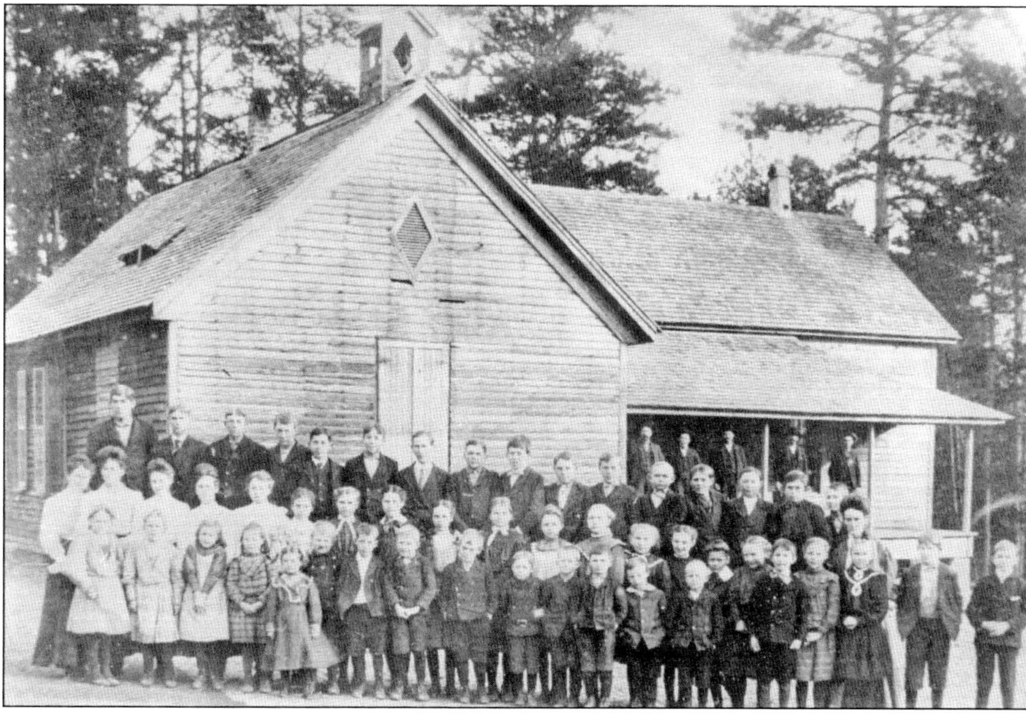

These are early class photographs of the Old Fairview School, formerly the Jeanette Stenhouse Academy. It was located on what is now Fairview Church Road but is no longer standing. (Both courtesy of Edwin Terry.)

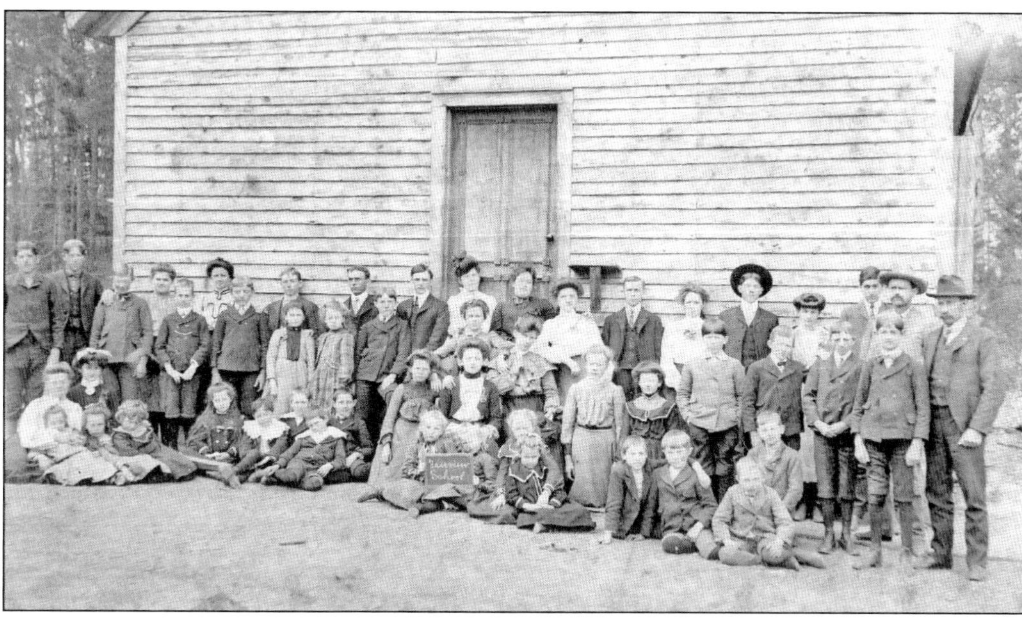

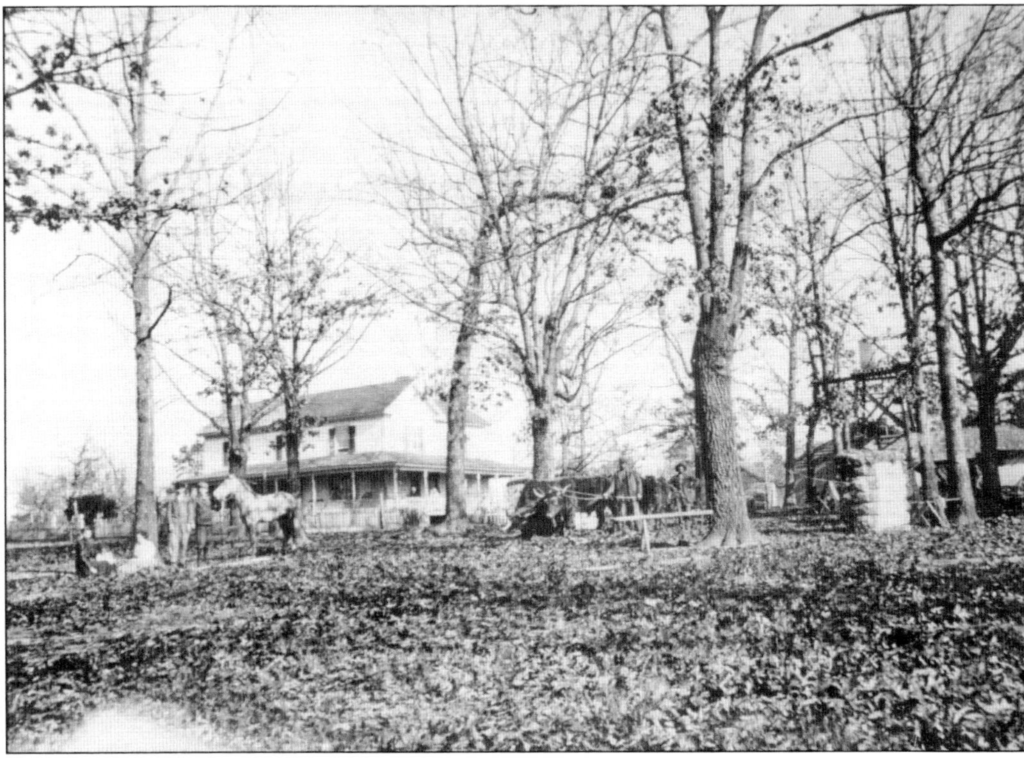

William Stewart Peden (1857–1944) was the son of David Martin Peden (1826–1893) and Caroline Susan Ann Harrison (1833–1919). His wife was Isabella Rixie Peden (1861–1958), a Peden who married a Peden. Her parents were James Scipio Peden (1821–1864), killed in the Battle of Atlanta (son of Alexander) and Elizabeth Stenhouse (1828–1912). Elizabeth was the daughter of Adam Stenhouse, brother of the first John Stennis (whose name was changed in America). The Stenhouse brothers came from Scotland and settled in the Fairview community. (Courtesy of Edwin Terry.)

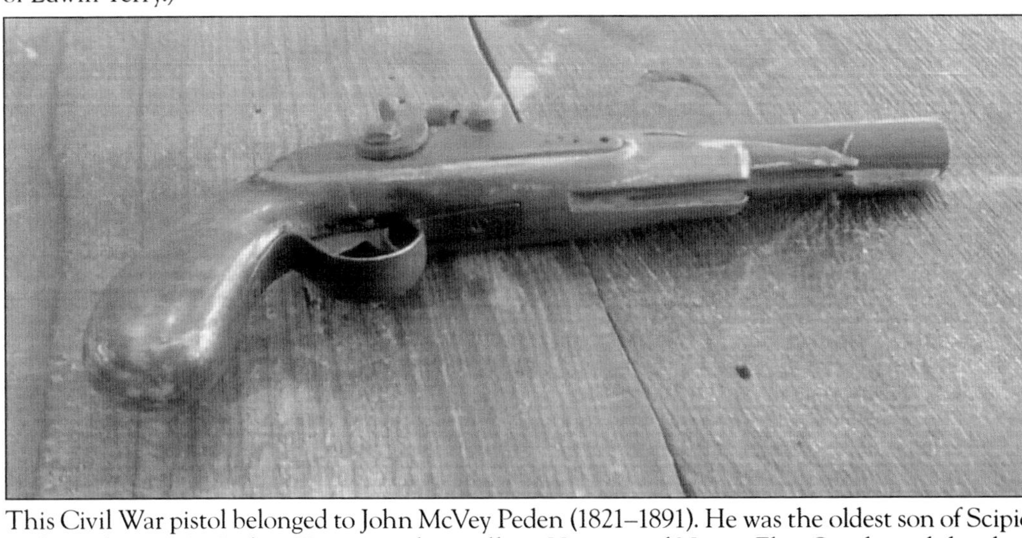

This Civil War pistol belonged to John McVey Peden (1821–1891). He was the oldest son of Scipio and Martha McVey Peden. He was in the artillery. He married Nancy Eliza Smith, and they had eight children. (Courtesy of Jackie Peden.)

John Ramsey Harrison (1845–1920) was born on family land in the Fairview community, residing there and in Fountain Inn. He served in the Palmetto Battalion of Light Artillery near Charleston and transferred to the 16th South Carolina Regiment, participating in many important battles. After the war, he was a successful farmer. Harrison started his political career in 1876. While serving for six years in the South Carolina House of Representatives, he was active on important committees and recognized as a leader. In 1892, he was elected state senator from Greenville County by a decisive majority after a hotly contested campaign. After two years in the South Carolina Senate, he was elected president pro tem. He ran for governor in 1896. (Courtesy of Mary Martin Tucker.)

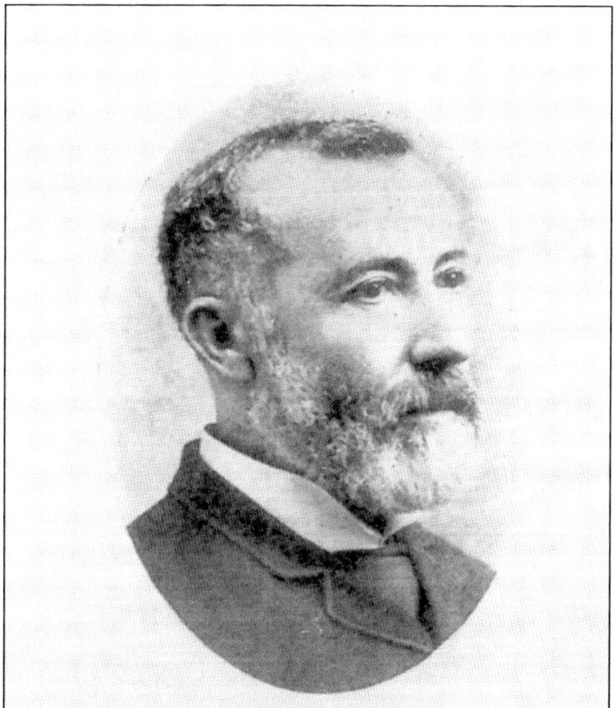

HON. JOHN R. HARRISON.

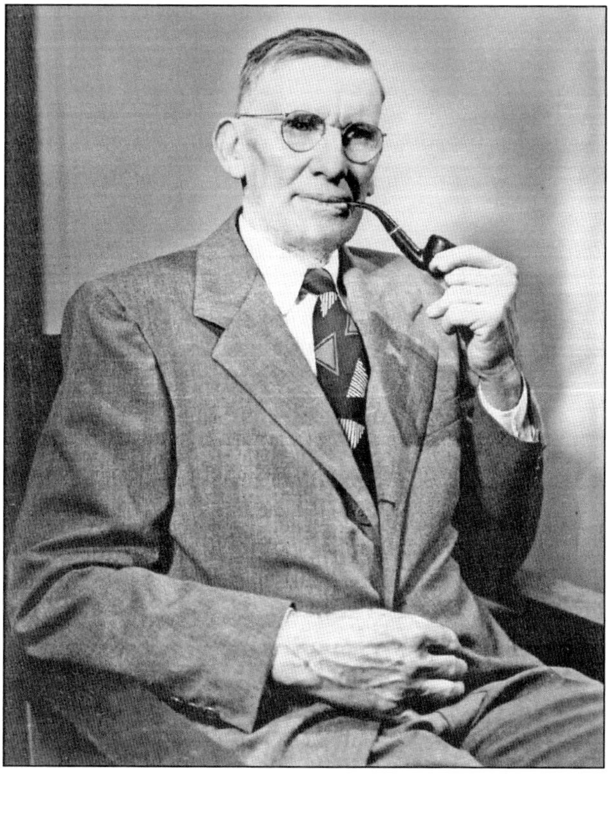

Angus McQueen Martin, born in Dillon County, South Carolina, on January 28, 1871, married Mary E. Harrison, oldest daughter of John Ramsey Harrison. In 1903, he moved to the Harrison family land in the Fairview community, living there until his death on December 28, 1967. He represented Greenville County in the South Carolina House of Representatives in 1915–1916 and 1933–1934. He was the grandfather of Mary Martin Tucker. (Courtesy of Mary Martin Tucker.)

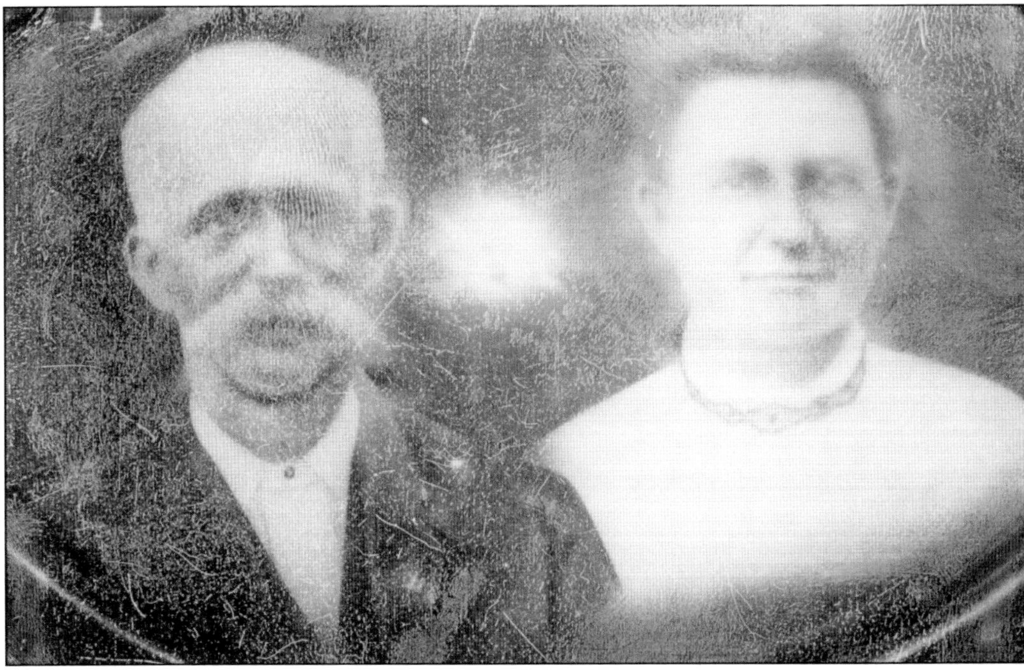

W.H. Lafayette Thompson (1856–1922) and his wife, Margaret Matilda Peden Thompson (1859–1938), are shown above. Their home was built around 1850 in the Hillside area. Margaret Matilda was the daughter of Andrew Milton and Elizabeth Eliza Fowler Peden (pictured on page 30). (Courtesy of Jackie Peden.)

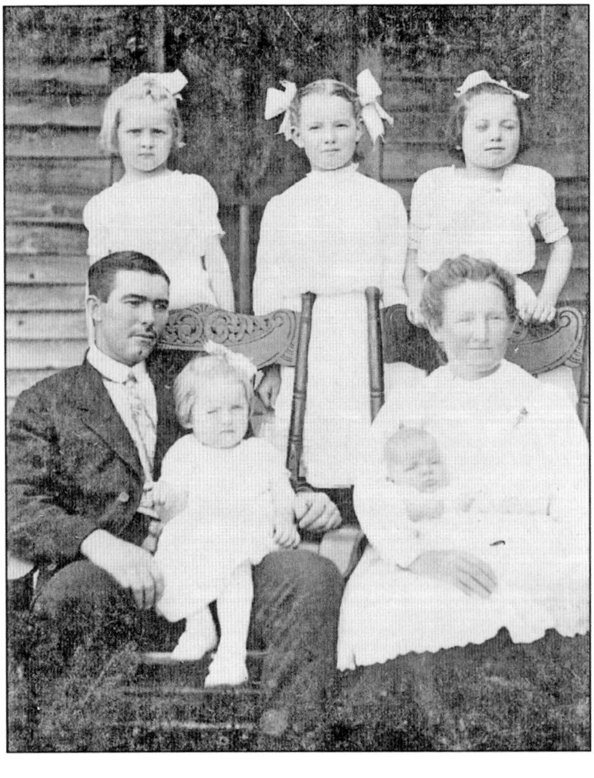

Mina Josephine Peden Thompson was the daughter of John Ballentine Peden (1844–1918) and Sara Ann Elizabeth Barton (1851–1913). Robert Vandiver Thompson was the son of W.H. and Margaret Thompson (pictured above). Mina and Robert Thompson lived in the Hillside community. They belong to the line of Andrew Milton Peden of the house of Alexander. From left to right are (first row) father Robert, daughter Ethel, and mother Mina (holding baby Fred); (second row) daughters Nettie, Muriel, and Irene. (Courtesy of Ann Vaughan.)

A monument to the country doctor stands in the Fairview Church Cemetery. Pictured at left in this photograph, Dr. Henry B. Stewart (1855–1947) designed it and had it erected. For 25 years, he rode a horse to make his calls; for 12 years, he drove a horse and buggy. He ushered 2,750 babies into the world. A year after graduation from medical school in Atlanta, he married Martha Eugenia Peden (1858–1932), daughter of Scipio and Martha McVey Peden. They had eight children. Dr. Stewart also donated a monument to "unknown slaves of the South." (Courtesy of James and Fair Stewart Rodgers.)

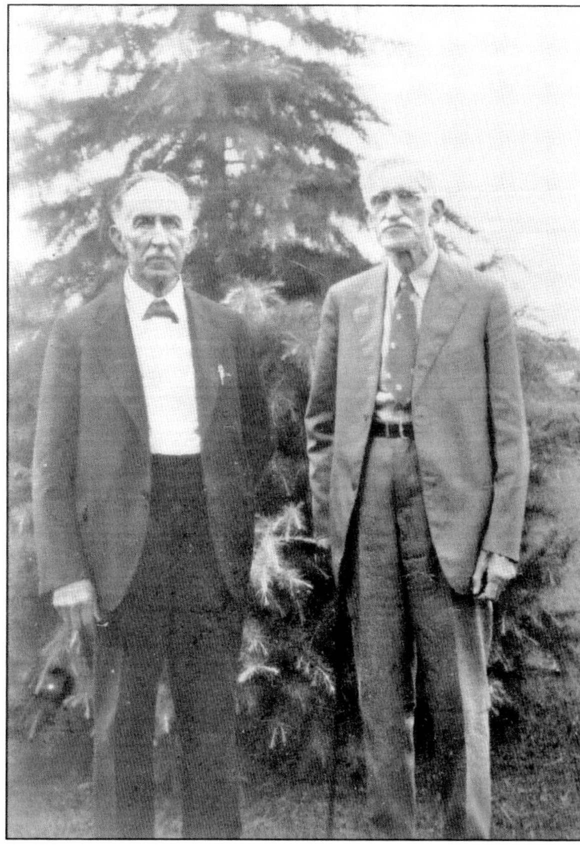

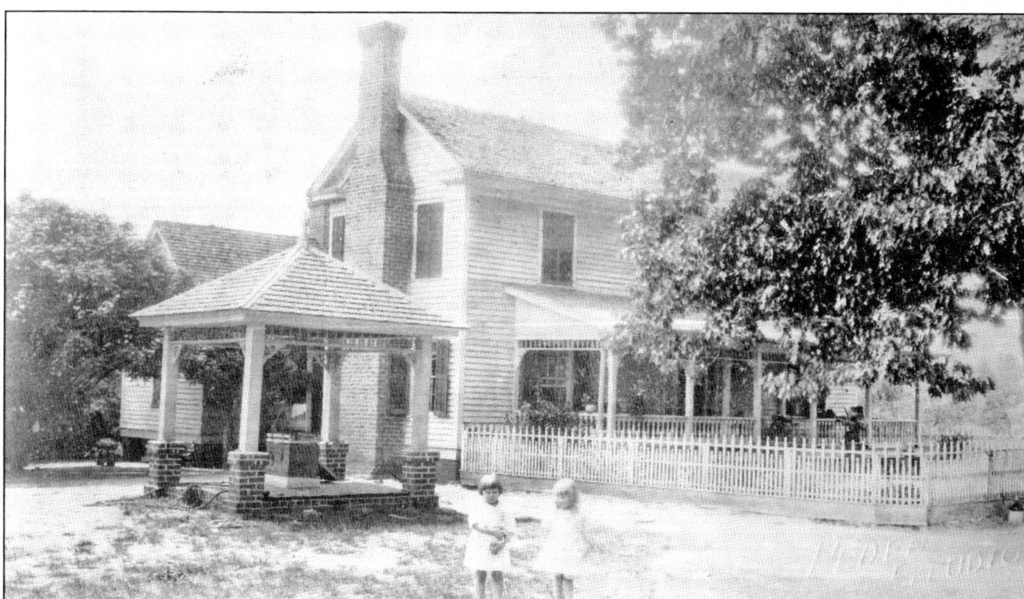

The Dr. Stewart home is located on Fairview Road. Until recently, three generations of the Stewart family had lived there. The last generation was Fair Stewart Rodgers. (Courtesy of James and Fair Stewart Rodgers.)

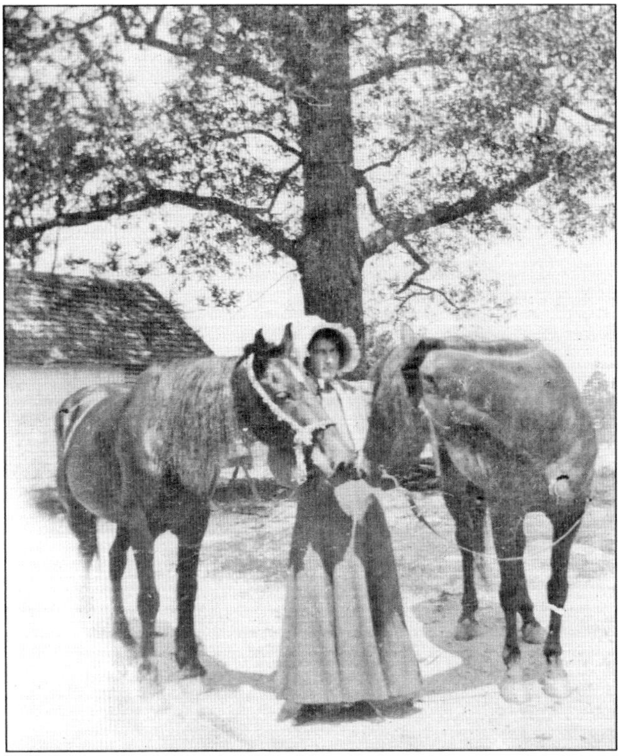

Cathy Stewart was the daughter of Rev. C.B. Stewart (1813–1890), pastor of Fairview. She is shown here at home with her horses. Reverend Stewart purchased Tullyton, also known as the Tully Bolling house, in 1858. It is located on Fairview Road with a historical marker, one of the few brick homes in the area. The 1840 home, built by Capt. Tully Bolling, is now occupied by Dr. Jim Richardson. Captain Bolling and his wife are buried at Fork Shoals Baptist Church. Cathy (Catherine Rachel, 1878–1954) married Charles Lindsay Peden (1879–1944). When Cathy died, her daughter Catherine (a cousin of Mary Lou Stewart Garrett) moved to Fountain Inn. Catherine never married but delighted in helping raise all the Garrett children and their cousins. (Courtesy of the D.H. Garrett family.)

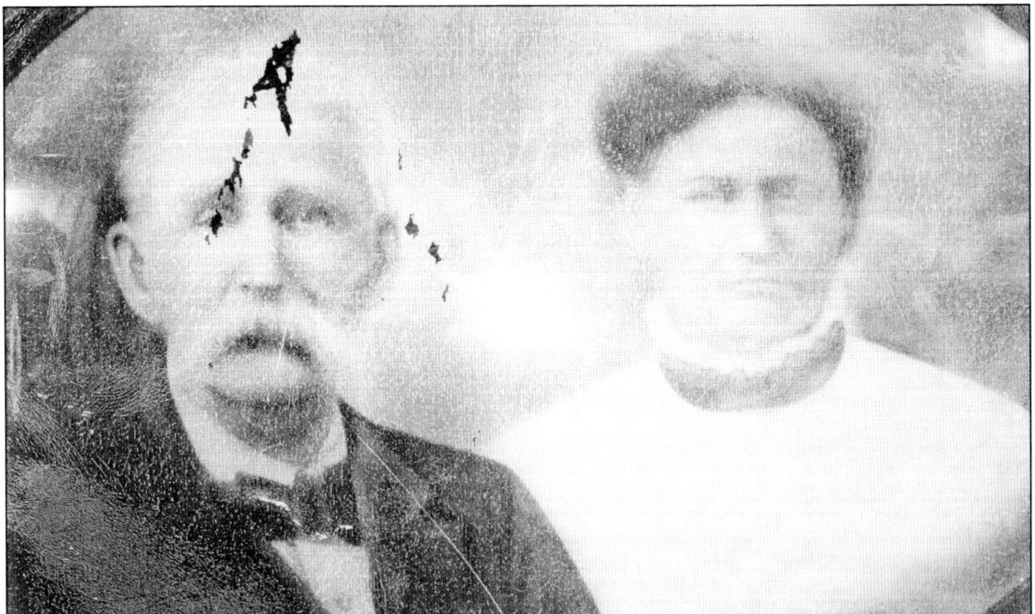

Andrew Milton Peden (1814–1878) is buried at Fairview. His widow Elizabeth Eliza (1820–1897) moved with family to Red Bay, Alabama. She had an unfortunate accident when she was with her dog that scared a cow. She died and is buried in Red Bay. Peden descendants still live there. (Courtesy of Jackie Peden.)

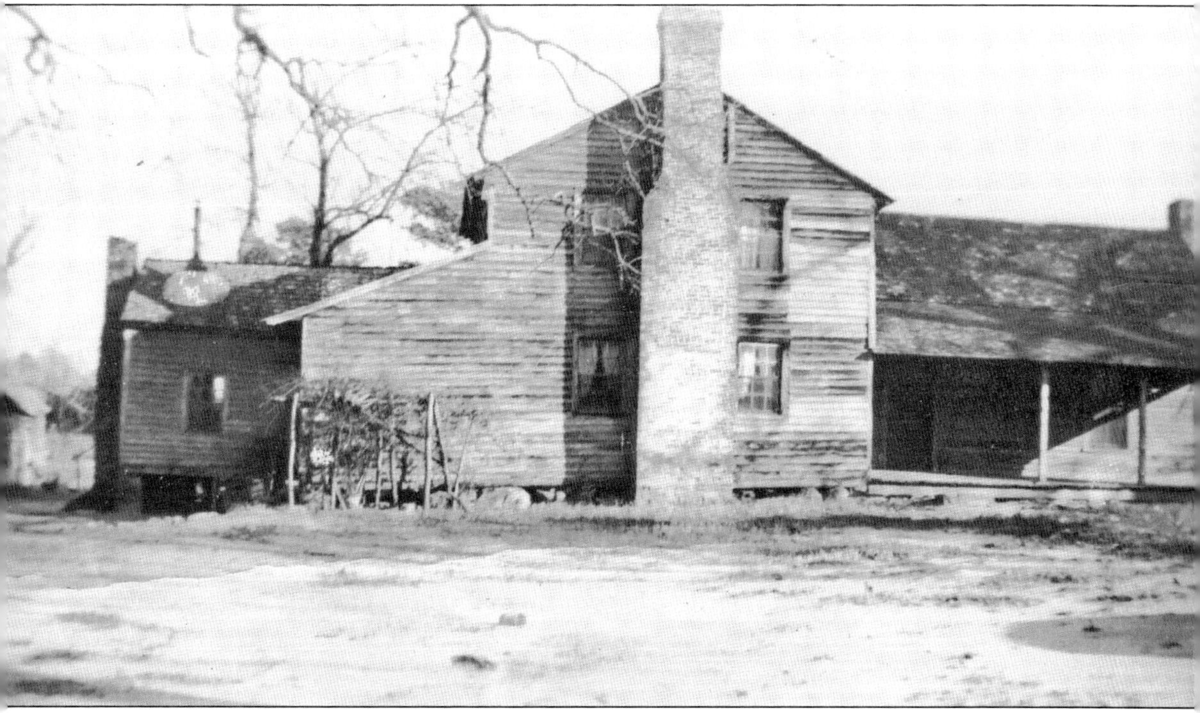

The John and Rebecca Peden Stennis home may be one of the oldest houses still standing in lower Greenville County. It was built in 1808 in the Hillside community. The land was sold to John Stennis by Solomon Hopkins, father of John and Jeremiah. Jeremiah (1795–1854) and his wife, Lucinda Babb Hopkins (1803–1886), are buried at Fairview. The back of their monument reads: "In memory of Solomon Hopkins and his wife Margaret. Born in England. Died about 1815. Buried near Hillside Church." (Both John and Jeremiah Hopkins were married to women named Lucinda.) The land was originally owned by William Choice, a Revolutionary War soldier who mustered out Alexander Peden. The Choice graves are nearby. Rebecca was a daughter of Alexander Peden. The Stennis home was constructed of logs weatherboarded over with oak, and the floors were of heart pine. Across the creek stood the home of John Stennis's brother, Adam Stenhouse. It is gone, as is Rebecca's brother Scipio's home that stood nearby. From the Stennis home, sons Alexander and Adam left for Mississippi, never to return. Dr. Alexander Stennis was the grandfather of longtime Democratic senator John C. Stennis of Mississippi. John and Rebecca's daughter, Mary Ann, moved back to the home place after her husband Samuel McKittrick was killed in the Battle of Atlanta. Her granddaughters were Caroline Sprouse Coleman and "Cinnie" Sprouse Stewart Thomason. (Courtesy of the D.H. Garrett family.)

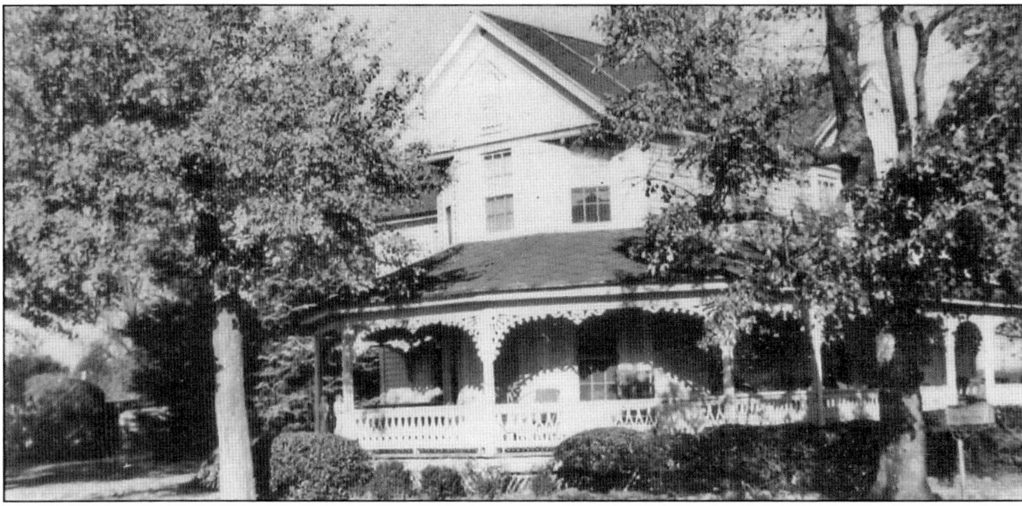

The 1849 Coleman home has been added onto numerous times. At one time the kitchen was separate, as was customary because of fire. The original owners were John and Anna Babb Coleman. John was a member of Wade Hampton's Cavalry and was killed the first day of battle at Trevellian Station, Virginia. He was buried there by neighbor Barnett Babb, who brought his possessions back. Anna was left with the family farm and five children. Robert, the oldest, was fifteen. Anna was buried at Rabon Creek Baptist Church. On the monument is a tribute to John. The house is located on Greenpond Road near Beulah Baptist Church. (Courtesy of the Caroline S. Coleman family.)

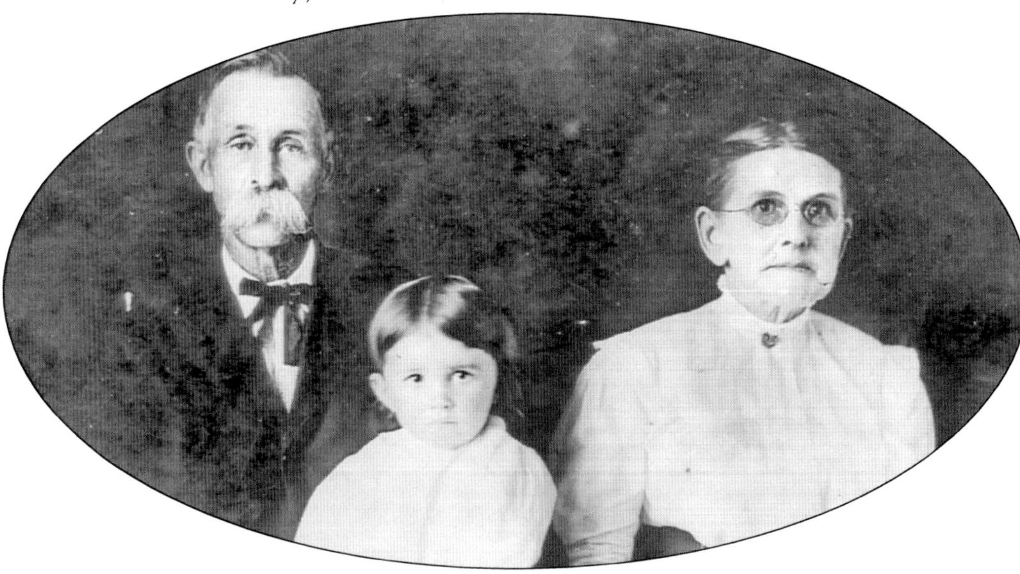

Robert and Isabella Abercrombie Coleman, pictured here about 1912 with their oldest grandchild, Agnes, lived in the Coleman house until the home near Fairview of their oldest son, Will, and his wife, Frennie Stewart Coleman, burned down. Robert and Isabella built a house in town at 423 South Main Street that stands today with a beautiful brick wall around it. Robert was a founder of the Beulah Baptist Church. He, Isabella, and daughter Lula Reddick are buried there. Will and Frennie moved back to the old home place; they were the last Colemans to live there. Will was a lifelong member of Beulah but is buried at Fairview with Frennie. (Courtesy of the Caroline S. Coleman family.)

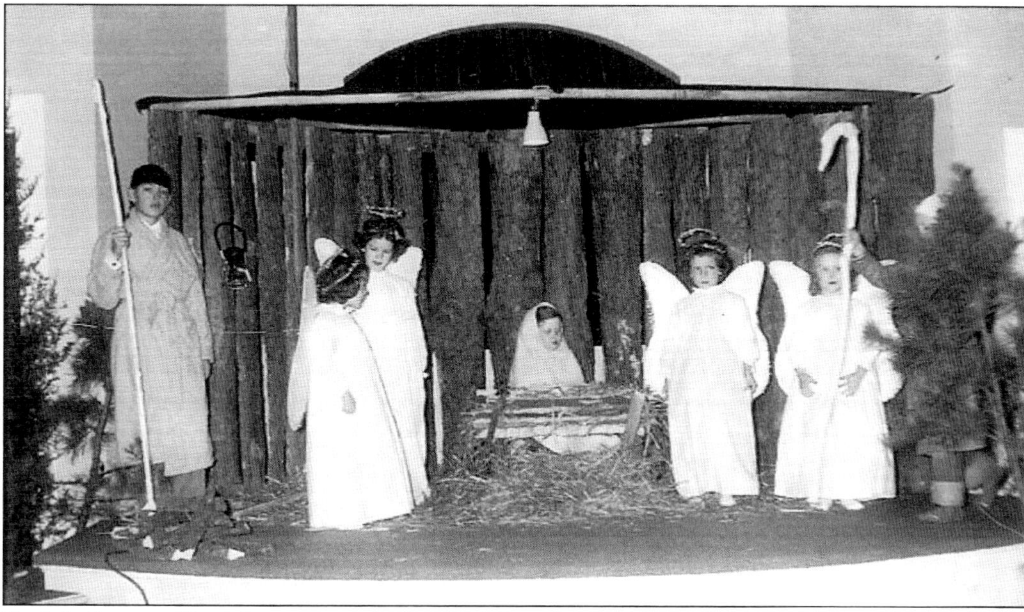

Beulah Baptist Church was organized in 1883 in the Greenpond community by Reverend J.K. Mendenhall, and S.S. Knight, Graves L. Knight, C.P. Nelson, E.N. Garrett, H. Vaughn, J.J. Shumate, and Martin Wood. The 29 charter members came from Poplar Springs, Rabon Creek, and Fountain Inn Baptist Churches. The first deacons elected were Thomas Babb, J.H. Nash, and Robert Coleman. The land was given by L.P. Armstrong. Until 1956, the church shared a minister with Rabon Creek. The first minister was Reverend H.R. Ezell. This is a photograph of an early Christmas pageant. (Courtesy of Jack Marlar and John Weathers.)

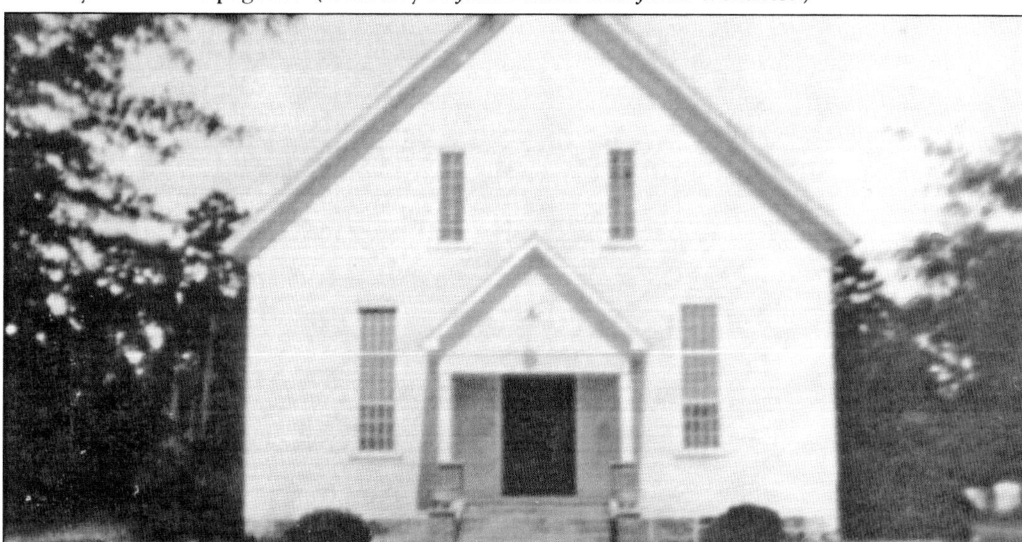

The Green Pond Methodist Church was organized in 1844 by Thomas Andrews. The first building was a one-room log cabin on land donated by Abraham Abercrombie. The name was derived from a green lake or pond nearby. The church was built near a spring and had a wide fireplace and hand-hewn benches. When it burned, a frame building had stood until 1890. Families who attended this early church were Abercrombies, Babbs, Owens, and Kelletts. Circuit riders served the old church about every three months. (Courtesy of Ann Vaughan.)

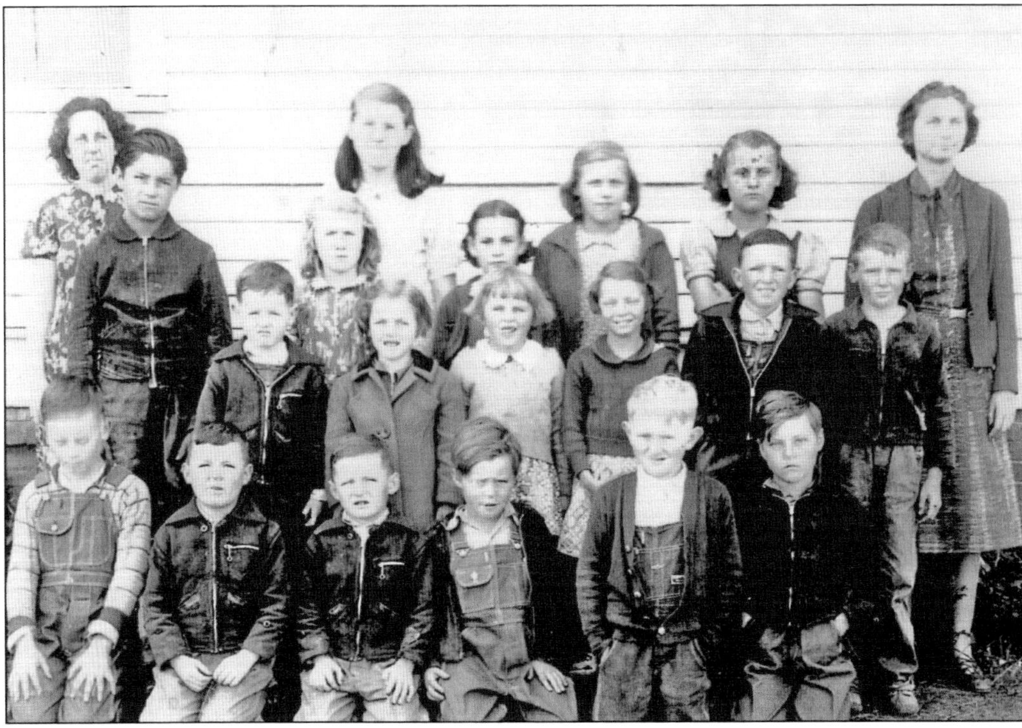

Eden Grammar School (first through sixth grades) was located on the left of Greenpond Road, south of Green Pond Church, about half a mile before Highway 101 in Laurens County. Ann Vaughan explained that in Greenville County it is Green Pond Road, while in Laurens County it is Greenpond Road. This picture was of the 1938–1939 class. From left to right are (first row) Fred Campbell, Bob Gray, unidentified, ? Banks, James Vaughan, and ? Banks; (second row) Marion Curry, Charlotte Hipp, Juanita Gray, Helen Babb, Billy Gault, and Edwin Babb; (third row) ? Banks, Martha Wham, Helen Gray, Viola Gray, Beatrice Gray, and teacher Koreta Farris; (fourth row) teacher Ethel Moore. (Courtesy of Ann Vaughan.)

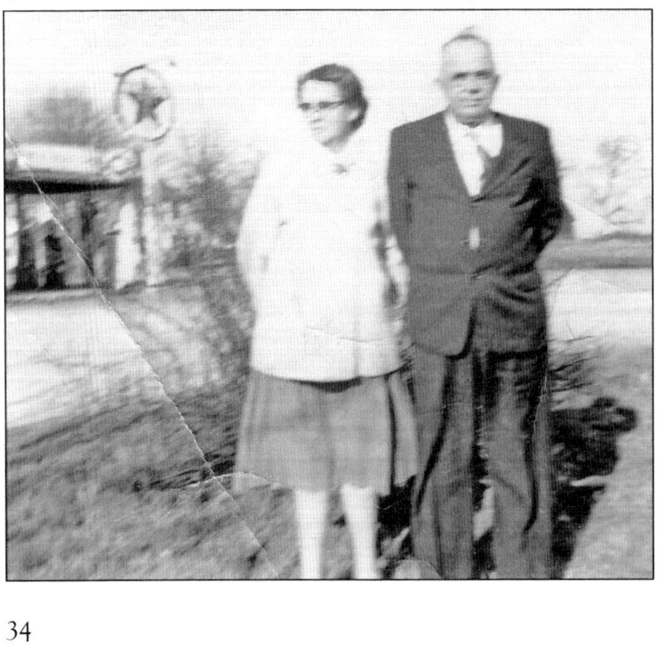

Willie and Mary Curry Bolt operated this country store and service station in the Green Pond community for 37 years. It was one of the oldest country stores in the area under same ownership. It began as a hot dog stand. They had cash and credit customers and never lost one. Their motto was "treat a customer like you would want everybody to treat you." Caroline S. Coleman wrote up this "human interest story" many years before her grandson Jack married the Bolts' granddaughter, Alice Tinsley. (Courtesy of Alice Tinsley Coleman.)

Robert McCarter (1914–1972) is in a beautiful baby dress made by his aunt Pearl McCarter Armstrong. (Courtesy of Ann Vaughan.)

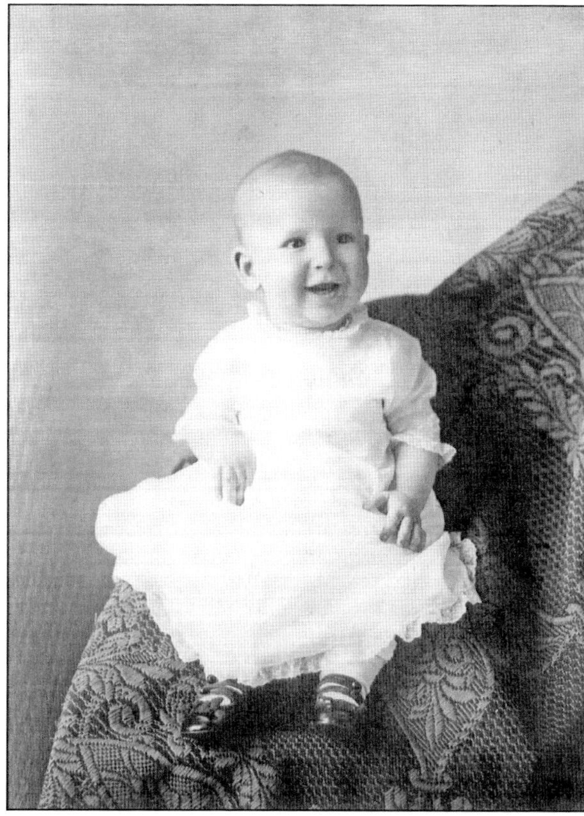

This portrait of the Robert Hugh McCarter family was made about 1906. From left to right are (first row) Robert Hugh McCarter, Martha McCarter, Mae McCarter, and Jane Elizabeth "Lizzie" Taylor McCarter; (second row) Hugh McCarter, John McCarter, Pearl McCarter, and Hilliard McCarter. (Courtesy of Ann Vaughan.)

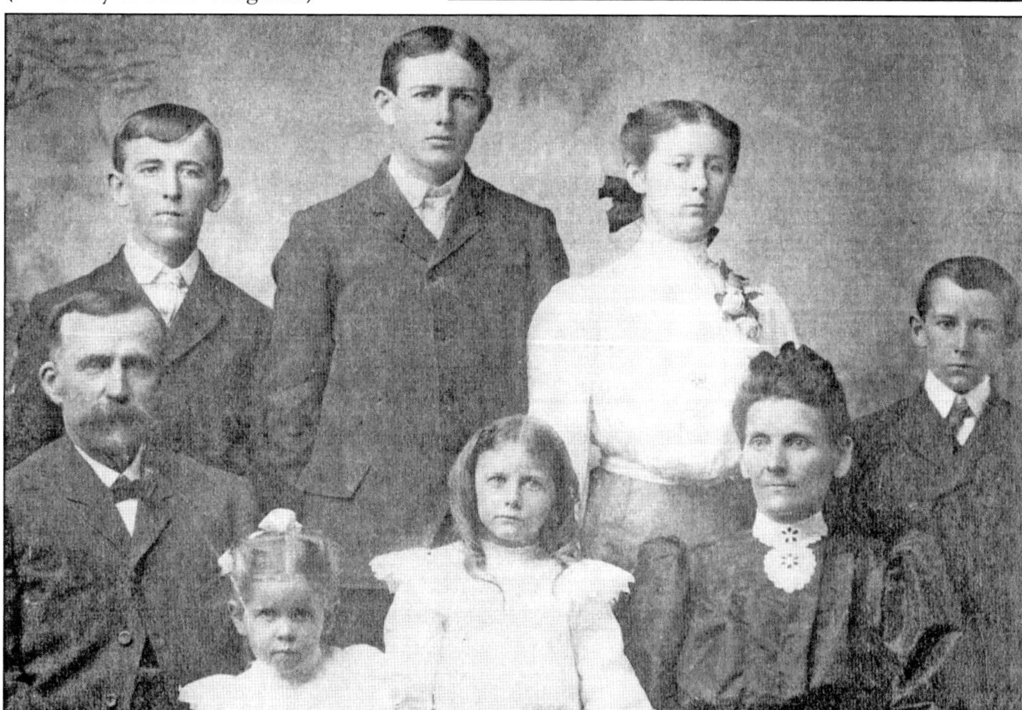

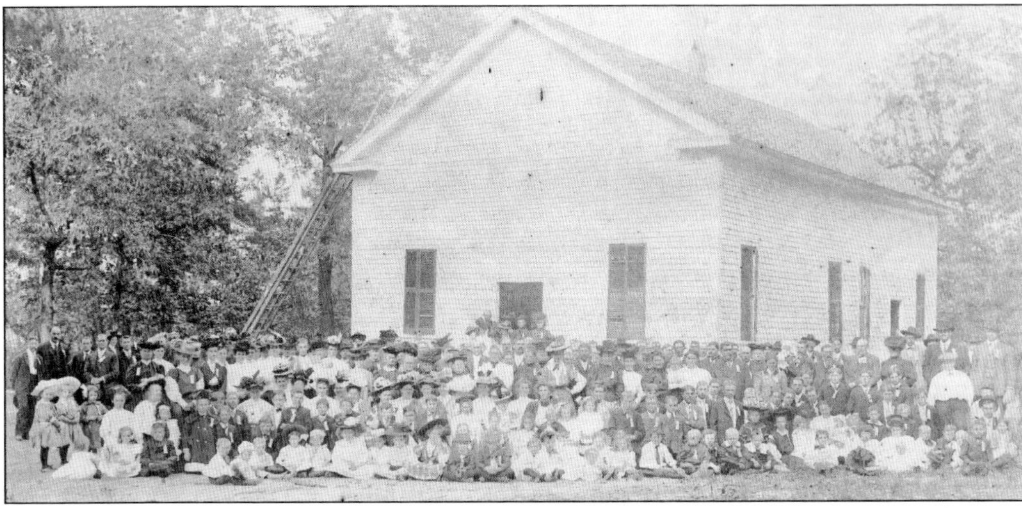

The first reunion of the descendants of Walter Stewart was held at New Harmony Presbyterian Church in October 1907. This photograph shows reunion attendees in front of the first frame church, which was destroyed by fire in 1932. When the congregation was established in 1844, Presbyterians and Baptists in this rural Laurens County community southeast of present-day Fountain Inn covenanted together to erect one building and share it on alternating weeks with special arrangements for fifth Sundays in the month. Nearly two centuries later, the same arrangement continues. The Presbyterian congregation is known as New Harmony; the Baptist is called Harmony. (Courtesy of Henry Fulmer.)

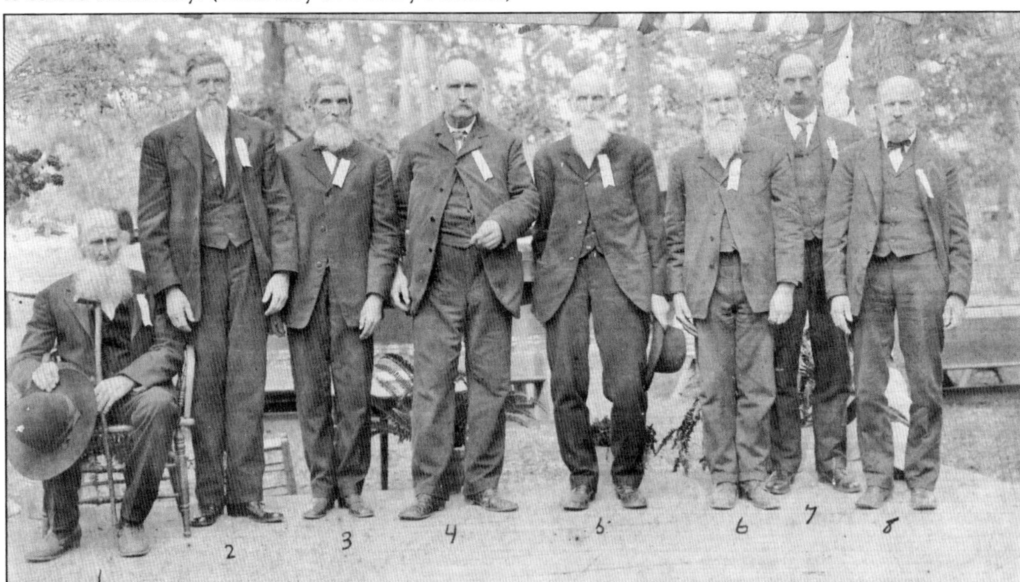

At the first reunion in 1907, the Walter Stewart clan was organized. The family association of descendants of Walter Stewart Sr. and his wives, Mary Ross and Isabel Bobo, chose William "Squire Bill" Stewart, seated at left, as chief and, standing from left to right, Robert Leland Henry, Samuel Dixon Stewart, John Wistar Simpson Stewart, James Preston Stewart, Samuel Turner Stewart, Robert Walter Stewart, and John Westmoreland Bradley as sub-chiefs representing the seven "houses" or lines of descendants through the sons of Walter Stewart Sr.: Samuel, John, Robert, James, Walter Jr., Clark, and David. (Courtesy of Henry Fulmer.)

Three

Going "Over Town"

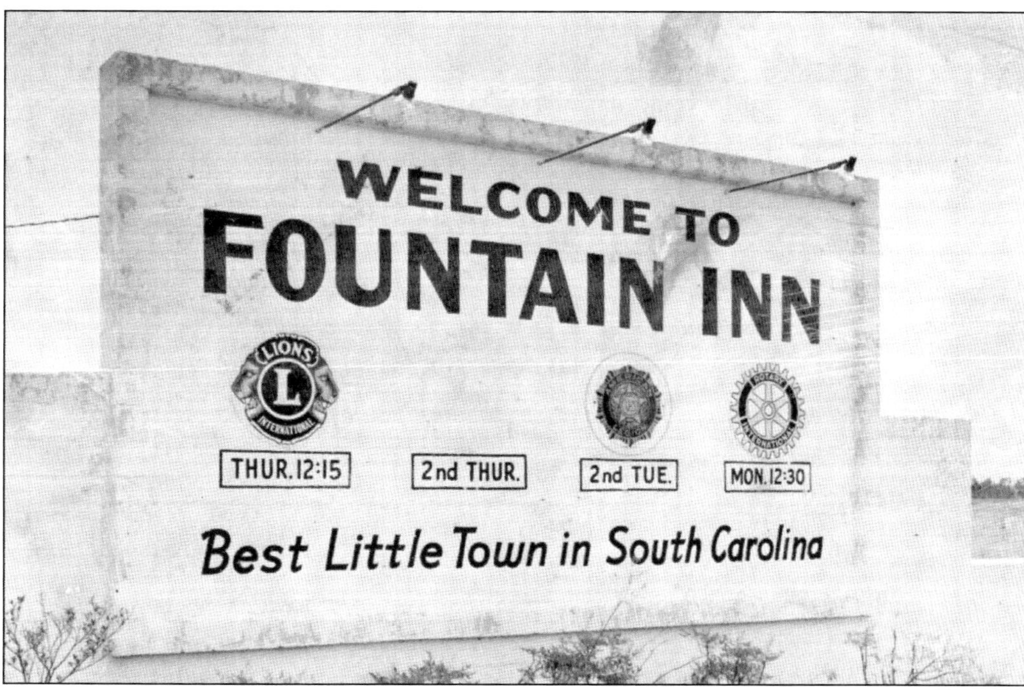

This sign and slogan were used for many years. It was designed and painted by resident Bogue Howard, who also ran the theater in downtown Fountain Inn.

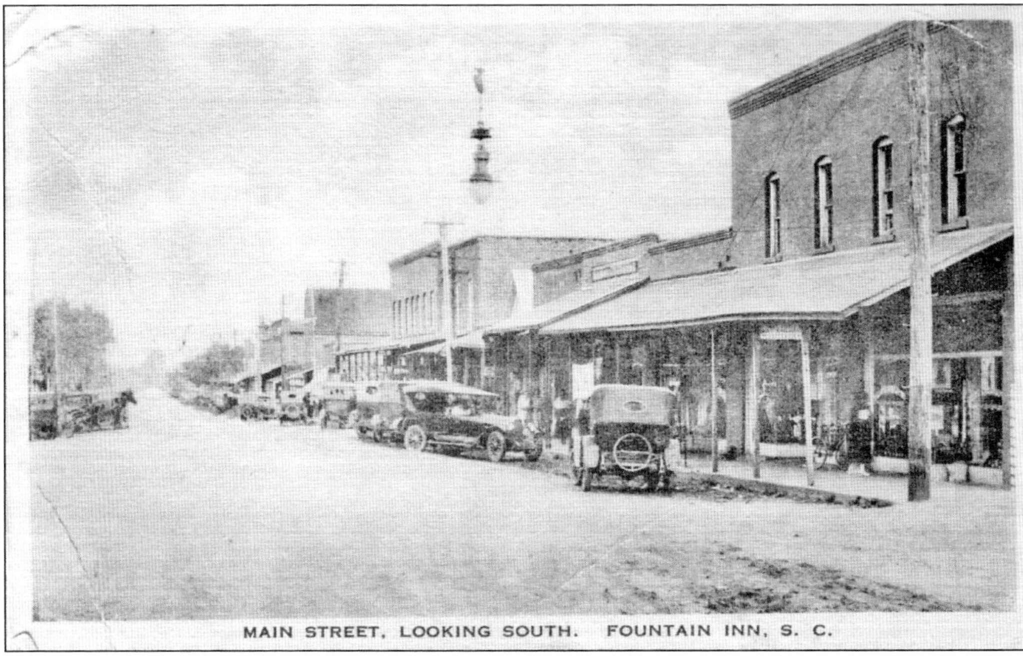

The image above shows Main Street looking south. There were no lined parking places in those days. Farmers still brought their wagons with horses or mules to town, even though automobiles seem to be the majority.

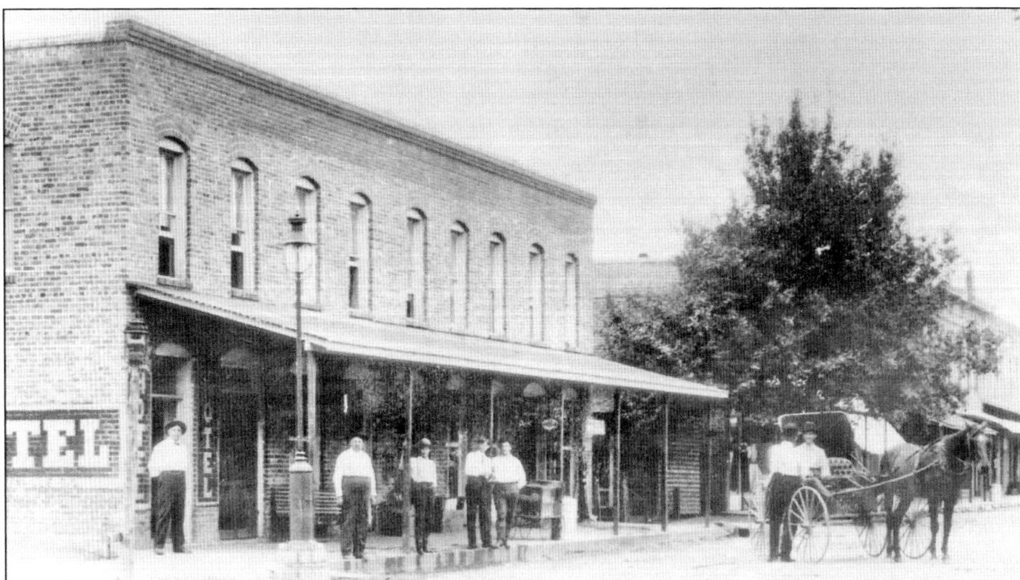

A hotel is shown in this photograph of Main Street. Some merchants in 1911 were A.G. Edwards, ? Armstrong, W.T. Vaughn, Ford Todd Cox, ? Richardson, ? Taylor, J.R. Kellett, ? Gilstrap, ? Rice, T.E. Nelson, T.E. Jones, James Stewart, ? Drummond, D.M. Garrett, W.C. Babb, A.R. Meadors, Ettie Winn, J.F. McKelvey, A.D. Cannon, Mrs. S.B. Bryant, W.Z. Davis, L.E. McKnight, ? Jackson, ? Parsons, ? Nichols, Mrs. Maroney, S.O. Babb, J.A. Fulmer, Y.R. Scruggs, ? Templeton, ? Limbaugh, ? Rhames, Robert Quillen, ? Roper, and ? Mahaffey. The 1880 Cannon Building on the corner of North Main and Trade Streets was listed in the National Register of Historic Places in 2005.

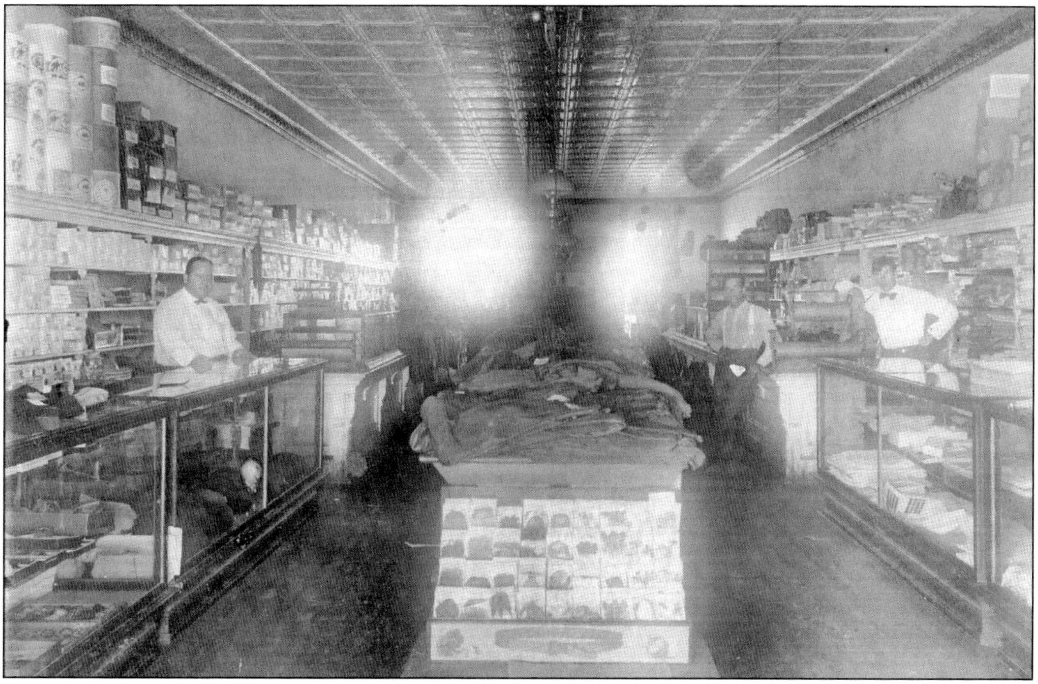

Drummond and Garrett sold general merchandise and advertised penitentiary-made shoes in the 1911 *Tribune*. In 1928, this business was listed as Drummond and Sons (the sons were J.H., J.C., and E.A.) and advertised as selling dry goods since 1908. At one time, Sam Drummond owned 107 South Main Street. The Drummonds also owned a filling station. (Courtesy of Juanita Adamson Moorman.)

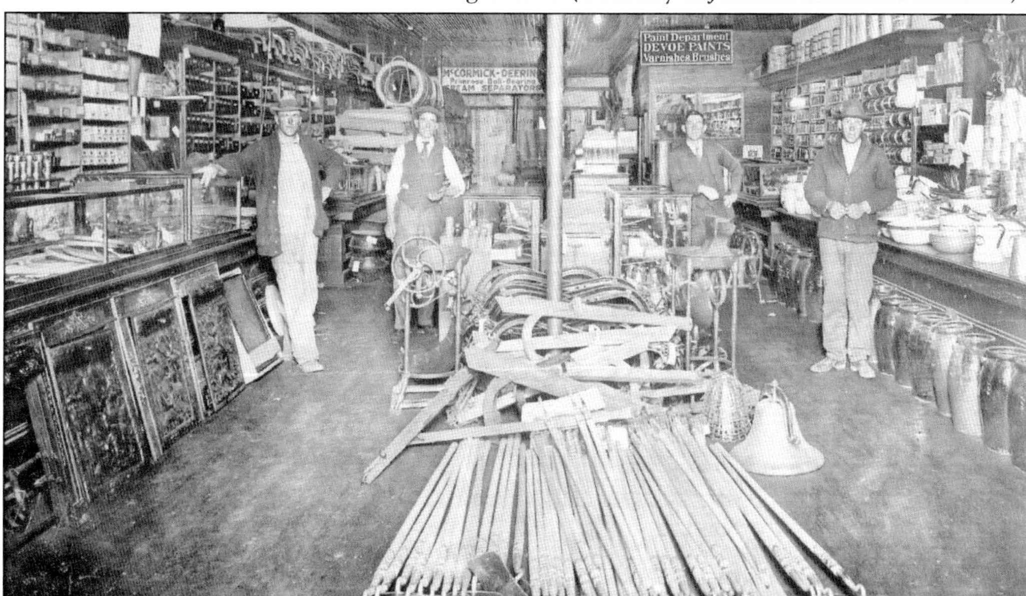

This photograph shows a general merchandise store. It carried a wide variety of goods. Note the crocks on the floor on the right. They may have come from Laurens. From 1878 to 1933, Joe "Jug" Johnson and his brother Harvey made utilitarian pottery used for storage and churns. Some of it is still with Fountain Inn families.

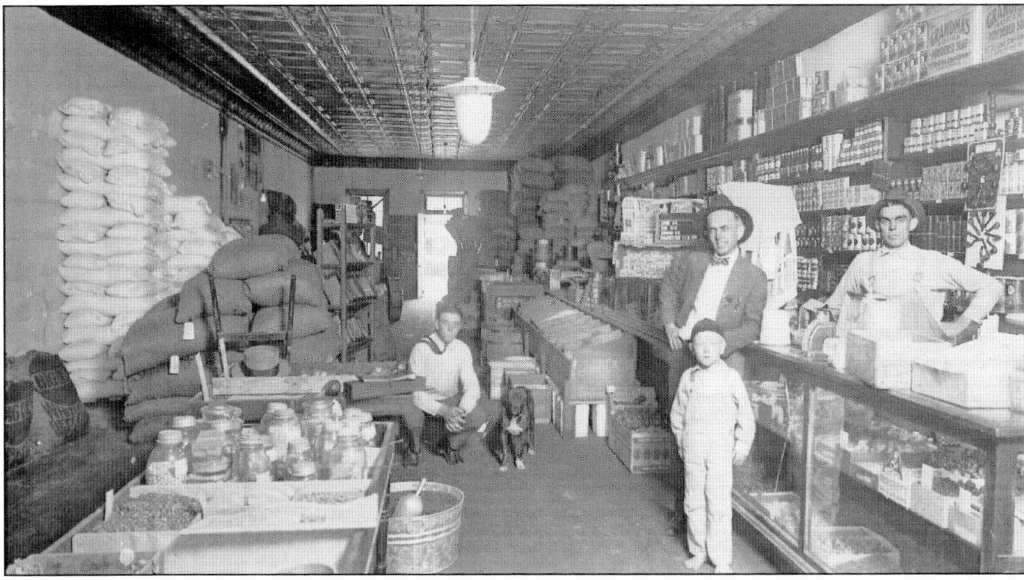

B.C. Givens, coauthor of *The History of Fountain Inn*, dealt in feed and seeds. He is standing here with young Boyne Givens, the son of O.B. (B.C.'s brother). O.B. and his wife, Janie, lived on the corner of Weston Street and Green Avenue. B.C. and his wife, Gladys, lived in the stone house on Weston Street. In 1933, B.C. advertised that he would no longer carry groceries. At one time, he owned a lot of downtown real estate around the northwest corner of Main and Fairview Streets.

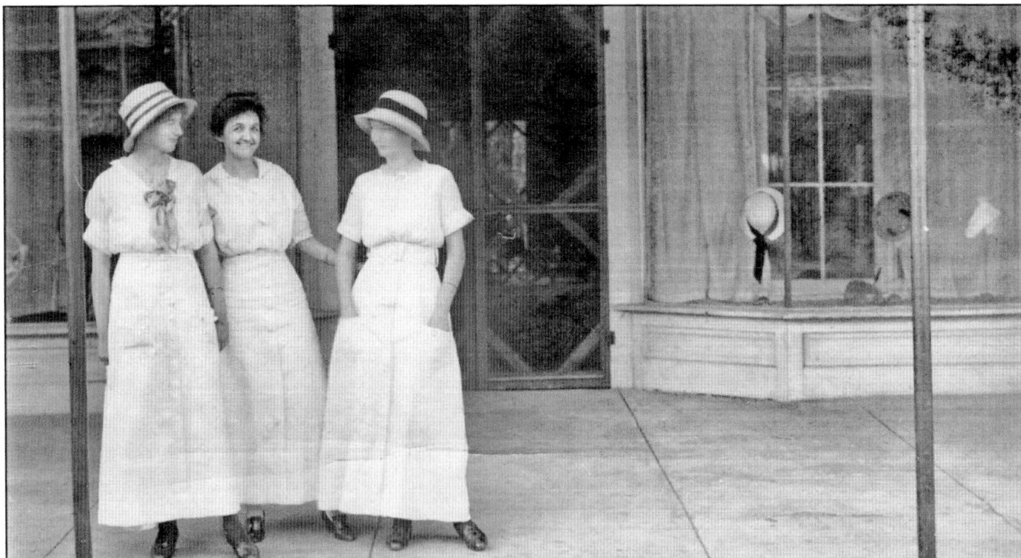

Over the years, there were many millinery shops. Ladies always wore hats. Donnie Cox, Robert Quillen's first wife, and her mother, Buena, owned a shop next door to the *Tribune* office. Ettie Winn's millinery shop opened in March 1912. Pictured above from left to right are Anne Farrow, Ettie Winn, and Estelle Farrow in 1923. Another milliner was Nan Usher Edwards, mother of Richard and grandmother of Nancy Yennie. Nan was trained at a milliner school in Atlanta. After working in Rich's, a famous department store, she came to Fountain Inn. The former Edwards home is on North Main Street next to the Fulmer house. (Courtesy of Juanita Adamson Moorman.)

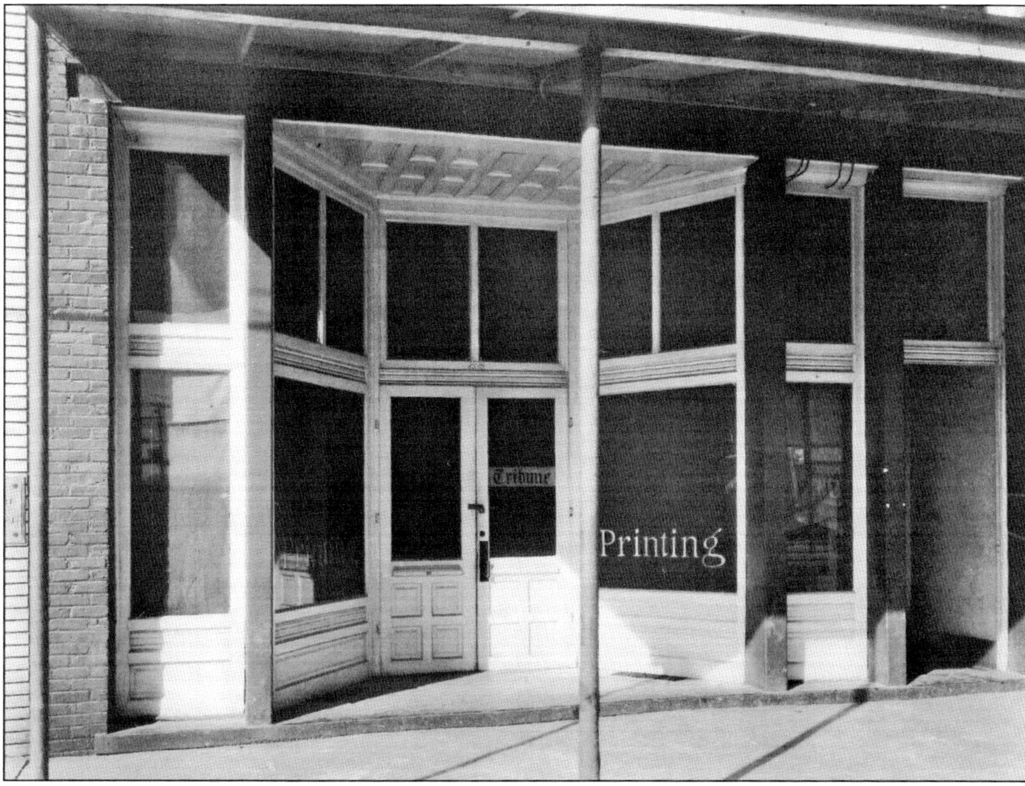

The first issue of the *Fountain Inn Tribune* was published on February 9, 1911, by Ford Cox and Robert Quillen. When Quillen became so busy with his syndicated column and cartoons, he sold the paper to West Kellett for $1. Quillen later became "homesick for printer's ink" and bought it back from Kellett for $2,000, so it is said. At Bob's death, the *Tribune* was sold to Mark Nelson, who had worked with Bob. Mark published the *Tribune* until his death in 1962. The photograph below shows Mark with Caroline S. Coleman in the *Tribune* office.

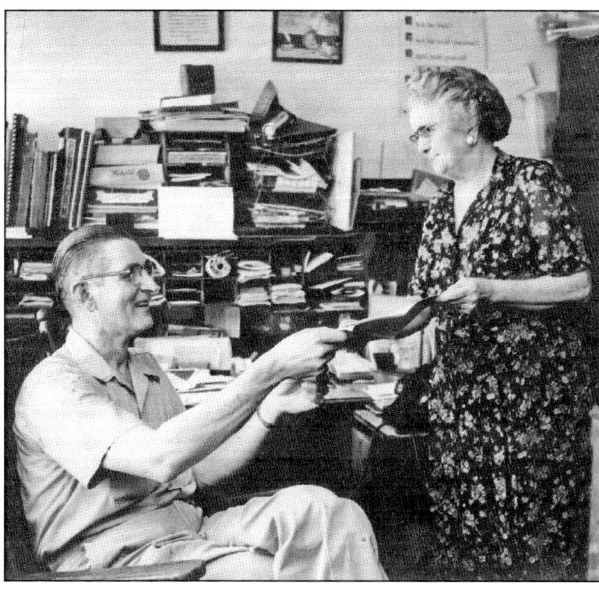

Caroline Sprouse Coleman (1883–1969) wrote "Little Town Talk" from 1912 until her death in 1969, longer than anyone writing for the *Tribune*. Robert Quillen was her mentor. She wrote feature articles for papers all over the United States, including the *Baltimore Sun*, *Charleston News and Courier*, *Detroit Free Press*, and *Philadelphia Enquirer*. Coleman was coauthor of *The History of Fountain Inn* and author of the 1962 book *Five Petticoats on Sunday*. A display of her memorabilia is located in the Fountain Inn Museum. Coleman was the grandmother of the author Caroline Sherman. (Courtesy of the Caroline S. Coleman family.)

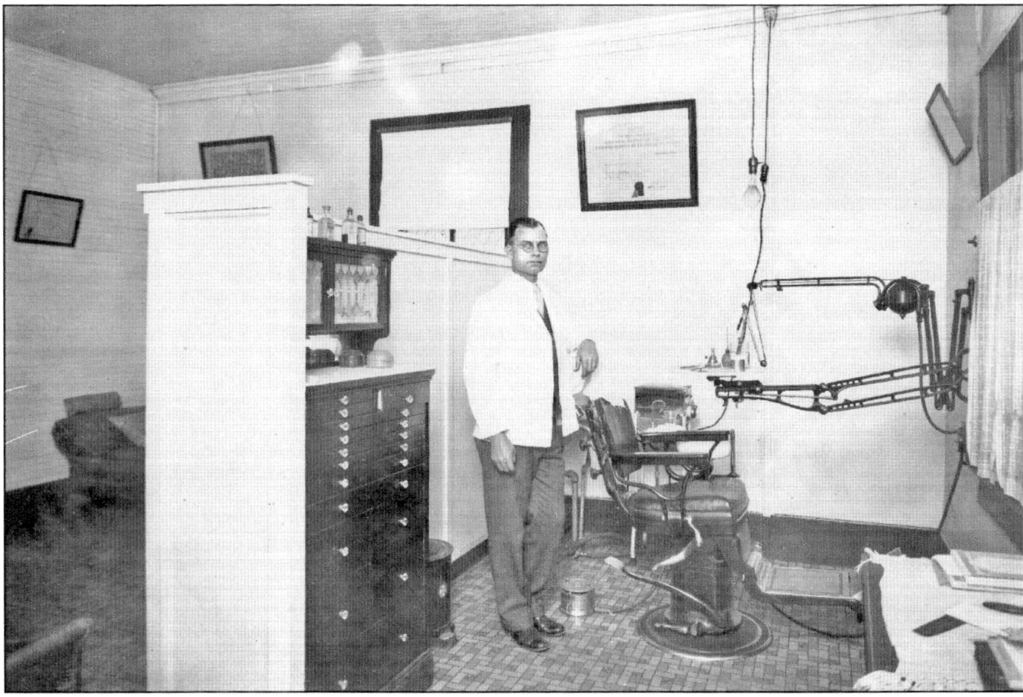

Dr. James Ambrose Fulmer Sr., known throughout Fountain Inn and the surrounding area as "Doc," was reared in the Piney Woods community near Chapin. Dr. Fulmer is pictured in the dental office in which he practiced for most of his four decades. Located on the second story of the Kellett Building at the southwest corner of South Main and Trade Streets, the office was accessed via a flight of stairs on the exterior of the building. Dr. Fulmer graduated in 1905 from the Dental Department of Baltimore Medical College and settled in Fountain Inn, where his brother-in-law H.B. Dominick was a school official. (Courtesy of Henry Fulmer.)

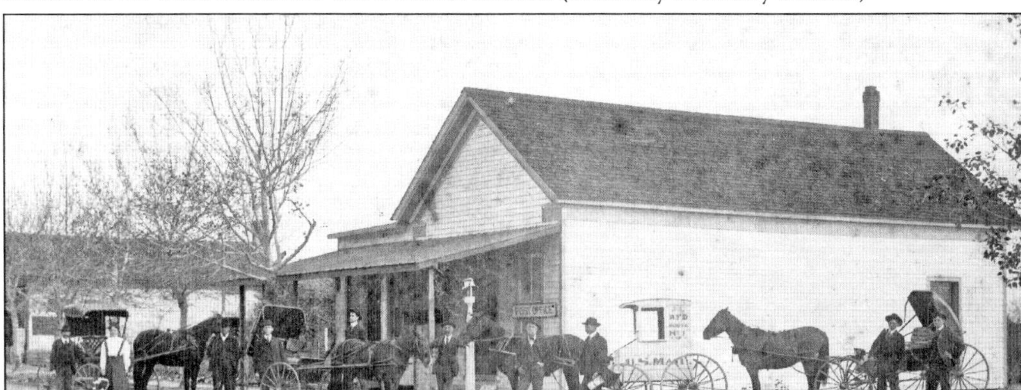

At the time of this 1904 photograph, the postmaster was J.A. Cannon. He served for 49 years. The assistant postmaster was Lee Marlar. Carriers were W.B. Stewart, Dennis Edwards, W.B. Childress, and S.L. Taylor. Substitutes were Emmie Stewart (Fulmer), James Adams, and Ben Cox. Before the times of rural free delivery, in 1901, there was Star Route, consisting of small rural post offices in general stores. Country folks could put up a mailbox and pay 25¢ a quarter for delivery. In 1900, W.B. Childress drove this Star Route in his horse and buggy. (Courtesy of Henry Fulmer.)

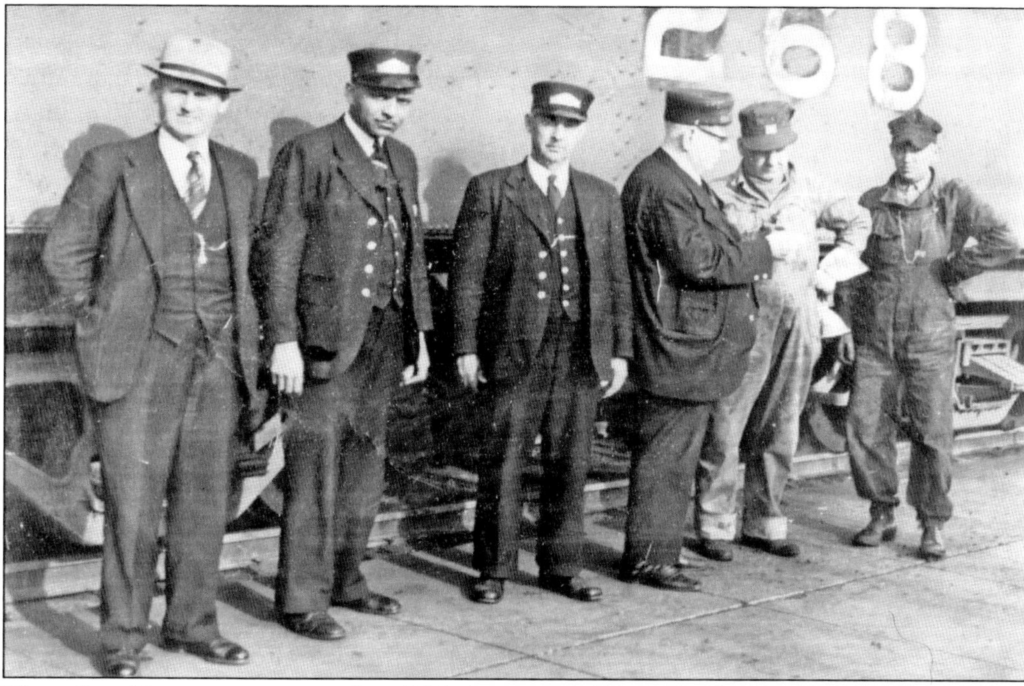

The railroad line was constructed in 1886, the year of chartering of Fountain Inn. It ran through a part of the original cemetery, and graves had to be moved. J.I. West and J.A. Cannon owned the land and gave right of way to the Charleston & Western Carolina Railway for the track and the depot. In the 1900s, all mail and freight for merchants was received on the train. It was major transportation for Fountain Inn. The 1909 Peden reunion mentions people arriving on the train. When the town stop was discontinued many years later, the 1903 depot was sold and moved. The farmer's market now occupies its space.

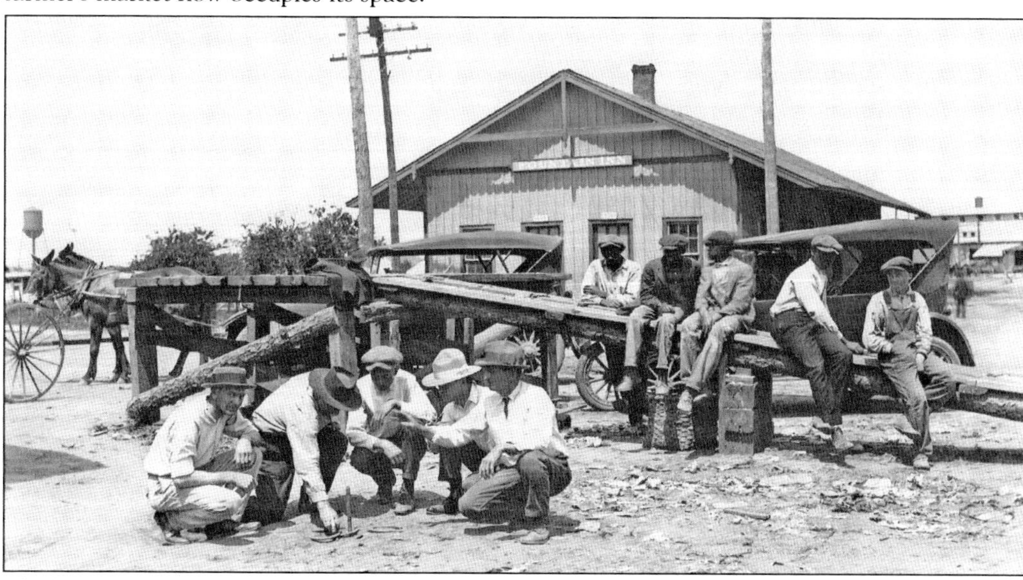

The longest serving depot agent was A.C. Crout. His wife, Bertha Crout, taught school and played the organ at the First Baptist Church. The Crouts had two daughters: Yvonne and Edythe Ann. Pictured above is a horseshoe game. Robert Quillen is fourth from left, kneeling.

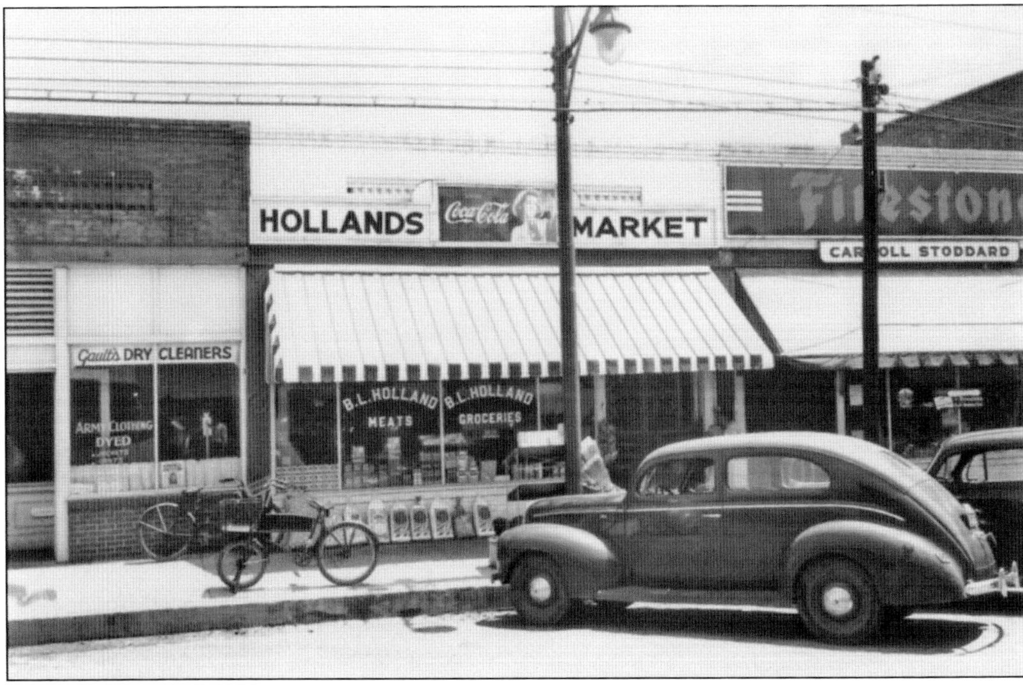

Reuben Benjamin "R.B." Holland was one of the first business owners in town. R.B. purchased a large portion of the east side of Main Street in 1886, just prior to the town being chartered. He established Holland's Market, which he and later his son Benjamin Lee ran for 75 years. After R.B., Bennie Lee and son Ben ran the business. Bennie Lee's home on Fairview Street still stands. Holland's offered a delivery service, allowing customers to place their orders via telephone with delivery by "Speck" Thompson. Holland's market was 114 North Main Street, the right-hand side facing north. Murk Gault's Cleaners, at 116 North Main Street, was on the left before moving to Jones and Weston Streets. (Courtesy of Susan Bowen and Carole Holland Davis.)

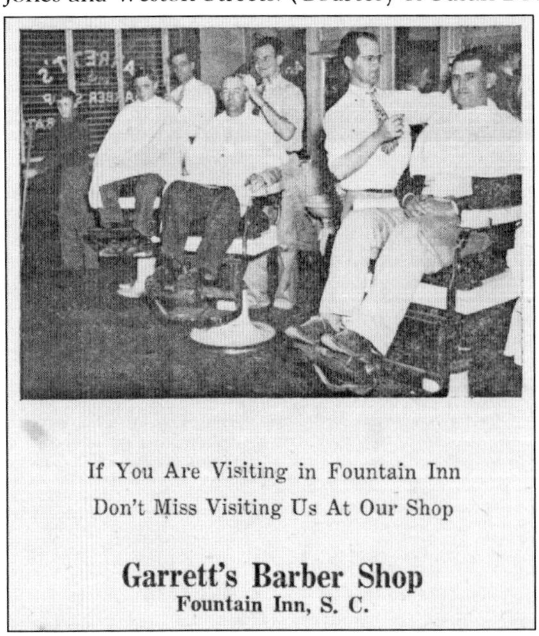

Garrett's Barbershop has been at 110 North Main Street since 1936. It is probably the only store in town that has not moved. It was owned by brothers Ben and Jeter Garrett Sr. and by now Jeter Sr.'s son Jeter. There have been many barbershops in Fountain Inn. In 1911, there were four. In 1928, Moore's was listed, probably owned by Mitchell Moore, father to James, who later had a shop with Jake Templeton.

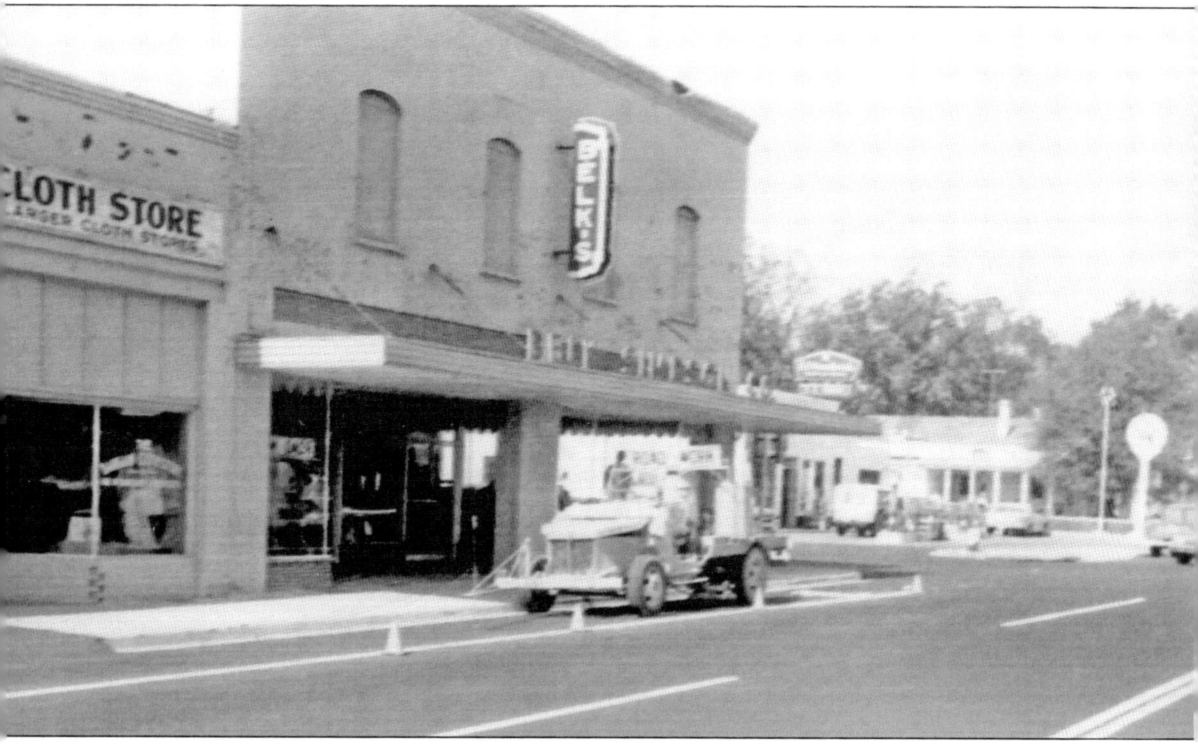

Belk's Department Store was located at 129 North Main Street on the corner of Fairview Street. The old building was known at one time as Belk's-Putnam, then Belk's-Simpson. Before Belk's, this building housed Jim DeBard's grocery, Givens-Thackston Hardware, Leake and Woods grocery, Fountain Inn Plumbing, and Western Auto. The Bargain Cloth Shop was next door at 127 North Main Street. Green's Filling Station and the Conway Jones home can be seen in the background, where a drugstore is now.

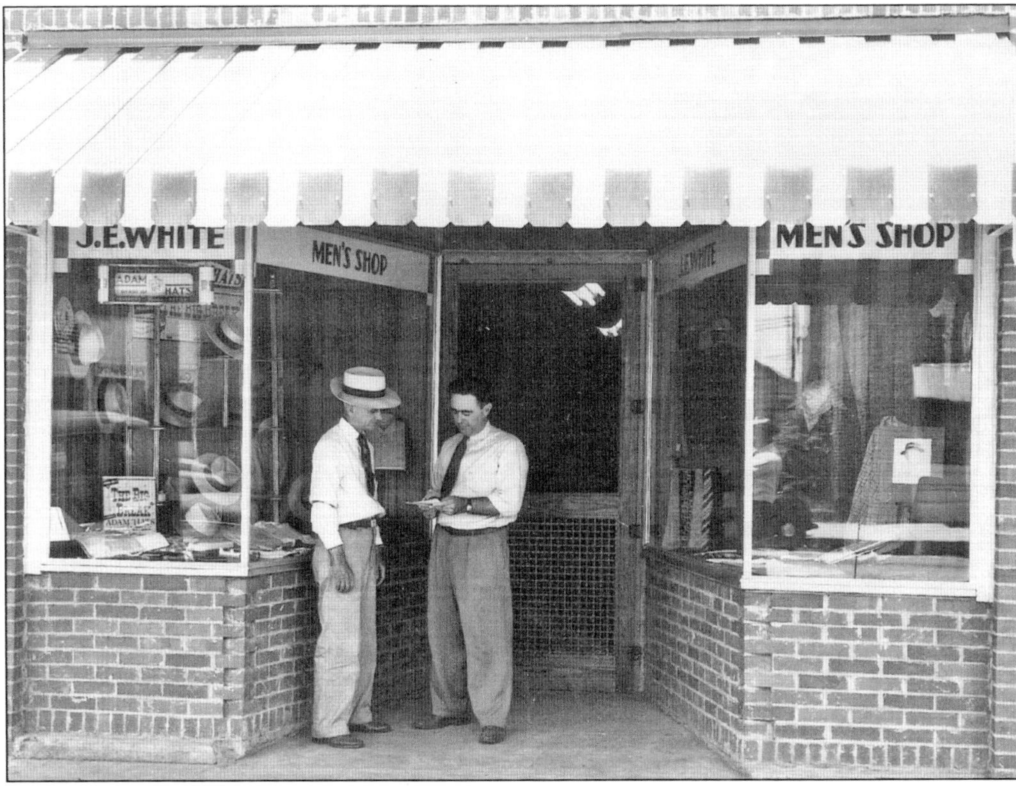

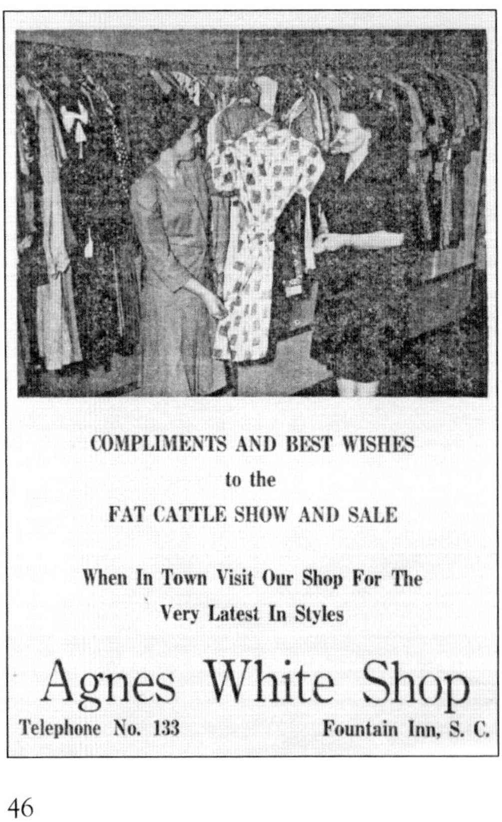

J.E. White's Men Shop was at 119 North Main Street from 1946 to 1986. J.E. "Pete" White (1909–1999) was the brother to Earl and Luther White, who owned a plumbing company. They were raised in the Durbin community. Pete first worked at Givens Hardware and a cotton warehouse in Greenville, before opening his shop. Previously this store was Lee Willis's restaurant, which sold hot dogs. B.C. Givens is pictured above on the left, and Pete is on the right.

Agnes Roberts White (1912–1990) was born in the Bethany community. She graduated from Simpsonville High School and Asheville Normal College in North Carolina, now Woodrow Wilson. Agnes White's Specialty Shop (1943–1974) opened during World War II. Merchandise was hard to come by then. Thomas Arnold, a buyer in New York City and founder of Meyers-Arnold, a large department store in Greenville, helped her negotiate with wholesalers. Her store was located in the former Purkerson's Drug Store. She was the wife of Pete White.

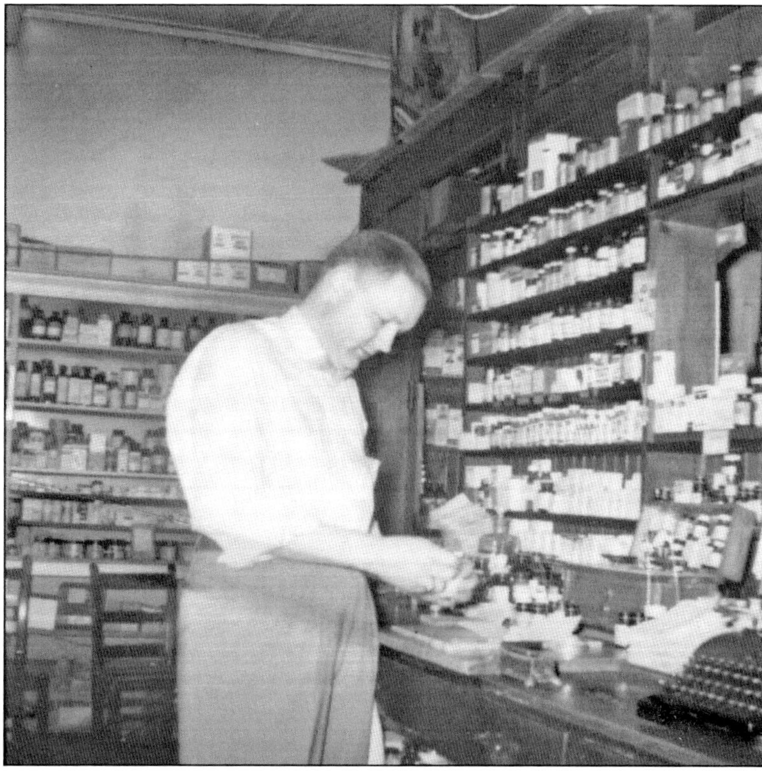

Dr. Charles Alberson, son of Dendy and Bessie Armstrong Alberson, purchased the Fountain Inn Drug Store at 104 North Main Street in 1953. In 1967, they moved to 100 South Main. Dr. Alberson retired in 2003 and closed the store. Five of the original shelving units are in the Fountain In Museum, where they house vintage copies of the *Tribune Times*. (Courtesy of the Charles Alberson family.)

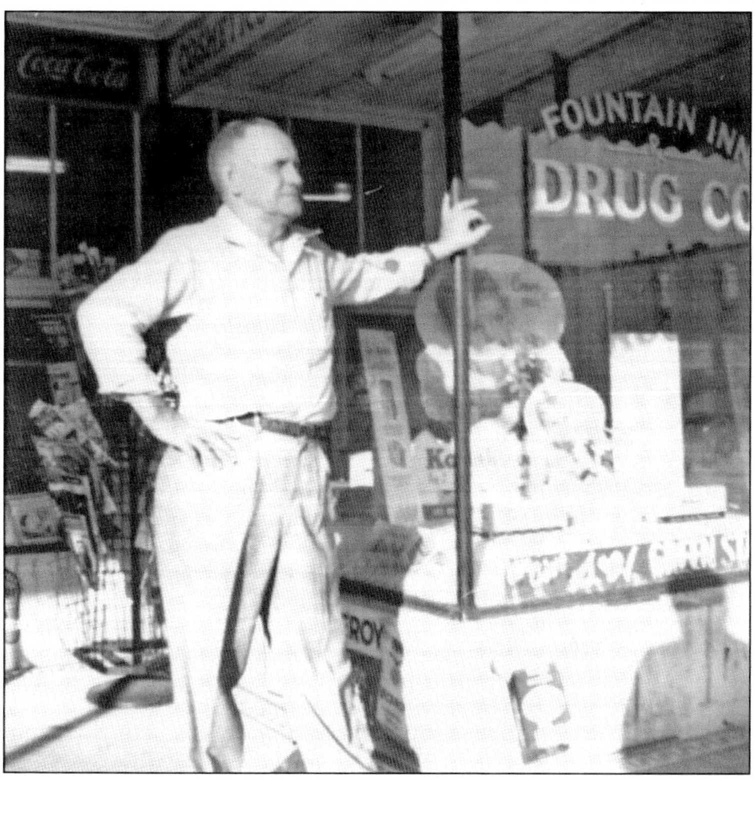

Peden McDowell was a fixture at the Fountain Inn Drug Store, where he worked many years for his brother-in-law, Dr. Jack Walton. Dr. Walton had purchased the store in 1936 when it was known as Reddick's Pharmacy. Dr. Walton was married to Minnie Lee McDowell. Peden's droll sense of humor, the soda fountain, and ice cream made the drugstore a favorite place for afternoon visiting. Tables in the back of the pharmacy had attached stools, and children delighted in twirling around on them. (Courtesy of the Charles Alberson family.)

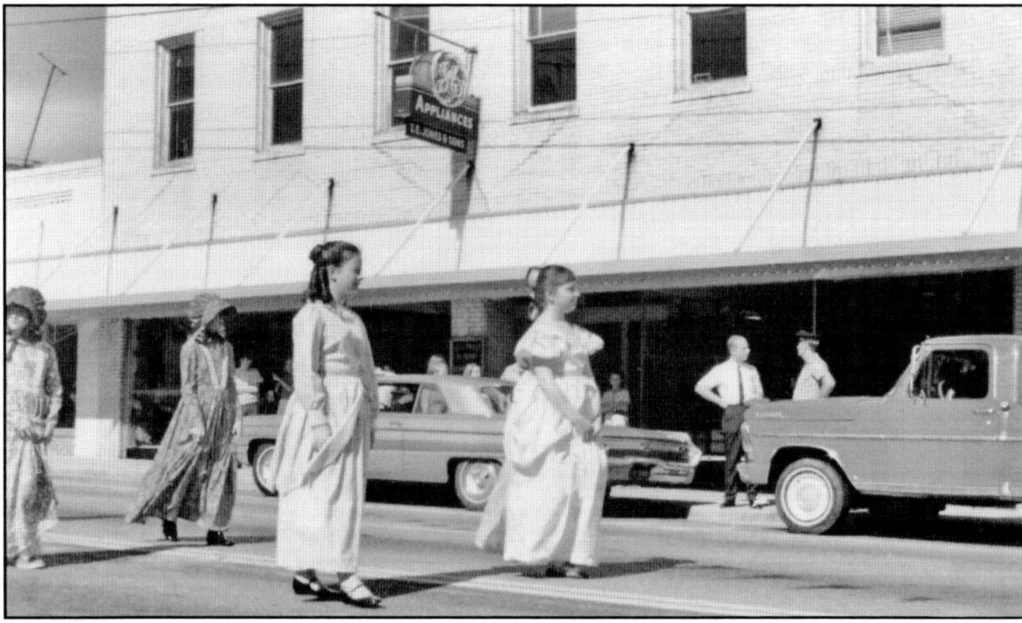

T.E. "Tom" Jones was born on a farm near Fountain Inn in 1870. A true entrepreneur with no formal business training, he began by selling clocks and sewing machines. He traveled throughout the county in a horse and buggy. Accumulating a fortune of $500, he opened his first furniture store in Fountain Inn in 1919. He married Lora Hughes and had nine children. They built a large brick home on Gulliver Street. Two sons, Conway and Paul, carried on the family stores. In 1966, the *Tribune* lists Conway's many accomplishments. He received his bachelor of science degree from Furman University in 1919 and in 1921 married Lilla Belle Howard of Simpsonville. They had three children, Virginia Ann, Conway Jefferson Jr. "Buddy," and Lilla Elaine. Conway is listed as chairman of the Emergency Relief Agency, chairman of the board of trustees of Greenville County Schools, chairman of planning for Hillcrest Hospital, president of South Greenville Fair Association, Citizen of the Year, member of the Southern Retail Furniture Association, American Marketing Congress director, deacon and trustee of First Baptist Church, Mason, charter member of the Rotary Club, and outstanding Rotarian. The large two-story store was located on North Main Street where the parking lot is now. There was a bench out front where older gentlemen could be seen discussing the news. The former Jones Store can be seen in the background of this picture of Horse and Buggy. (Above, courtesy of the Cannon family; below, courtesy of Elaine Jones Carver.)

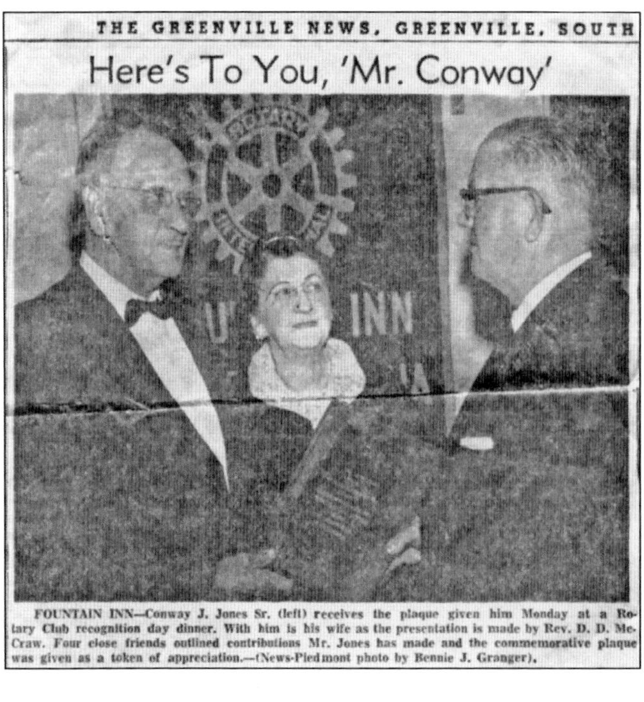
THE GREENVILLE NEWS, GREENVILLE, SOUTH

Here's To You, 'Mr. Conway'

FOUNTAIN INN—Conway J. Jones Sr. (left) receives the plaque given him Monday at a Rotary Club recognition day dinner. With him is his wife as the presentation is made by Rev. D. D. McCraw. Four close friends outlined contributions Mr. Jones has made and the commemorative plaque was given as a token of appreciation.—(News-Piedmont photo by Bennie J. Granger).

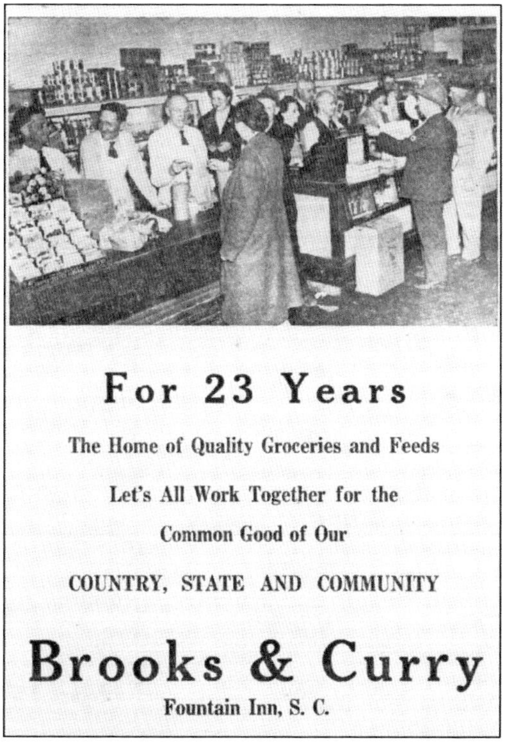

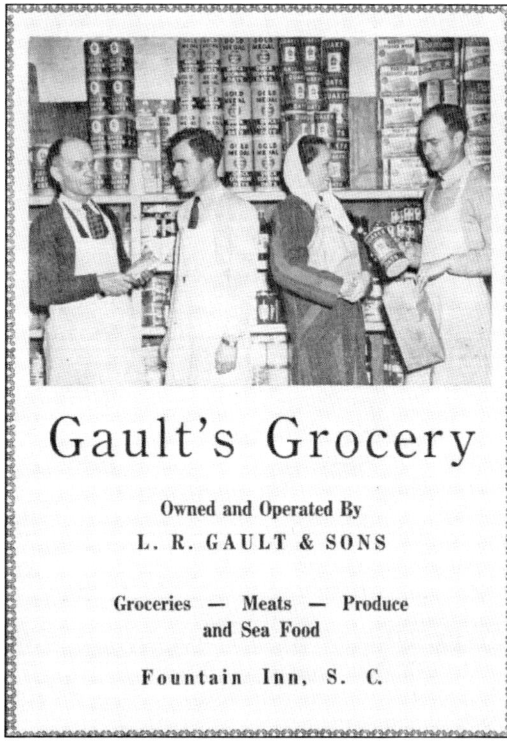

Brooks and Curry Grocery store was located on Main Street in the same block and on the same side as Given's Hardware and the White's Stores in the 1950s. Marvin and Warren Curry were owners. Later, it became Curry and Farrow. Shown here at Gault's Grocery, from left to right are Lester (father), Paul (son), a customer, and Sam (son). In 1953, they opened Gault's Clothiers on South Main Street. Paul became mayor of Fountain Inn in 1960 and served a total of 19 years.

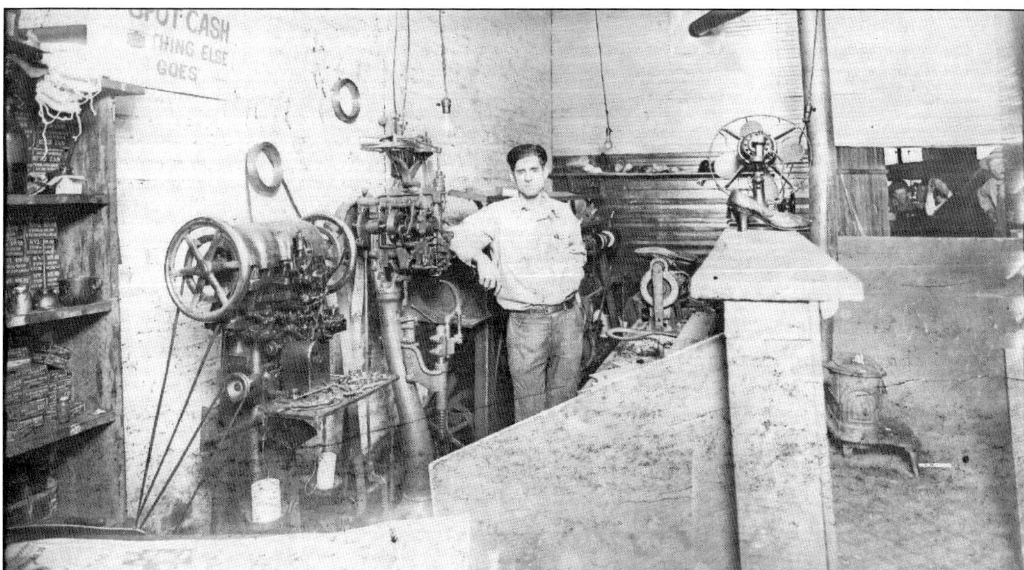

Clint Smith is pictured in his shoe repair shop on Main Street. Son Junior joined him after World War II. (Courtesy of Jayne Smith Thompson.)

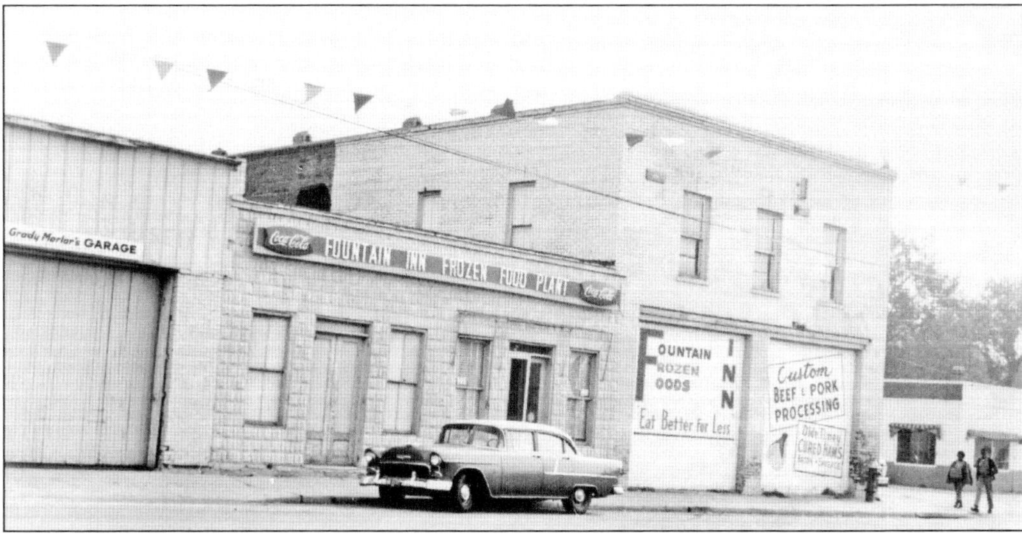

Fountain Inn Frozen Foods opened in 1944 at 117 South Main Street in the McKnight Buildings. It was a service to the community for cutting up meat, wrapping, and storage. Each family who rented storage had a key to go to their unit. There were no home freezers then, and the freezing compartments of family refrigerators were small. S.B. and Edna Thomason Rouse managed their business for 14 years. Above the Locker Plant, accessed by a flight of stairs that are still there, was the telephone switchboard operated by Janie Dodson, mother of Betty Jane Gault. Marlar Garage was located to the left, and that space is now a walk-through from the back parking lot to Main Street. Shown below standing in the Marlar Garage are Clint Smith, Grady Marlar, Willis Marlar, and Elbert Marlar. At one time, the fire truck was kept there. Later, when Willis Marlar opened a new garage, this space became Grady Marlar's Garage.

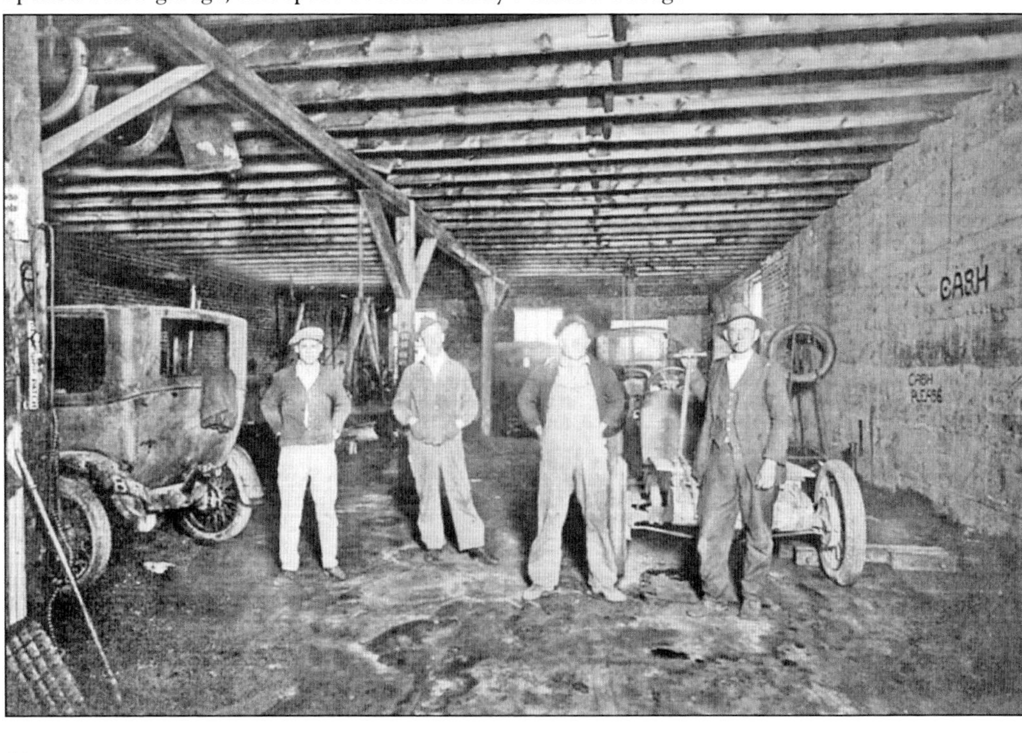

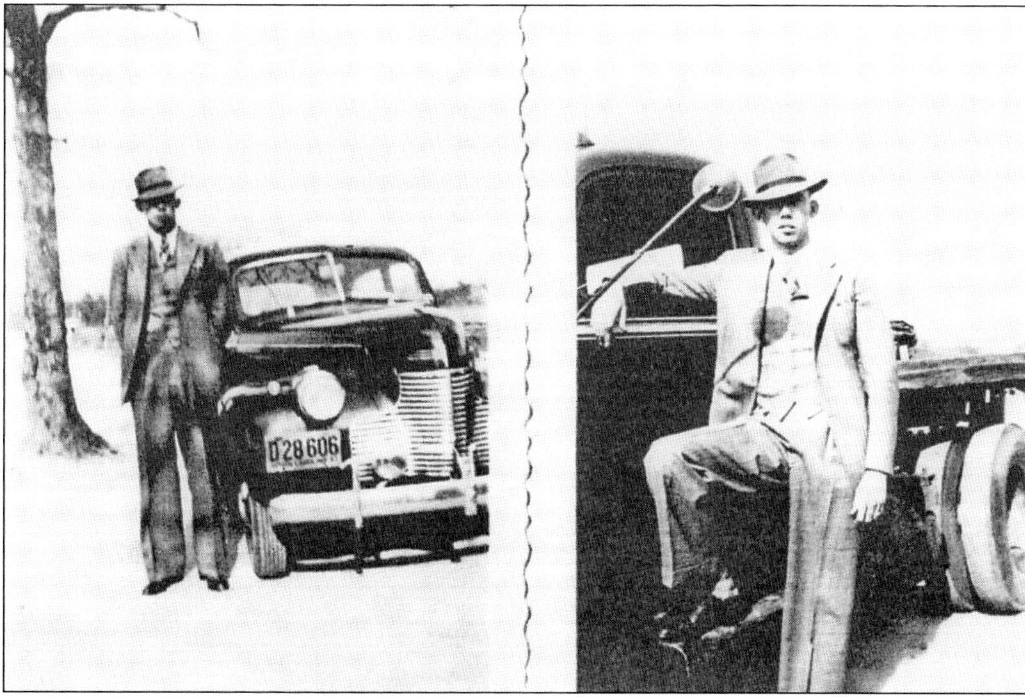

In 1931, David Hunter Garrett took over his family farm at 17 after his father, Tobe Hunter Garrett, passed away. He left high school since he had to help his mother run the farm. Gordon Garrett, David's third son and family historian, said his father told many stories of his life back then. Like much of the South, the fields were worn out from growing cotton and had ruts and gullies in them. He and his mother, May, got the farm back on a good basis and made what money they could during the Depression. (Courtesy of the D.H. Garrett family.)

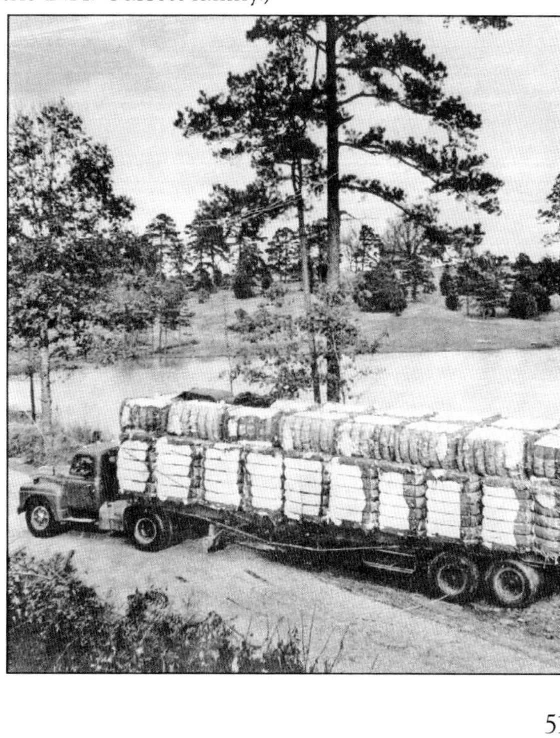

To earn extra money and fulfill a deep desire, David bought a truck and started David Garrett Hauling. He parked on Jones Street at the corner of Main Street. Janie Dodson, the telephone operator, was his unofficial dispatcher. Someone would call for David, and she would lean out the window and yell for him. In the early 1950s, David and Blake Garrett Sr. got together when Blake heard about house trailers used when the Savannah River Power Plant was being built. They planned to buy the trailers, haul them to Fountain Inn, and resell them. They went to George Wenck at the local bank for financing, and he became their partner. So was born Garrett, Wenck & Garrett. They sold mobile homes for several years. Later connections were made with Frank Outlaw, who founded Bi-Lo. (Courtesy of the D.H. Garrett family.)

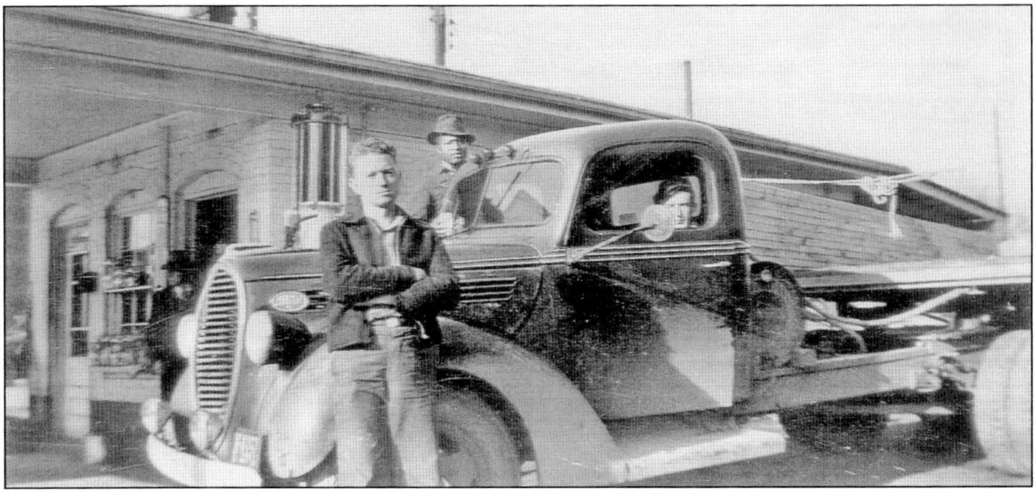

This is David H. Garrett's first truck, driven by his first employed driver "Tee" Thackston. They hauled fertilizer, cotton, sugar, and other commodities for neighbors and merchants. "Hack" Fowler is standing in front and Bud Bailey in back. By the early 1940s, David had two trucks. (Courtesy of Sarah Margaret Thackston.)

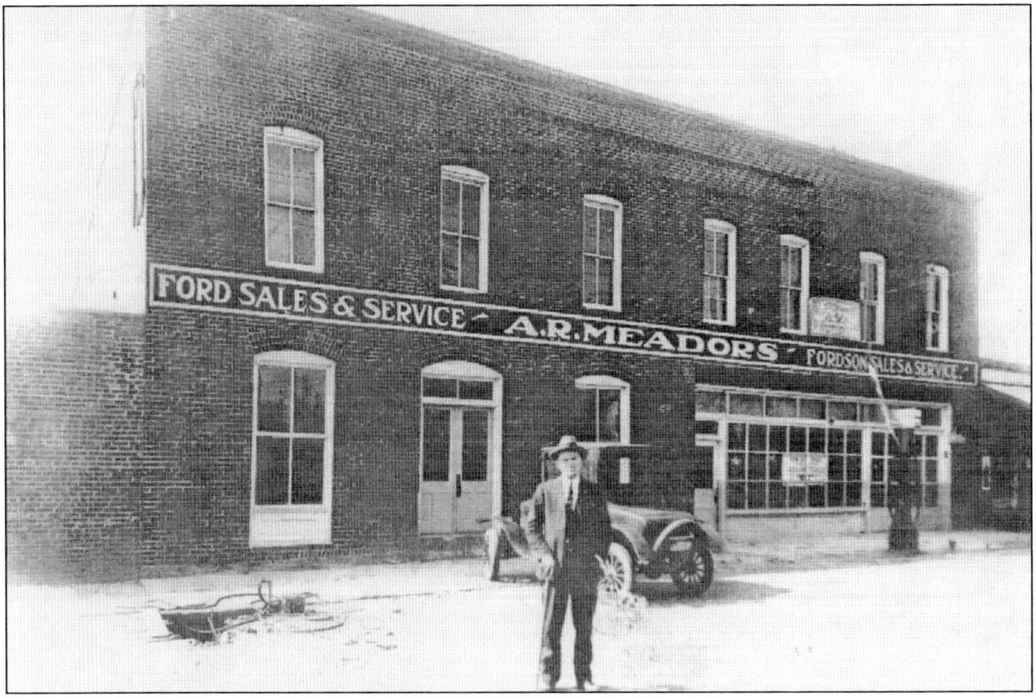

Two automobile dealerships were located in town on Main Street. In 1928, the Ford dealership on South Main Street was owned by A.R. Meadors. Later the Fountain Inn Motor Company was primarily a Ford dealership owned by the Berry Woods family. Berry and Grace Chamblee Woods were pillars of the First Baptist Church. The building is still on South Main Street. It has been renovated and is in use but not as a dealership. The Woods family lived then and now on Old Fairview Road just past the Sam Coleman family. The bridge is out, so the road is closed to through traffic. The Kellett family owned the Chevrolet dealership in the Kellett Building on the corner of Trade and South Main Streets.

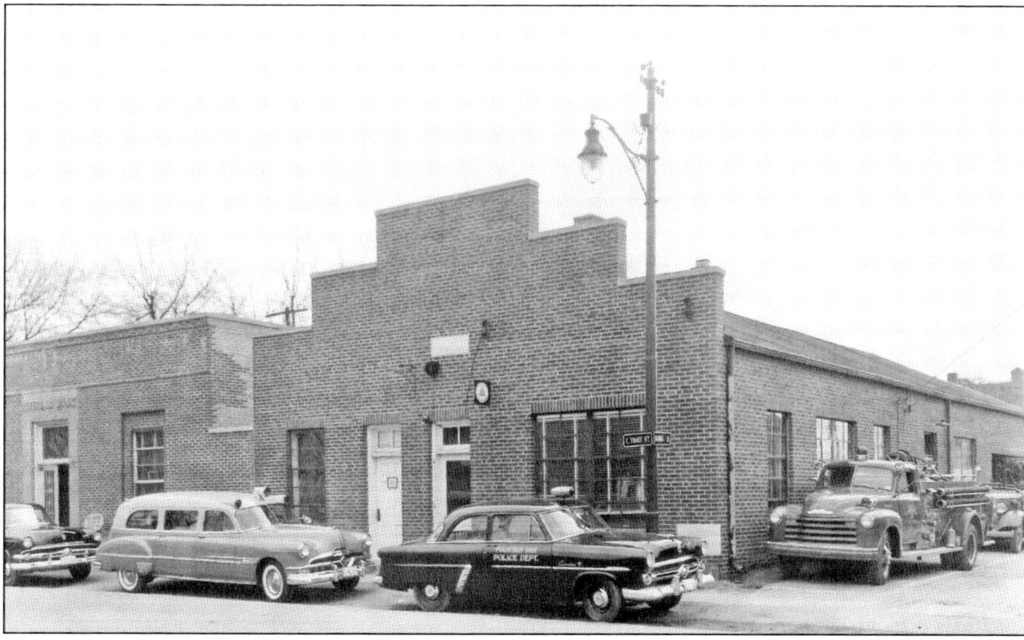

The photograph above shows Citizens Bank to the left, the library (white door), city hall, the police station, the jail, and a fire truck located at 107 Trade Street at Weston Street. In 1965, Lillian Karelitz and a group called Friends of the Library contacted the head of the local Beaunit Mills Plant. Lillian was able to secure a new library from the mill if the town provided the location. The Fulmer/Butler Garrett home was torn down and a new brick building constructed on the corner of North Main Street and Quillen Avenue. In later years, the city hall complex was located on North Main Street at the former home of Robert Quillen, and the fire department is on the site of the Frank Edwards home. The new library, contributed by resident Melvin Younts, is located on the grounds of the former Tom McGee home, next to the former Fountain Inn High School, now the Younts Center.

Gibb Armstrong (left) and James Earl Land (right) were two of Fountain Inn's favorite police chiefs. In the early days, the jail was a wooden building located on Trade and Depot Streets across from what is now the Fountain Inn Museum. There is a small empty lot there now, previously the location of Alberson's Coal Company. Later, a brick jail was built nearby.

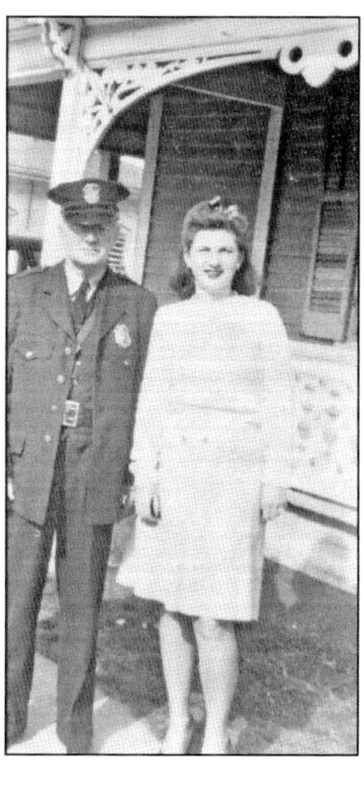

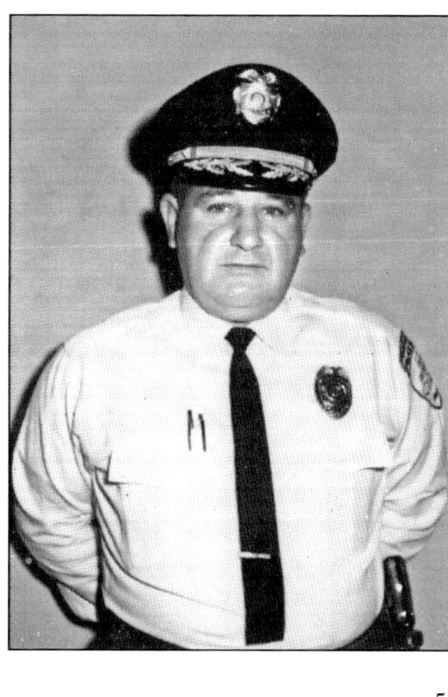

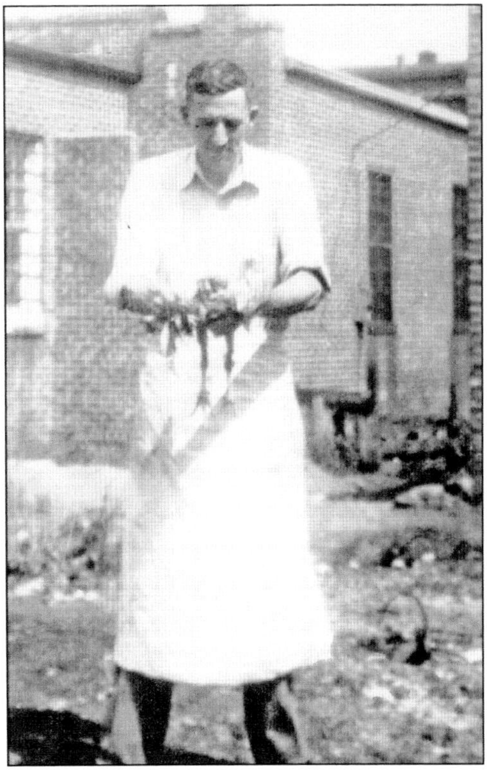

Ern Rodgers advertised his café at 105 North Main Street in the *Tribune* in 1928. In 1929, Robert Quillen lauded the café, saying it served between 500 and 600 people on Sunday and that it was modern and clean. In the 1950s, when Ern was older, it was a small restaurant. The authors can still picture his sister, Ethel Casey, her famous high heels clicking in through his door and ordering a hot dog after working at the post office.

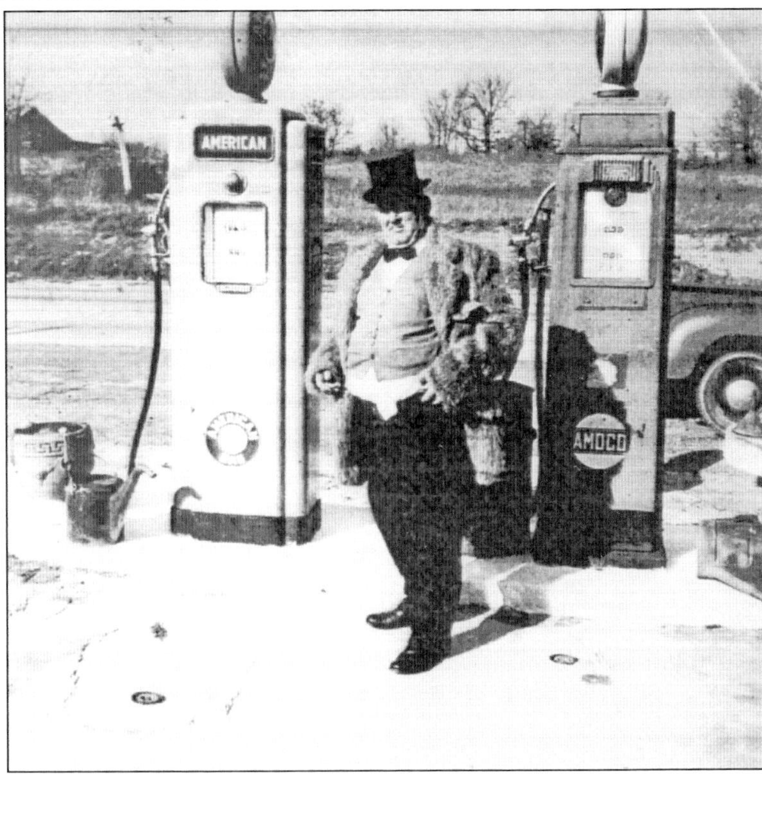

Lee Willis was a popular dealer of antiques or most anything one wanted to buy. At one time, he had businesses on various places on Main Street. He sold gas and had a restaurant. His final store was on North Main Street close to Howard Drive. His son, Tommy, was a talented artist and illustrated *The History of Fountain Inn.*

Susan Bowen's grandfather Wells Holland, son of R.B. Holland, owned and operated Holland's Restaurant, affectionately known as "Greasy Corner," from 1927 to 1969. Wells was known for the best roast pork sandwiches and hot dogs. Susan's grandmother Nettie Tumblin Holland made the famous pies and cakes served there. This building was destroyed by fire in 1971 and was torn down to make way for Rotary Park on the corner of South Main and Jones Street. Wells had three sons: Susan's father, Rev. Wells Daniel "Dan" Holland Sr., longtime city councilman Frank Holland, and Keaton Holland. Dan worked in the café until he left home to go to college. (Courtesy of Susan Bowen.)

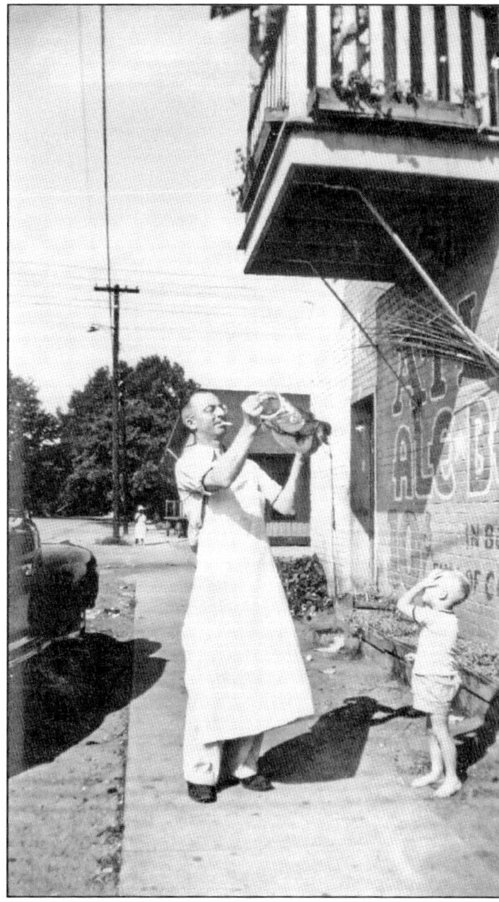

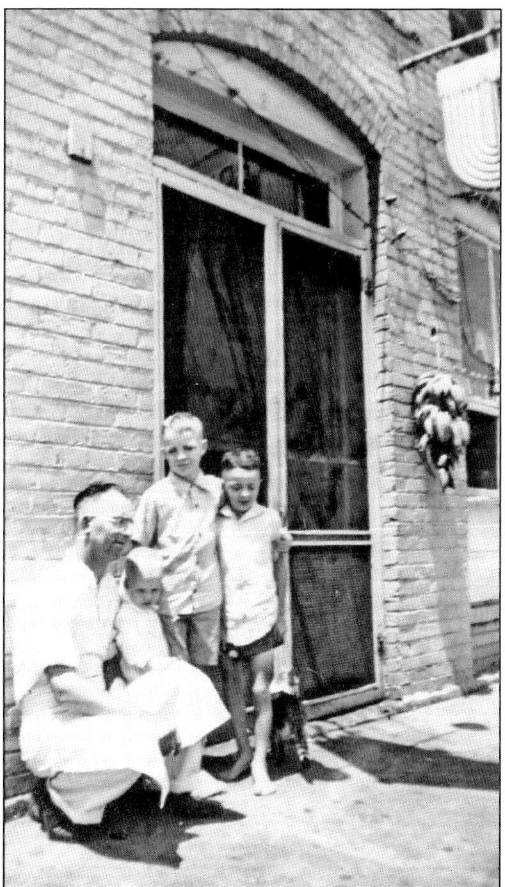

In the early days of the restaurant, the Holland family lived upstairs and rented several rooms out to boarders. In the above photograph, one can see the balcony and, in the background, the train depot. In 1942, they bought a house and 16 acres at 423 South Main Street but continued to rent the upstairs of the restaurant to boarders. Outside of the restaurant, Weldon "Wells" Holland sold produce and fireworks during the holidays. Susan Bowen has memories of going into the café as a child and filling her pockets with candy from the old-fashioned jars, as well as looking at all of the old Coke and Orange Crush coolers and signs, the old jukebox, and the stool where her daddy sat to cut onions for hot dogs. (Courtesy of Susan Bowen.)

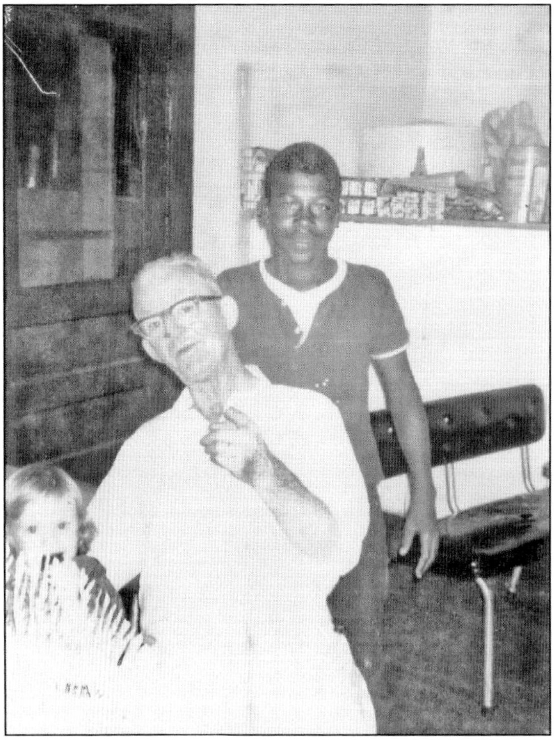

There are many stories of folks who came to the café. One of the most notable was Al Capone, who came through Fountain Inn with his bodyguards on their way to Florida. As the story went, Capone ordered a roast pork sandwich. After stating that it was the best he had ever had, he ordered a second one for the road. Another story involved the KKK coming into the café late one evening in full hooded attire. Wells Holland, hearing them coming, hid a black lady, Little Laura, who worked in the kitchen, so no harm would come to her. Pictured at left are Susan as a child, Wells, and Johnny Shell. (Courtesy of Susan Bowen.)

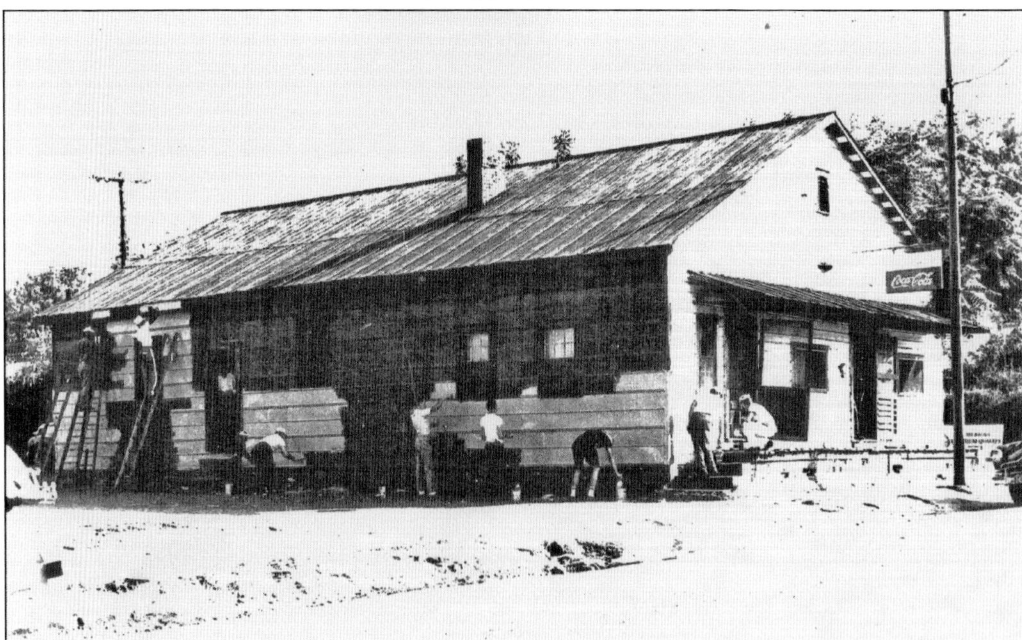

During segregation, the Dixie Café catered to the black folks in the area. It was located in town on the corner of South Weston and Jones Streets. On the weekends, it was quite a lively spot, with music playing and patrons having a good time. Several ladies have said that they were not allowed to go in there. It was a little raucous and not a place for good girls, so their fathers said. (Courtesy of Emmanuel Sullivan.)

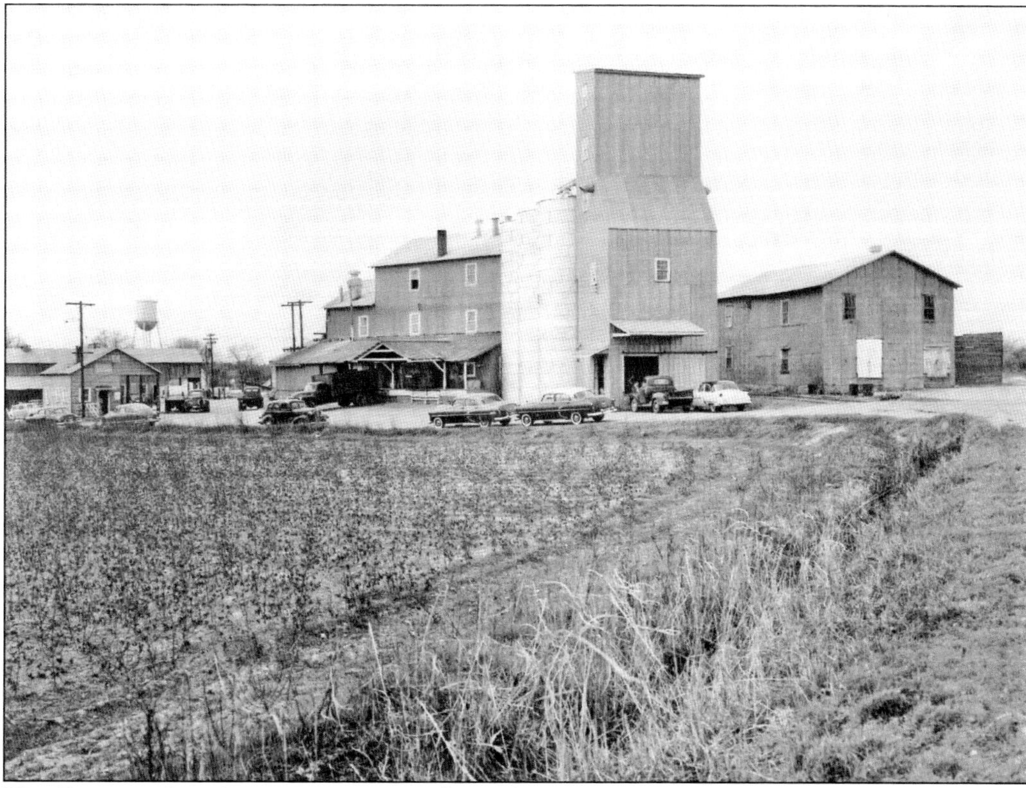

The Fountain Inn Ginning Company, shown here in 1950, was located on Wall Street across from the train depot. It was owned by Lacey Cooper and Charles Bell Sr. Charles Sr. married Lacey's daughter Louise. The milling company is also shown here. It was built in 1941 and was owned by F.G. Ellison. It was the only flour mill in Laurens or Greenville County. It made flour, ground cornmeal, and mixed feed.

Charles Young Garrett, born in 1884, was best known for his Pine Oil business. He did not manufacture this but purchased it in drums, bottled it, and shipped it to many states. This business began in Georgia in 1926, but C.Y. moved back home in 1932. At one time, he had 140 people working for him. Residents in their 60s, 70s, and 80s remember Pine Oil as a cure for all cuts, scrapes, insect bites, and infections. A bottle of Pine Oil is in the museum along with a walnut corner cupboard owned by C.Y. Garrett. It was willed to nephew Lloyd, who in turn left it to the museum. The cupboard was originally owned by the Pickeral family of the Bethany area, for which the famed Pickeral Hole and Pickeral Hole Farm (owned by the Shumate family) were named.

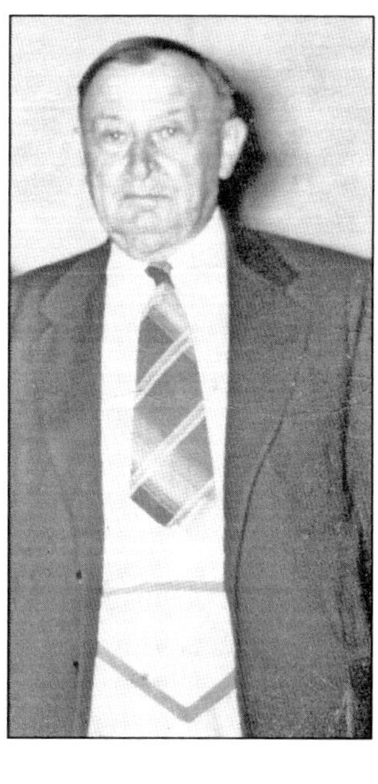

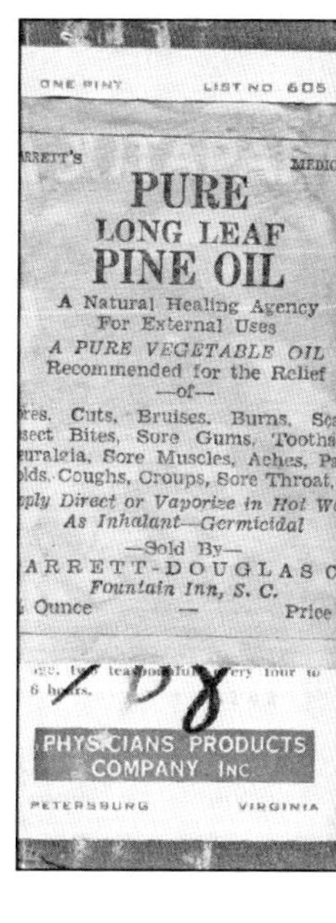

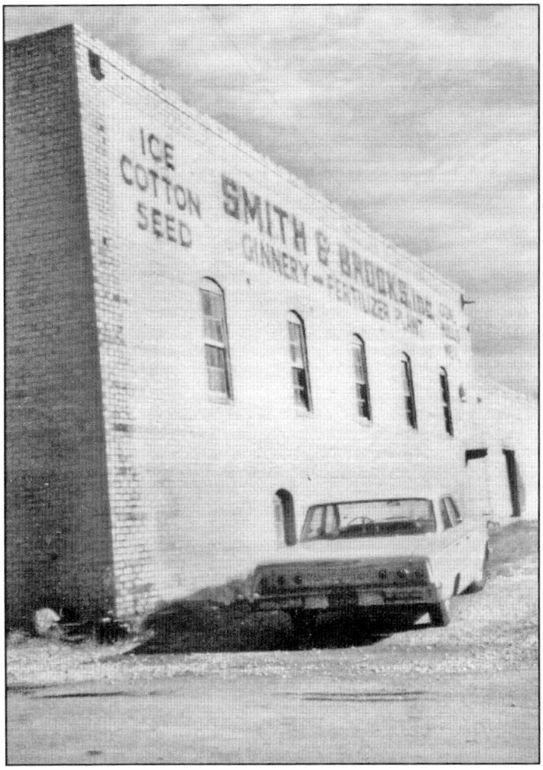

In 1891, Fountain Inn Oil Mill and Cotton Gin opened with five owners on South Main Street and Highway 418, where a shopping center and bank are now located. After the oil mill burned down, the cotton gin continued; it was reputed to be the second oldest in the state. T.D. Woods operated it for several years, then J.A. Barry became an owner. Barry's family lived on North Main Street. In 1946, newcomers from Lexington, North Carolina, Walter Smith and friend Stuart Rabb, purchased the business. They operated the business for 10 years. When Rabb retired, J.T. Brooks became a partner. It became Smith and Brooks. Coal, meal, hulls, fertilizer, and fuel oil were sold. When Walter Smith Sr. died in 1981, Walter "Buzzy" Smith Jr. closed most of the business. "King Cotton" was no more. There were very few farms left in the area that needed these services. (Courtesy of Buzzy Smith.)

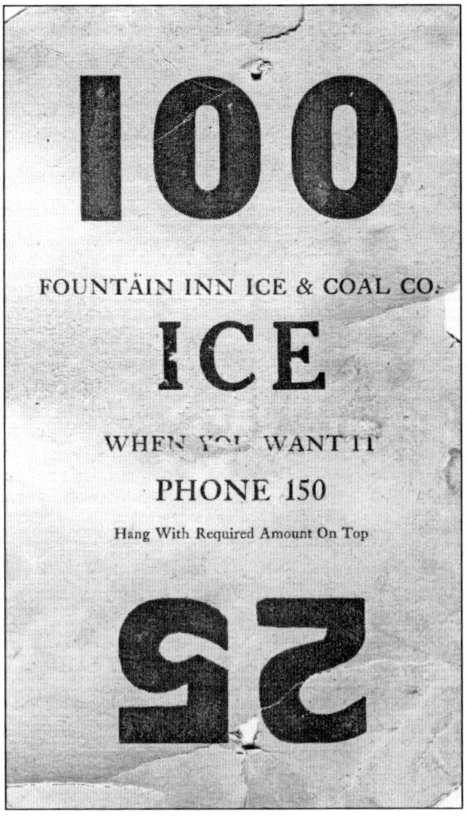
100

FOUNTAIN INN ICE & COAL CO.

ICE

WHEN YOU WANT IT

PHONE 150

Hang With Required Amount On Top

25

The ice plant and coal company were integral parts of the business. This tag was hung by customers on their door to designate how much ice should be left in their icebox. Later ice was provided to peach packing sheds. In the summer, many local folks brought their watermelons to the ice plant to be cooled for picnics. Coal was delivered to customers for their stoves or fireplaces. (Courtesy of Buzzy Smith and Randy Willis.)

Pictured in this 1950s newspaper clipping are employees Fred Sprouse and Raymond Hellams, farmer Frank Bobo, Walter Smith (co-owner of the gin), and Everette Bobo, Frank's son and a farmer from Gray Court. Everette's daughter, Rita, would marry the Smith family's cousin Stewart Garrett, whom she met at the Sprouse reunion at the American Legion Park. (Courtesy of Rita Bobo Garrett.)

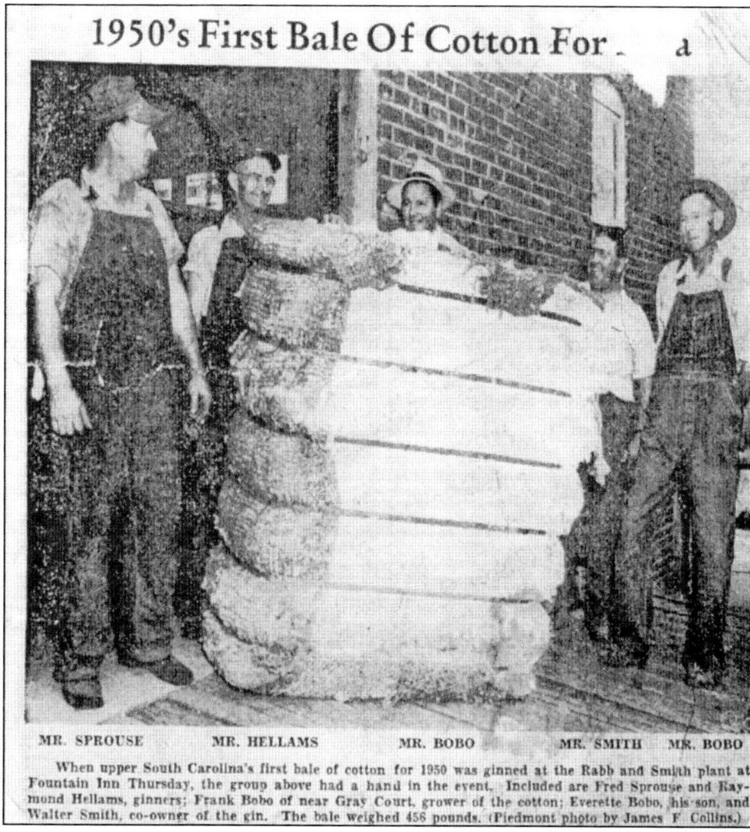

1950's First Bale Of Cotton For . a

MR. SPROUSE MR. HELLAMS MR. BOBO MR. SMITH MR. BOBO

When upper South Carolina's first bale of cotton for 1950 was ginned at the Rabb and Smith plant at Fountain Inn Thursday, the group above had a hand in the event. Included are Fred Sprouse and Raymond Hellams, ginners; Frank Bobo of near Gray Court, grower of the cotton; Everette Bobo, his son, and Walter Smith, co-owner of the gin. The bale weighed 456 pounds. (Piedmont photo by James F. Collins.)

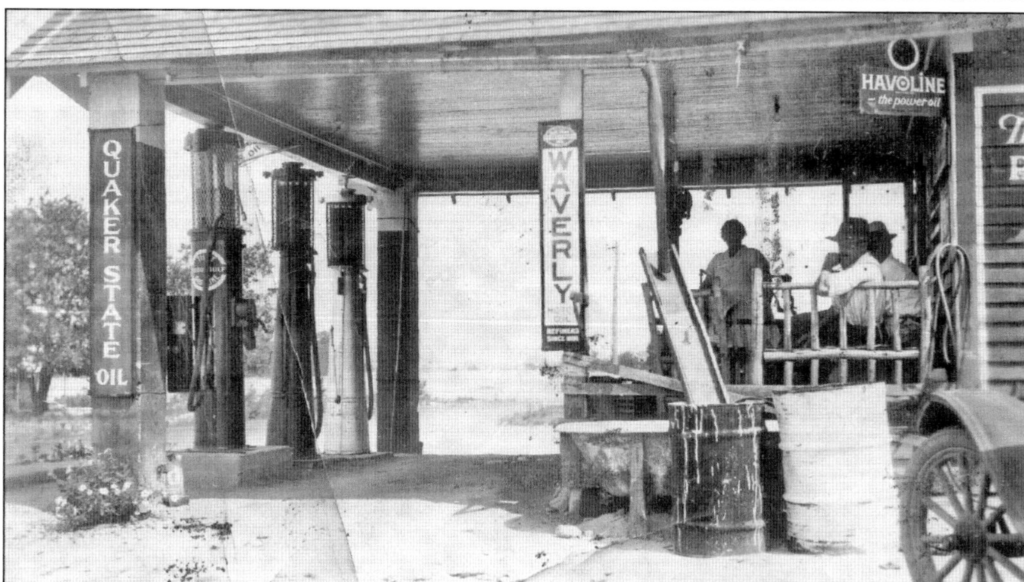

Jayne Smith Thompson tells that Jones Store was a Laurens County voting precinct. The store was located beside the Jones home on the old road from Fountain Inn to Owings and Gray Court. Glenn Stoddard lives in the Jones home now. Marion Jones married Junior Smith, the older son of Clint and Lula Smith. Jayne is the daughter of Junior and Marion. (Courtesy of Jayne Smith Thompson.)

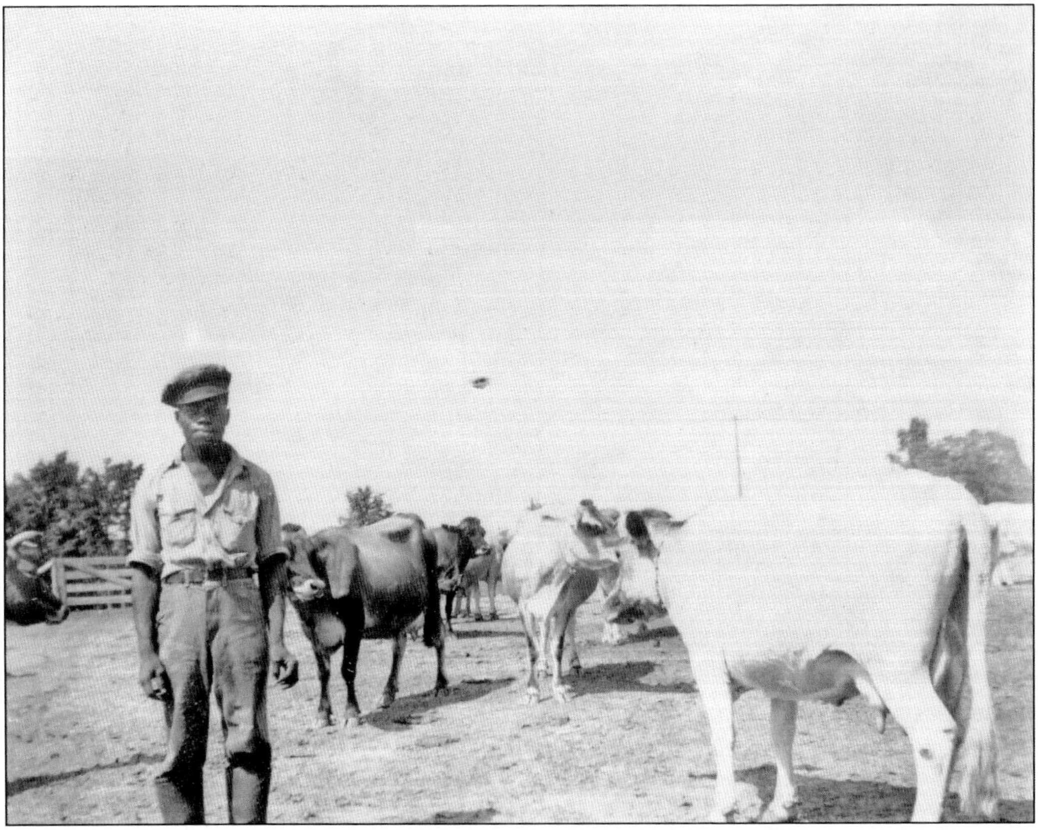

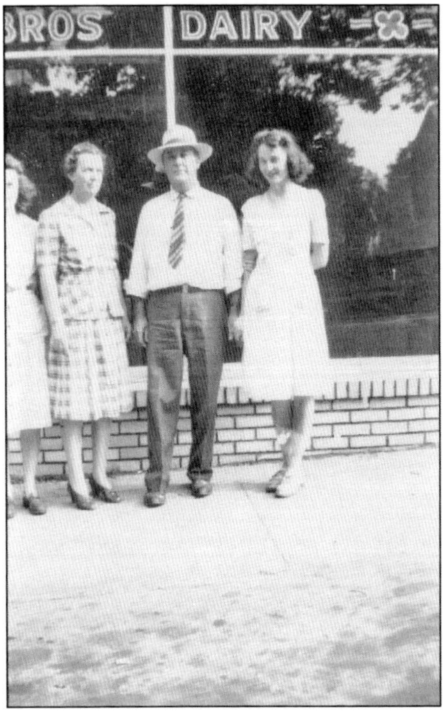

The Leake Dairy farm was located north of Fountain Inn. The store was located on Pendleton Street in Greenville. Frank Leake Sr. was married to Allene Culbertson. They had one son, Frank Jr., who carried on the business. Soybeans were grown on the farm in the 1950s. Frank Jr. married June Harrison. The Harrison family were large landowners in the Upcountry with an interesting, extensive history. Harrison Bridge Road is named for them. In the left photograph, from left to right are an unidentified employee, Allene, Frank Leake Sr., and another unidentified employee. (Both, courtesy of Mike and Carol Leake.)

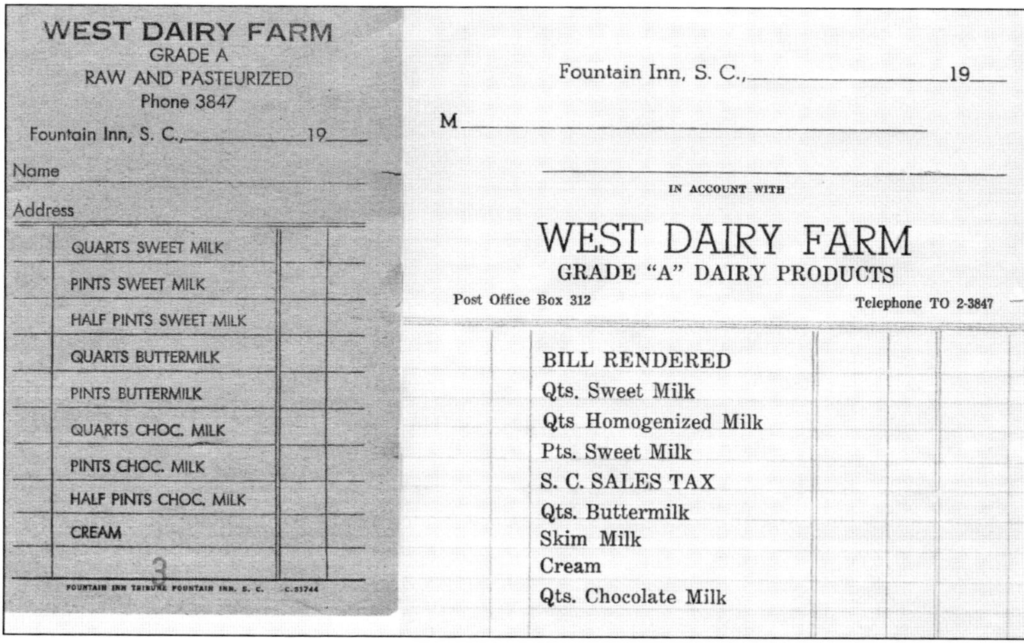
WEST DAIRY FARM
GRADE A
RAW AND PASTEURIZED
Phone 3847
Fountain Inn, S. C.,________19____
Name
Address
QUARTS SWEET MILK
PINTS SWEET MILK
HALF PINTS SWEET MILK
QUARTS BUTTERMILK
PINTS BUTTERMILK
QUARTS CHOC. MILK
PINTS CHOC. MILK
HALF PINTS CHOC. MILK
CREAM

Fountain Inn, S. C.,________19____
M________
IN ACCOUNT WITH
WEST DAIRY FARM
GRADE "A" DAIRY PRODUCTS
Post Office Box 312 Telephone TO 2-3847
BILL RENDERED
Qts. Sweet Milk
Qts Homogenized Milk
Pts. Sweet Milk
S. C. SALES TAX
Qts. Buttermilk
Skim Milk
Cream
Qts. Chocolate Milk

West Dairy was owned by Bob West. It was located off Howard Drive. Bob was related to the Leake family and later sold his business to the Leakes, working for them as a salesman. Bob provided door-to-door service to Fountain Inn and Simpsonville for many years. His sons, Floyd and Jack, worked with him as youngsters. Bob maintained a log book that was used to keep account of all of the customers, a receipt pad for orders, and calendars given to customers. Bob's wife, Dahlia, had come to Simpsonville from Georgia as a teacher and taught for many years in the school system. She was an avid antique collector. (Both, courtesy of Floyd and Jack West.)

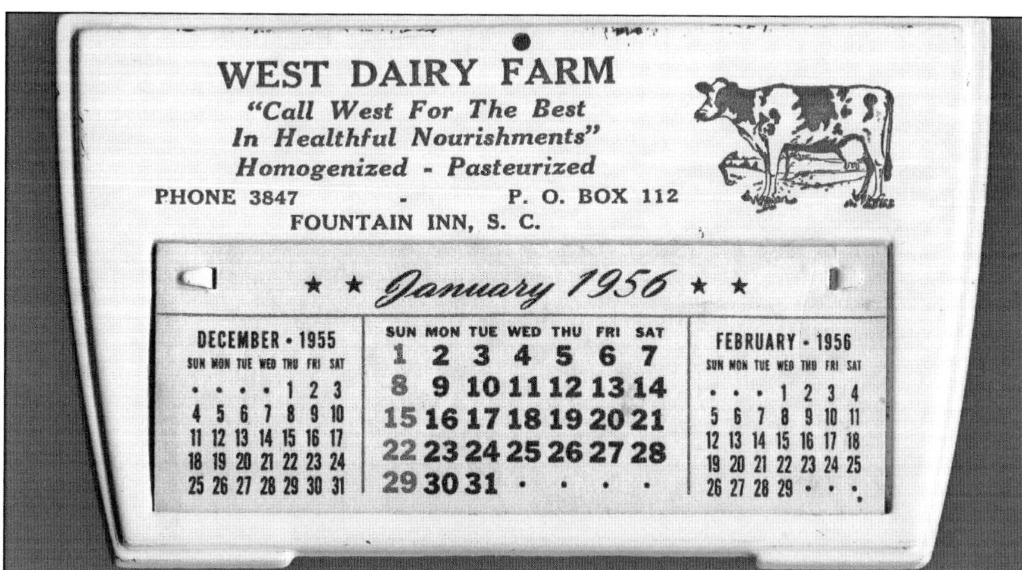

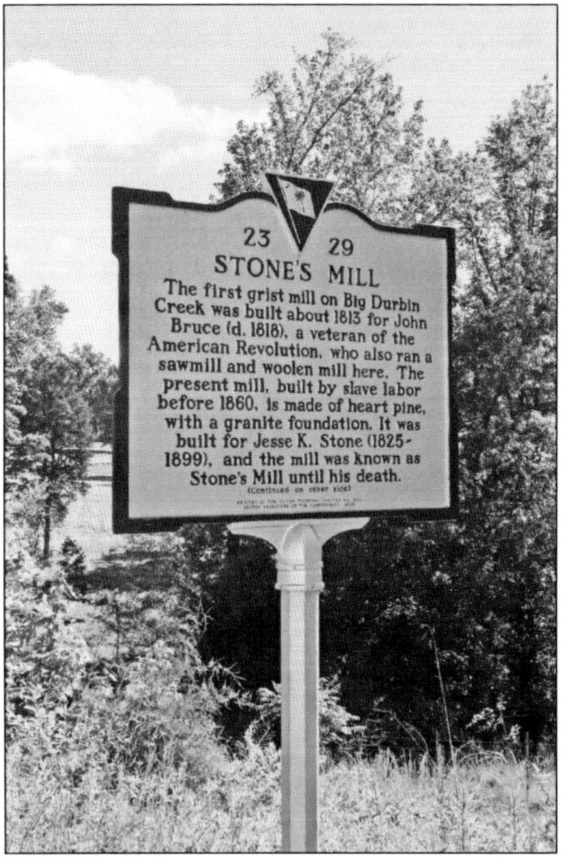

The markers tell the story of this mill. The Stone family that owned the first mill lived on Fairview Road in Simpsonville on what was later Sheriff Bob Martin's property. The mill is now known as Jones Mill and is owned by Charlie Garrett. Another mill was Nash's Mill on the creek between Fairview and Beulah. There was also a covered bridge over the creek. (Left, courtesy of Ron Urso.)

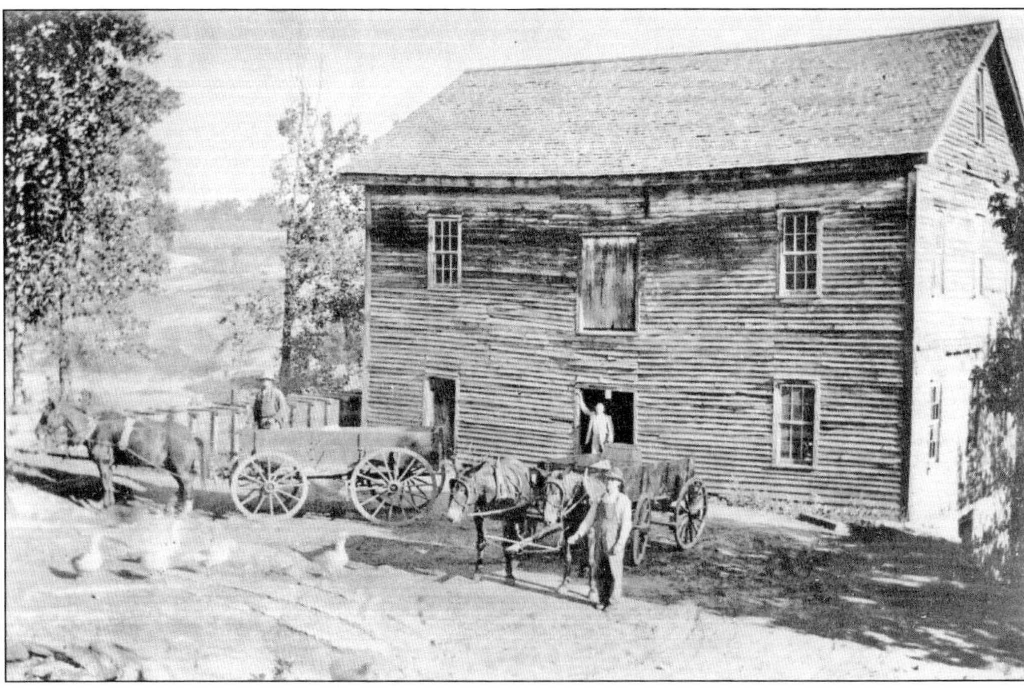

Four

The Oldest Town Community

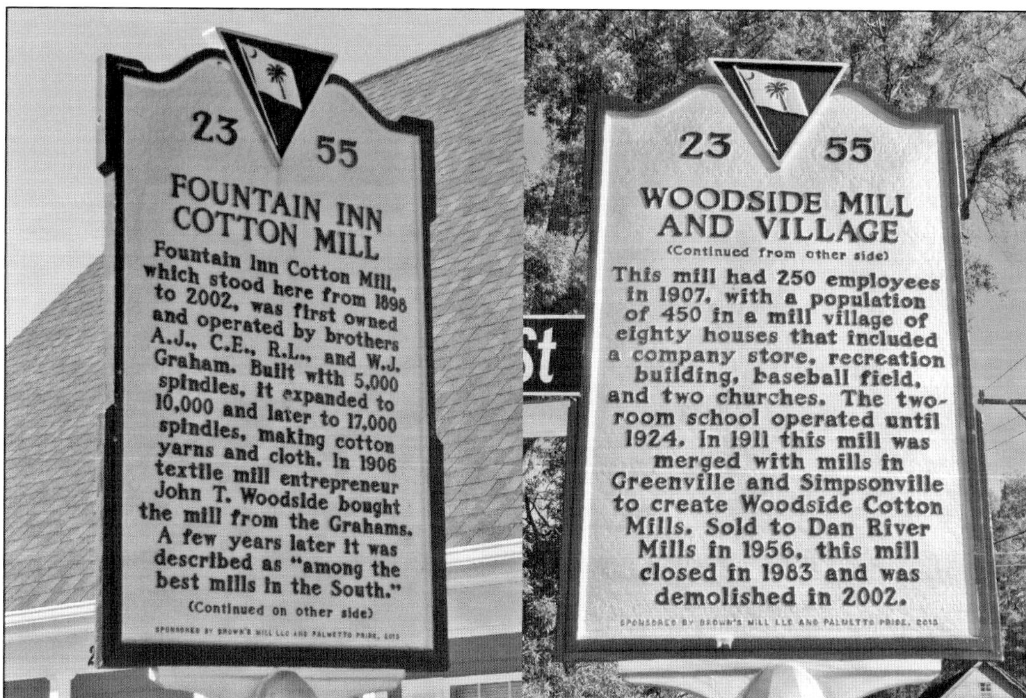

The Fountain Inn Manufacturing Company was originally owned by the Graham family, then sold to the Woodside family. John T. Woodside, a 1906 owner, had close ties to Fairview Presbyterian Church. His parents were members before his mother helped to found Lickville Presbyterian Church, closer to their home near the Augusta Road, in 1882. John T. and many of his brothers and sisters were baptized at Fairview. (Courtesy of Ron Urso.)

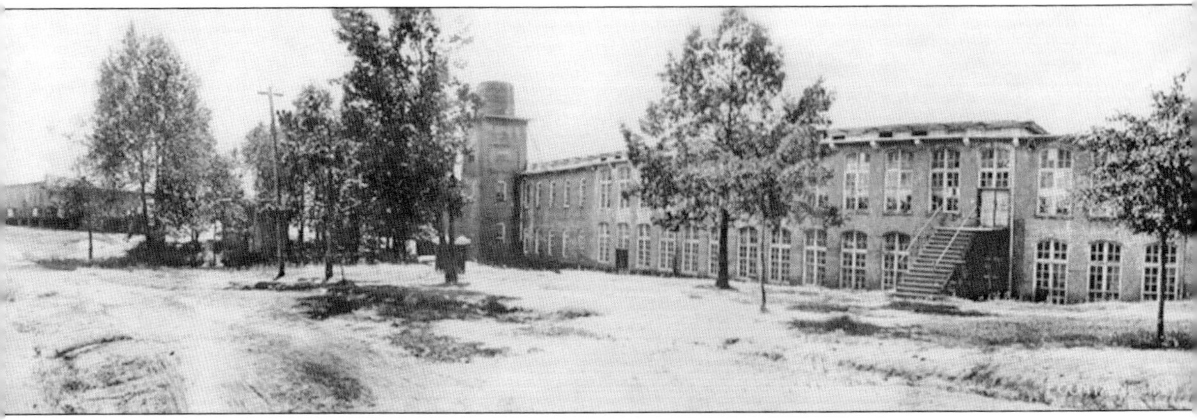

According to the 1999 Historic Resources Survey of Fountain Inn for the Greenville County Planning Commission, the Fountain Inn mill village was unique. Built in 1910 with 67 homes, both single family and duplex, it was near town and did not need a company store. People shopped in Fountain Inn. However, a school existed for a while on the property where the Wesleyan Church is now located, and the remnants of a swimming pool are still there. Sadly, the historic mill with its handmade bricks was demolished in 2002, but mill homes have been saved. Archie Huff Jr. in his book on Greenville describes the rise and fall of the cotton mills and the life of the mill worker. (Both, courtesy of Marshall Williams.)

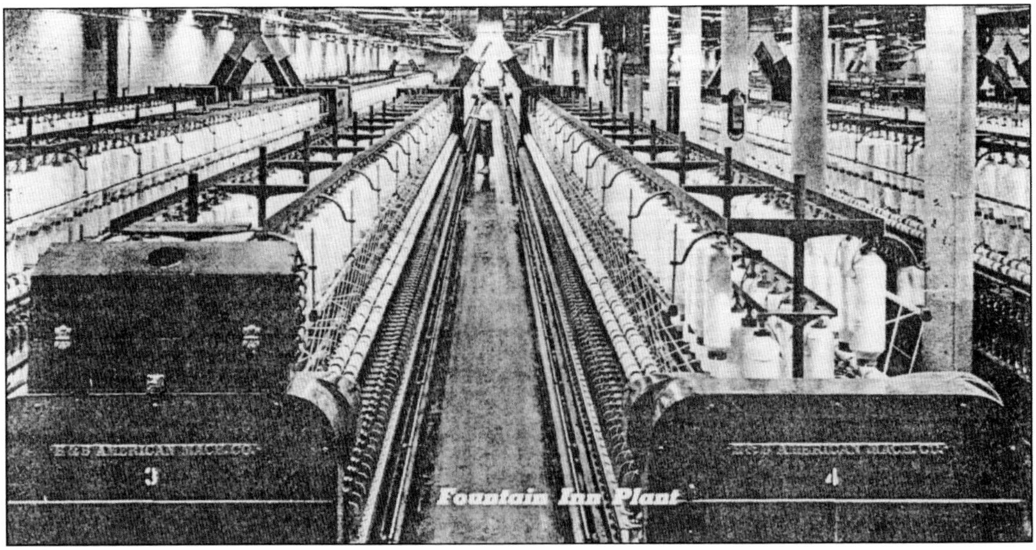

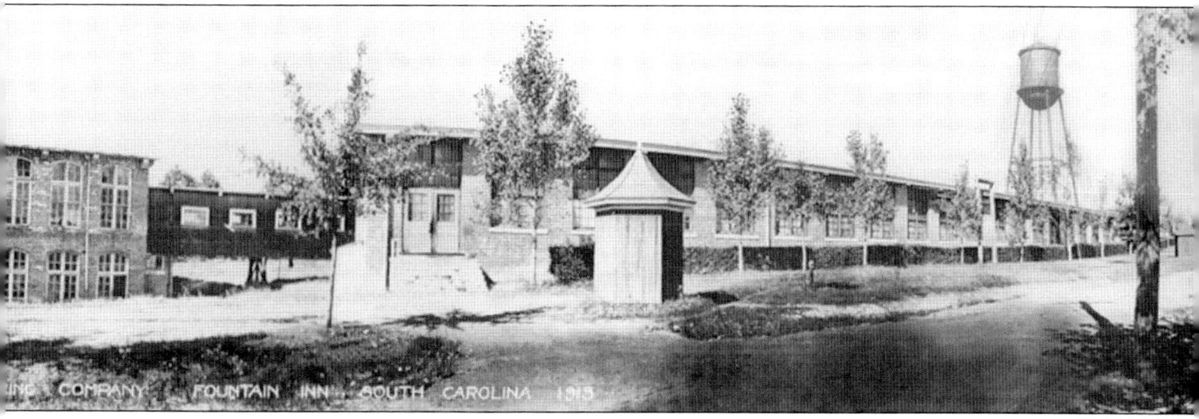

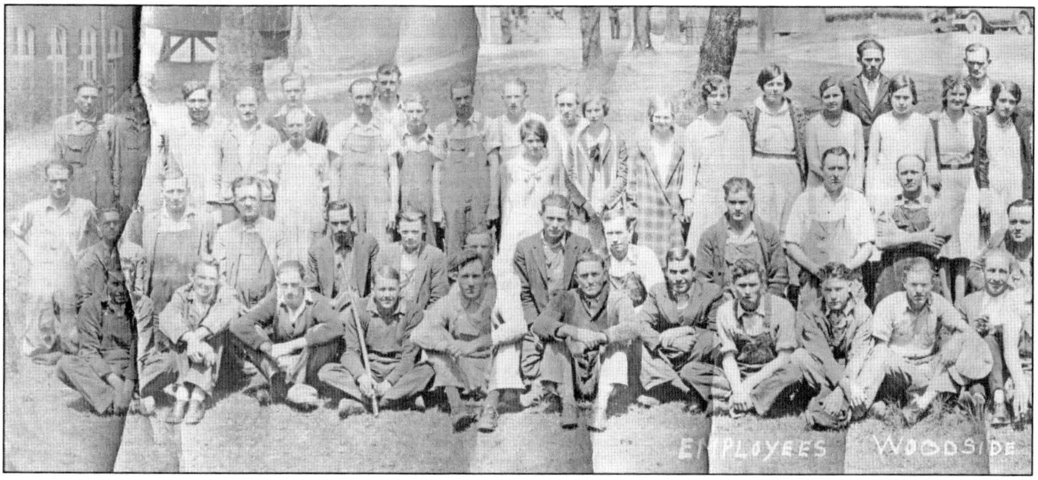

Employees of the Woodside Mill and their families lived in the mill village in Fountain Inn. These photographs are from April 1931. (Both, courtesy of Marshall Williams.)

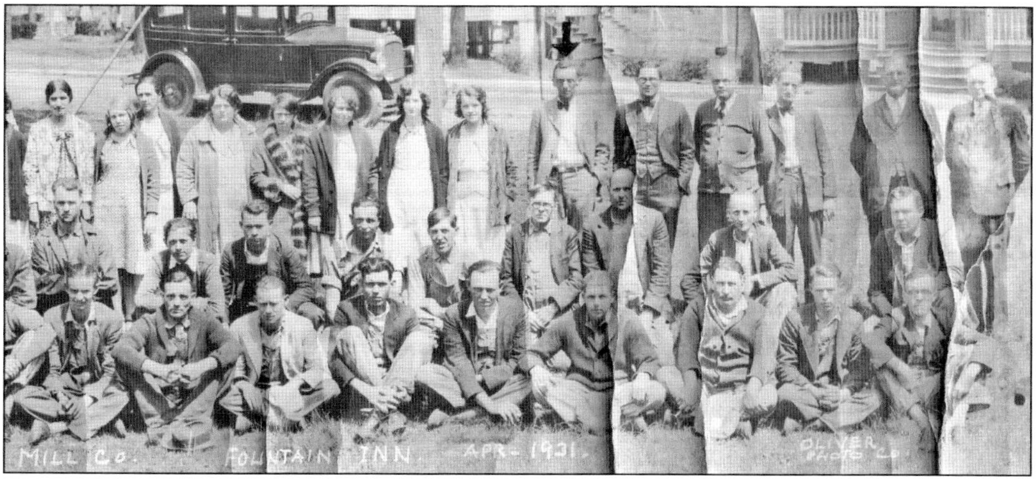

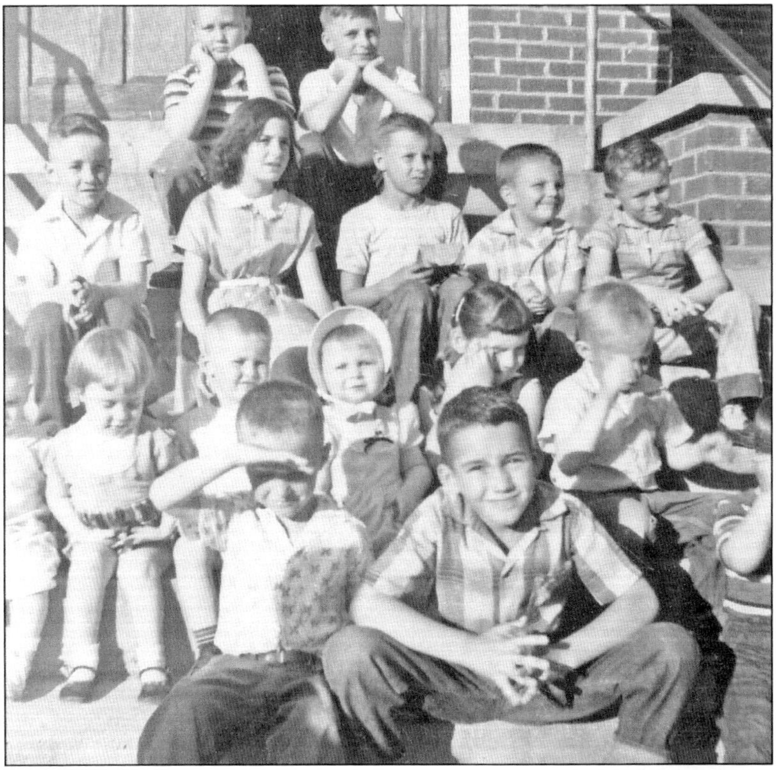

In April 1957, a group of children is seen sitting on the steps of the Wesleyan Church in the mill village. The church was founded in 1916. (Courtesy of Matt Smith.)

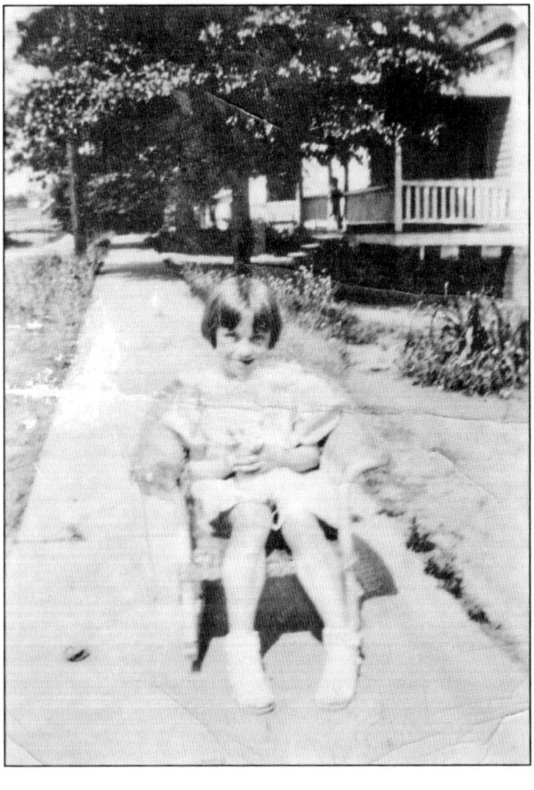

Bobbie Davis, daughter of Harvey Davis, a supervisor at Woodside Mill, is shown in front of the first mill house on Fairview Street next to the old mill. (Courtesy of Peggy White Nickson and Bobbie Davis Wilson.)

Charlie C. Ellisor, Chuck Ellisor's grandfather, opened the Mill Store in the middle 1920s on the corner of Fairview Street and Woodside Avenue. It was a community store but never owned by the mill. People could buy dry goods and groceries on credit and pay Ellisor on pay day. When the Depression hit, Ellisor lost his money and goods were auctioned off, even the receivables. He still ran the store after the Depression. Ellisor died in 1945. After World War II, Chuck's father purchased the store back with money from the GI bill. His mother, Viola (1898–1970) continued running the store. By that time, it had become more of a café. "Granny Viola" made hot dogs with chili, of course, and hamburgers and fries. Their trade secret recipe used leftover coffee in the chili. Chuck's father discovered this one day when the water was frozen. In 1962, Granny retired, a beloved and well-known figure. Chuck's father and family moved back in 1960 to the big house to take care of her. James Earl Land ran the restaurant for a while. In 1992, Chuck received the property from his father, and in 2015, he gave it to his sons, Chris and J.B. (Both, courtesy of Chuck Ellisor.)

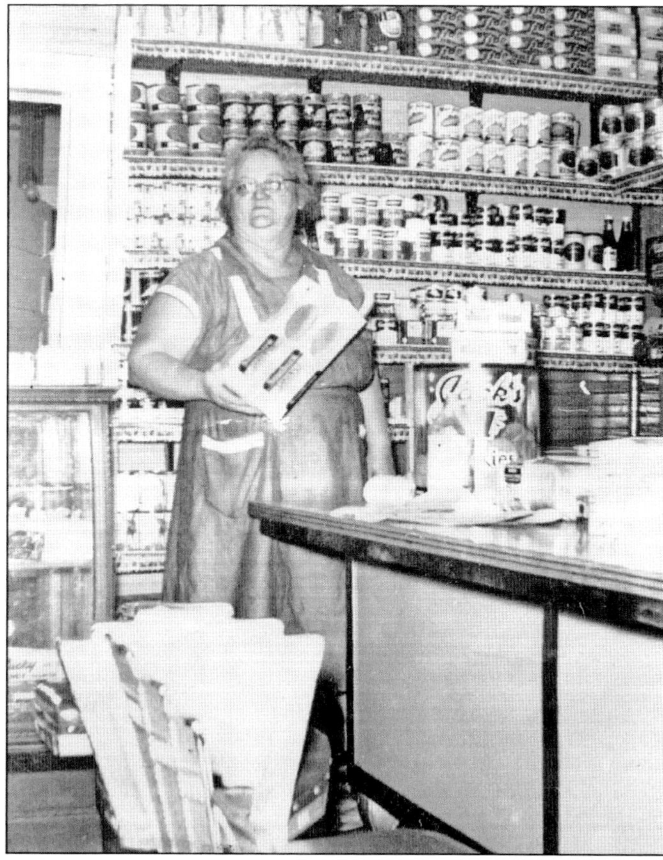

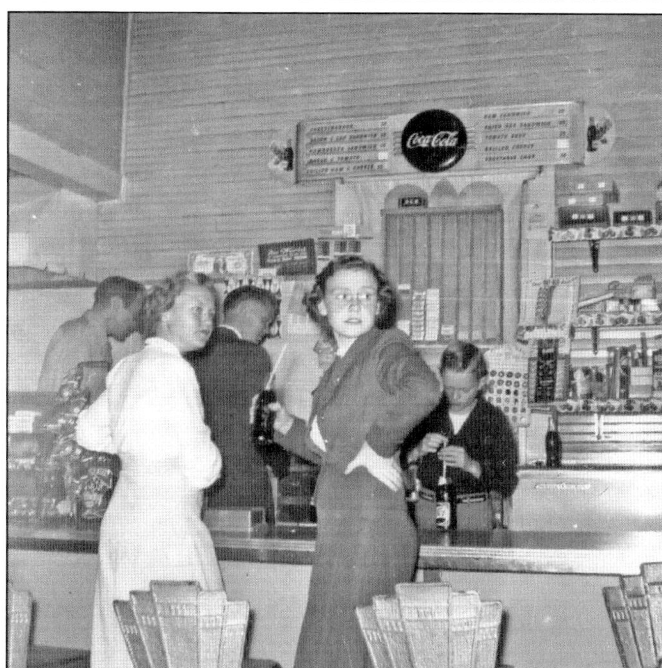

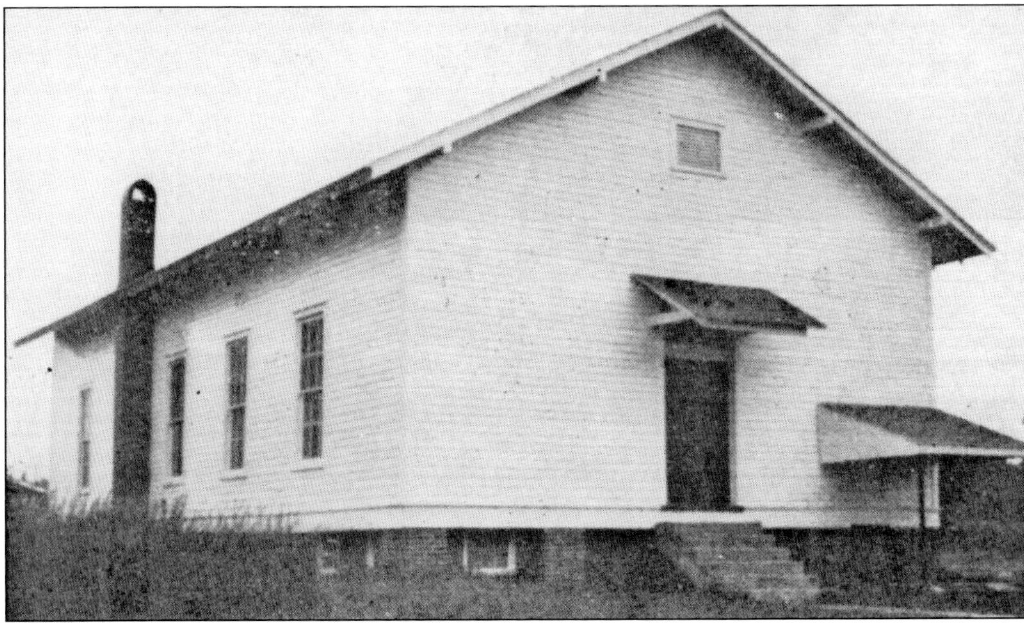

The Fountain Inn Wesleyan Methodist Church was started as a tent revival in 1916 by Rev. J.M. Hames, a holiness evangelist of the Wesleyan Methodist denomination. The first building was probably a large barn located behind the mill superintendent's home on Fairview Street, provided by the Woodside Mill owners. Rev. D.O. Powers was the first pastor. The barn became the mill community center when the present church was built on Church Street, now Woodside Avenue. There was a swimming pool by the church. Remnants are still there. In 1938, Woodside Mill deeded the church building to the trustees for $1. In 2016, the centennial celebration was held. (Courtesy of Matt Smith.)

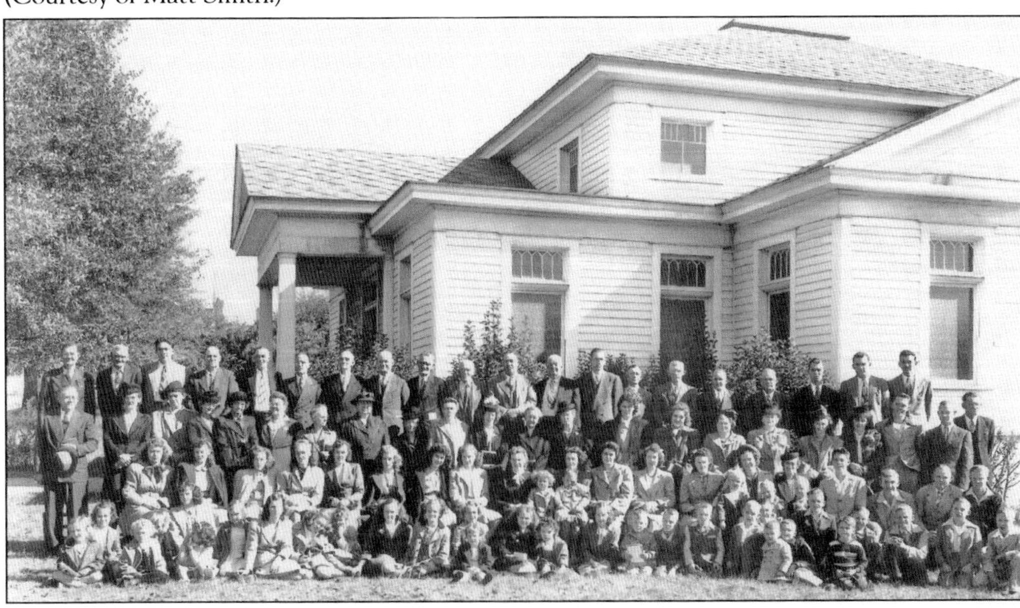

The Second Baptist Church had joint services until 1919 with the Fountain Inn Wesleyan Methodist Church. The Baptists relocated to a frame building on Fairview Street. A fire destroyed the building in 1947. The present building, now another church, was constructed in 1948.

Five

Town Churches and Cemeteries

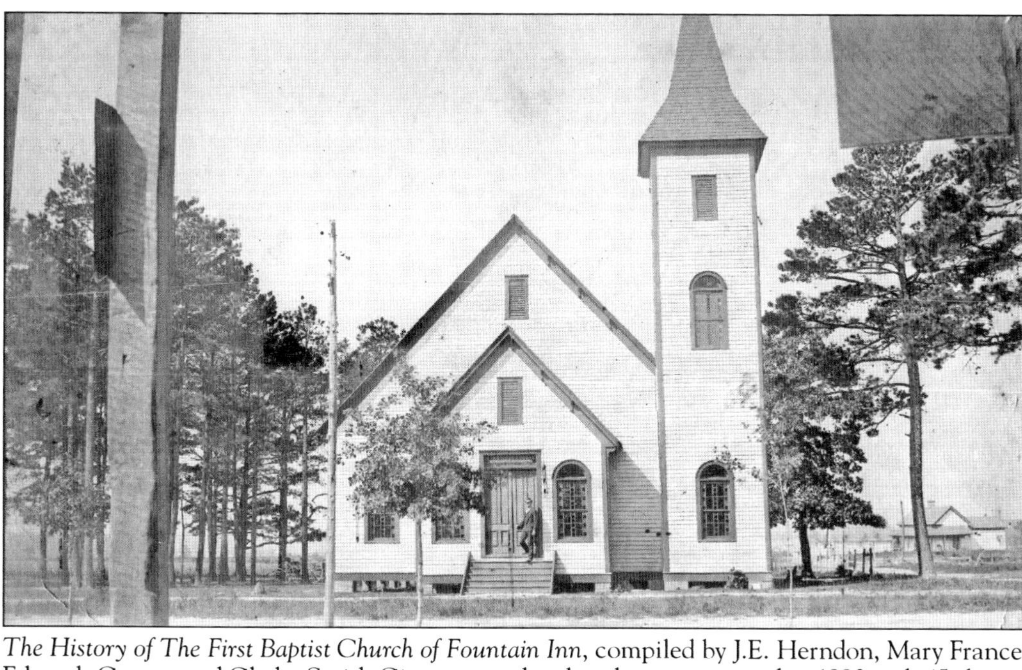

The History of The First Baptist Church of Fountain Inn, compiled by J.E. Herndon, Mary Frances Edwards Garrett and Gladys Smith Givens, says the church was organized in 1880 with 45 charter members. It is the oldest church in town. The Jones, Simmons, Howard, Vaughan, McGee, Nelson, Wood, Long, Sloan, Winn, Garrett, Stroud, Bramlett, Gary, and Calton families made up the membership.

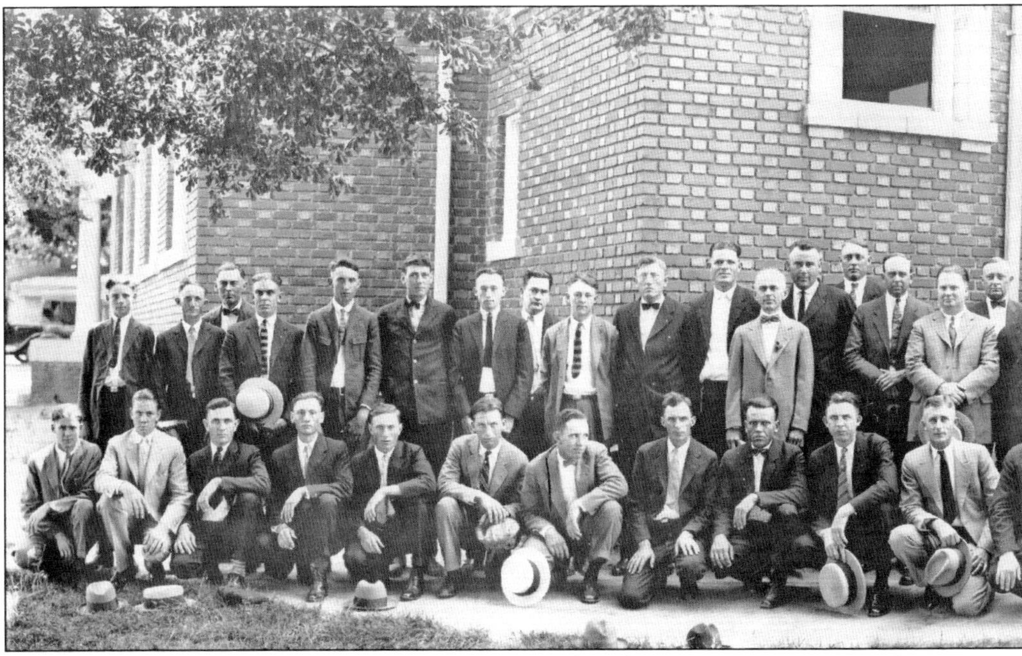

It is interesting to note that under the First Baptist Church government, "any member engaging in dancing or an amusement leading to the dancing Step, or card playing will be called to account for such conduct." Also "we cannot tolerate the practice of distillation and vending ardent spirits, except for medical purposes." The first meeting place was the Masonic Building behind Main Street, bounded by what is now Depot Street and the railroad. In 1892, a new building was constructed on the corner of Main and Fairview Streets. Worship continued in this building until about 1910, when the old frame building was moved to the present site of the church on Hellams and Weston Streets. In 1919, the first brick church was built on that site.

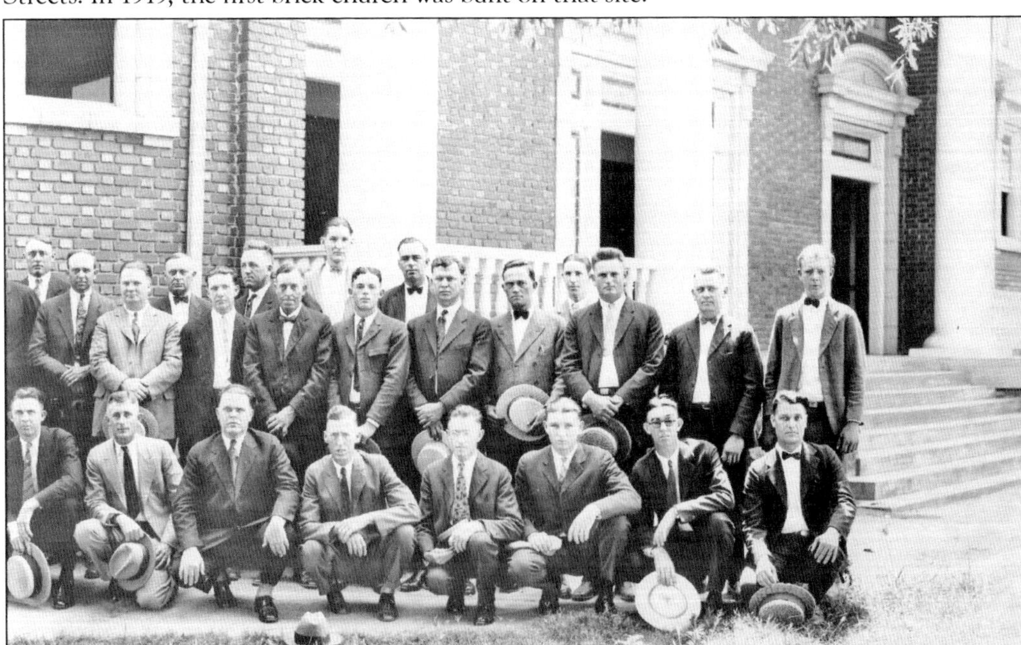

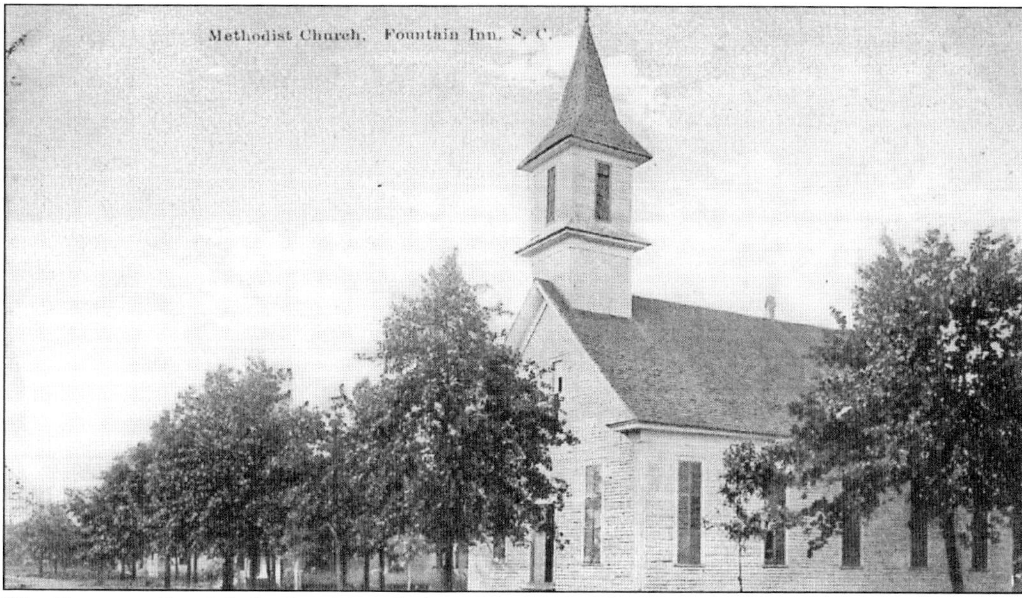

The Fountain Inn Methodist Church (now Trinity Methodist) was organized in 1887. Services were held on Main Street. The first church was erected on South Weston Street in 1888–1889 on land given by J.I. West and J.A. Cannon. Longtime member J.T. Brooks described the church with white clapboard siding, a steeple, and a bell tower. A large wood stove in the center of the building sat in a sandbox. Some of the men would sit close enough to use the box as the spittoon. On the opposite sides of the church, there were two benches along the walls. One side was for the choir; the other was the "Amen" corner. Early families included Brooks, Cannon, Garrett, Maroney, Armstrong, Hellams, Kellett, and Burdette. In 1923, a brick structure replaced the old wooden building. It was destroyed by fire in 1947. By 1948, the third church building was completed. For a time, the minister preached at Greenpond and Owings Methodist Churches in addition to his duties at Fountain Inn.

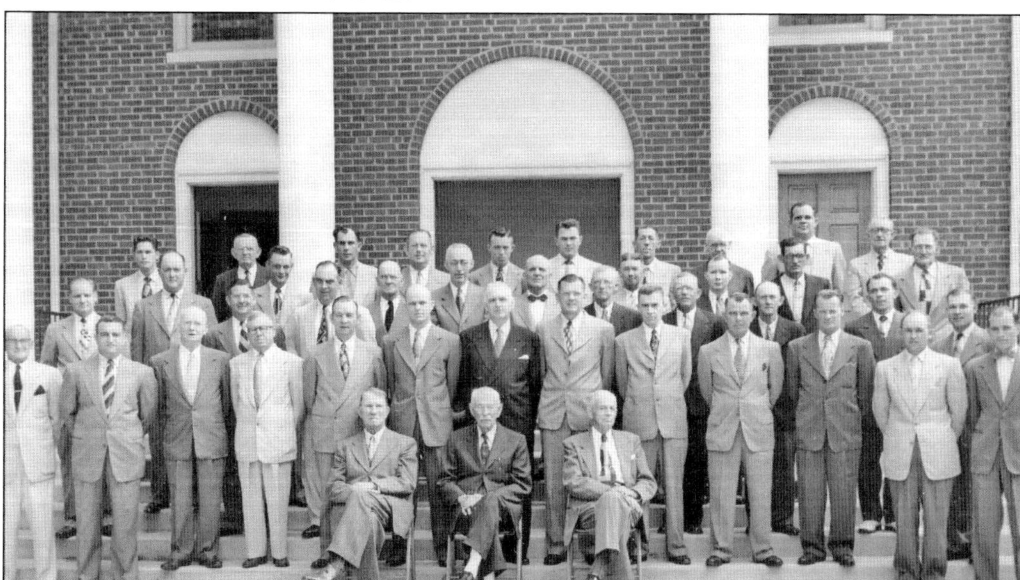

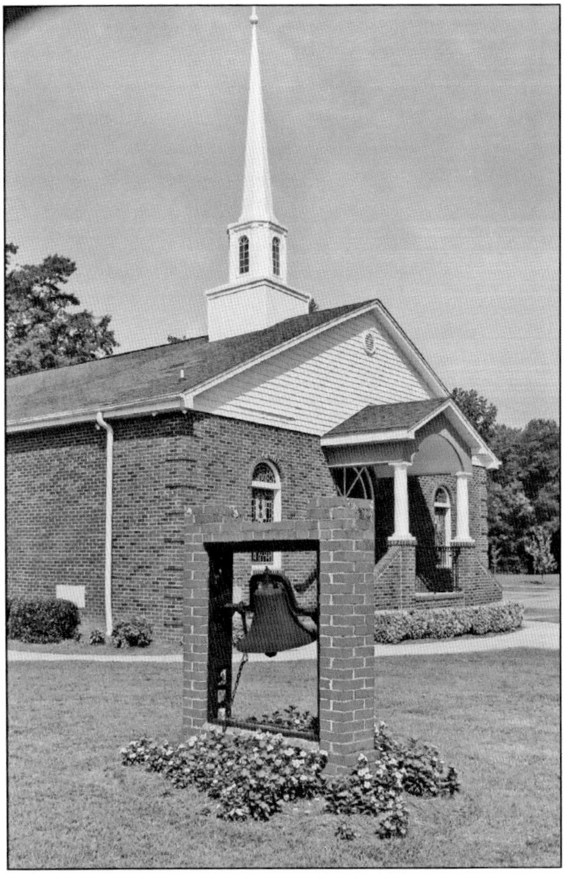

Mount Zion Baptist Church, organized in 1888, began as a brush arbor and a log building about three miles south of town, on the "Brown Line." Two acres of land were purchased from S.S. Knight. Later the church moved to its present site on Mount Zion Drive. The early organizers were led by Rev. June Canady and assisted by the Gilliam, Garrett, Tucker, Chiles, Williams, and Bates families. In the 1800s, a black cast-iron bell was purchased. It weighs over 500 pounds and has a rich, deep sound. The bell was moved from the original grounds by wagon and installed in the tower. A designated person would pull a rope to notify members it was time for church or a funeral. In 1982, it was erected on the grounds. The baptismal pool, measuring six by ten feet, came into being about 1910. The men of the church constructed this concrete enclosure for baptizing new members in the faith. Baptism would take place on Friday during revival week in August. Candidates would line up and enter the pool as the congregation sang the old hymns. (Both, courtesy of the Putman, Young, and Jones families.)

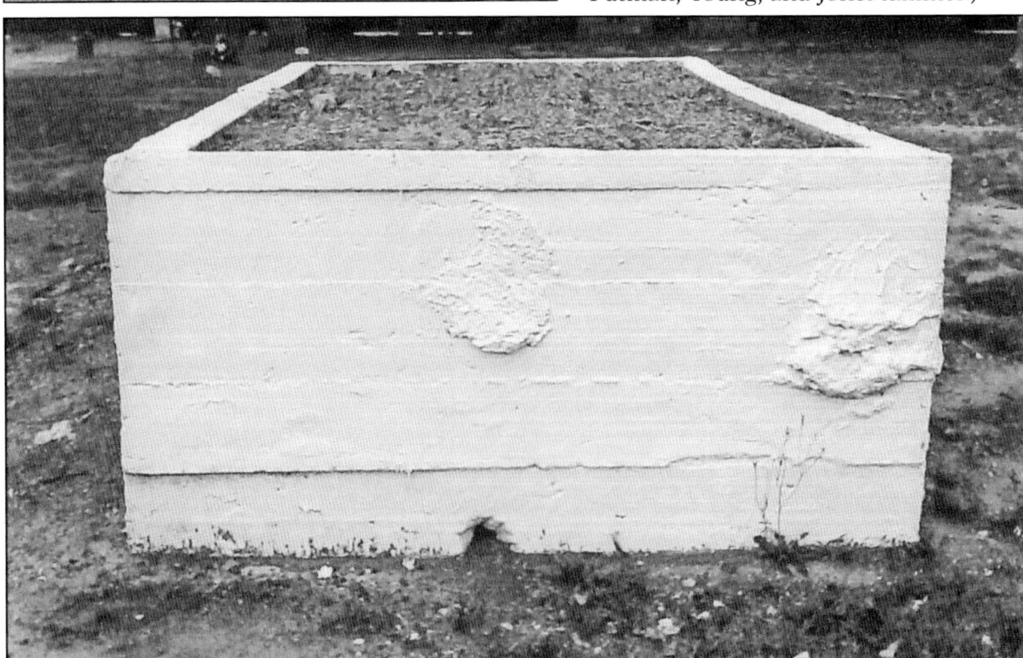

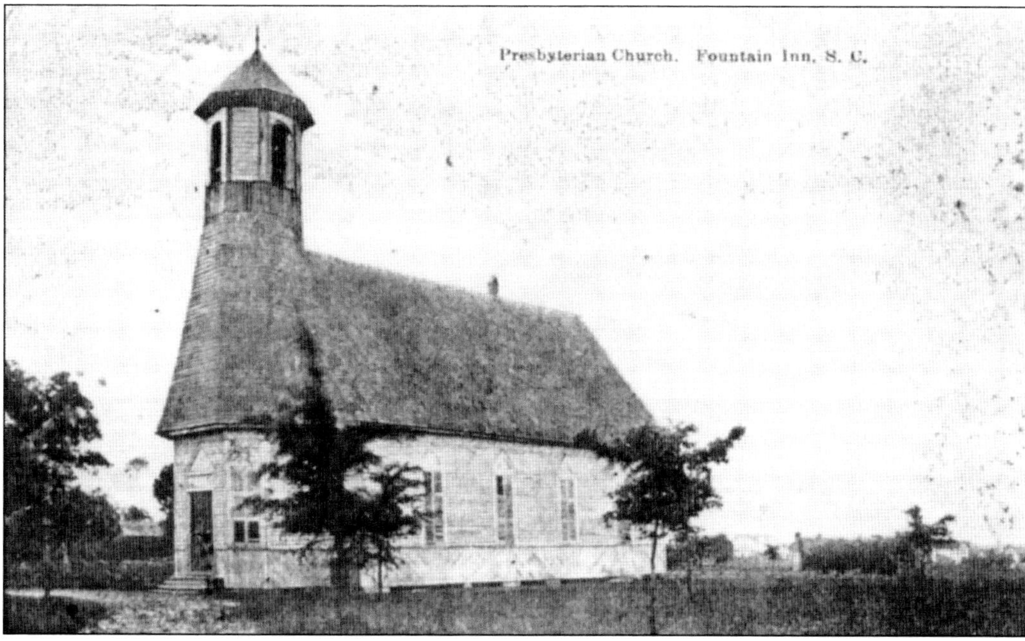

Fountain Inn Presbyterian Church, on North Main Street, was organized in 1889 with 14 charter members, 13 of whom came from New Harmony Presbyterian Church below Fountain Inn. Early members were the Scruggs, Hitch, Martin, Bradley, Bryson, Stewart, and Garrett families. The first church was an inexpensive frame building erected in 1891. The second building was made of brick in 1910. Additional building programs have taken place since then. In 1960, the church sought a full-time pastor. Until then, the pastor had also served New Harmony.

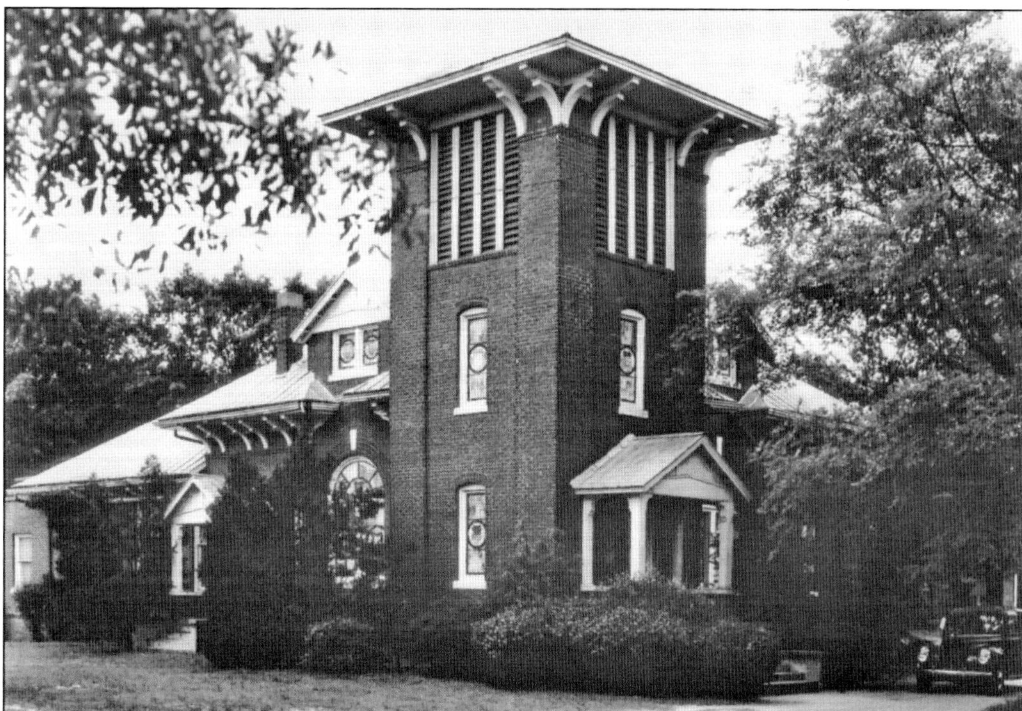

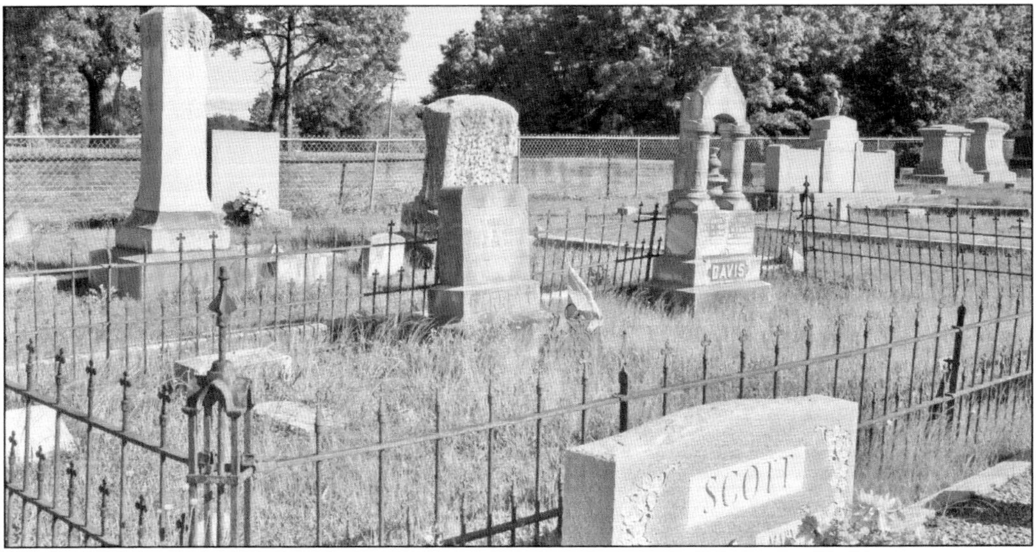

The city cemetery was established in 1890, four years after the city was chartered. It was originally located on what is now Depot Street beside the First Baptist Church. In the 1920s, it was moved to its current location on Highway 418. A charter member of the First Presbyterian Church, Lafayette Martin, contributed the land. Many of the first families of Fountain Inn are buried there. A historical marker was erected by the city in January 2016. (Courtesy of Ron Urso.)

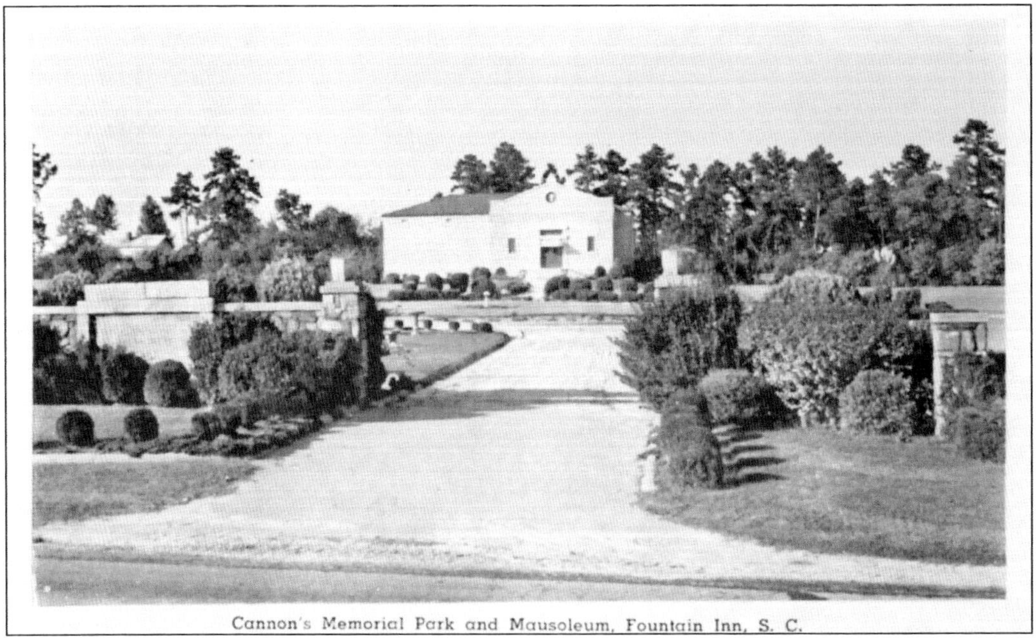

In 1876, J.A. Cannon, postmaster and store owner, started stocking coffins from Atlanta in his store. His son Dick's 1909 embalming license was said to be the oldest in the state. A horse-drawn hearse was purchased, and later the old Cannon residence on South Main Street was converted into a modern funeral home. In the 1940s, the family opened Cannon Memorial Park above the town, and in 1954 the first community mausoleum in South Carolina was erected. Dick's son James recalled that he drove an ambulance for the family business when he was 15 and was happy to sell this part of the business.

Six

Readin', Writin', and 'Rithmetic

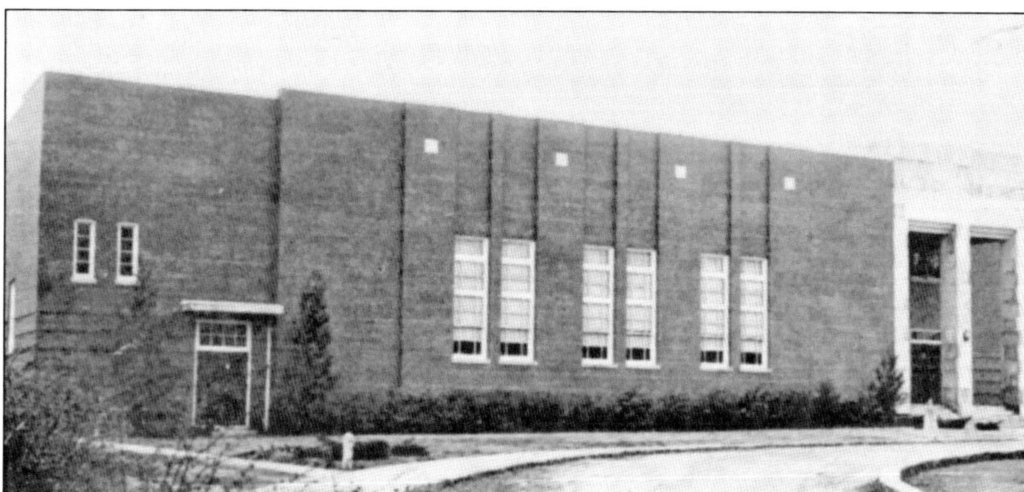

This former high school, serving grades 8 through 12, was built in 1939 on North Main Street. In those days, there was no junior high or middle school. It is an example of New Deal–era moderne design undertaken by the Public Works Administration, and is one of the notable designs of the Greenville firm of Beacham and LeGrand. The building served as a high school for only 17 years before the consolidated Hillcrest High School opened near Simpsonville for the three towns of Mauldin, Simpsonville, and Fountain Inn. Fountain Inn, in 1957, no longer had its own high school. The building became the elementary school. In 1997, a new elementary school was constructed, and the town purchased the building from the Greenville County School District. It serves the town by featuring a resident orchestra, a theater company, and traveling acts. In 2013, the building was renamed the Younts Center for Performing Arts and began a multiphase remodeling project, funded by residents Melvin and Dollie Younts. The building was listed in the National Register of Historic Places on June 3, 2009.

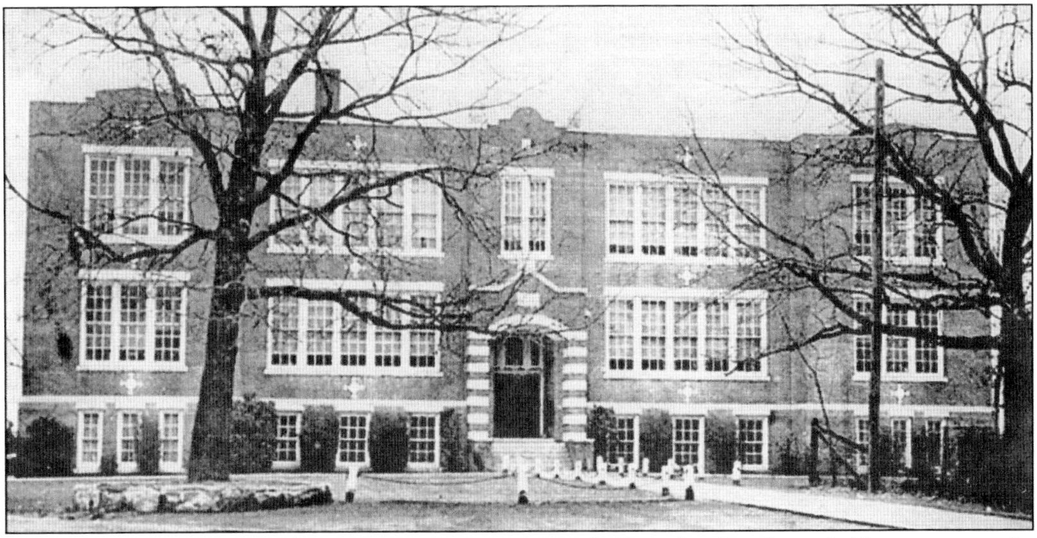

This former school, erected in 1919, at one time housed all grades for white children in town. In 1939, it became the grammar school for first through seventh grades when the new high school opened on Main Street. This school was located behind Trinity Methodist Church on South Weston Street. There was no air-conditioning and no window screens. Kids rode their bikes or walked, even from several miles outside town. In the early 1950s, some kids were bused in when small country schools were closed. James Taylor, a local resident, was the principal for many years. As was common in those days, he did not believe in "sparing the rod and spoiling the child," but all respected him and grew up into good citizens. He was a well-known artist and taught art.

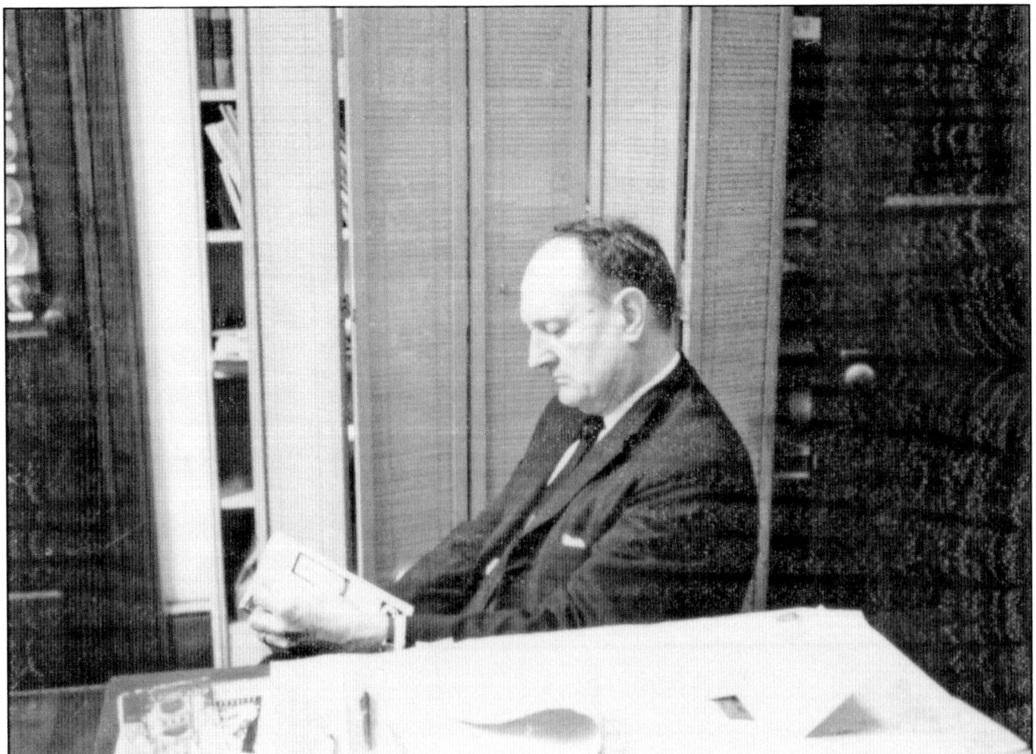

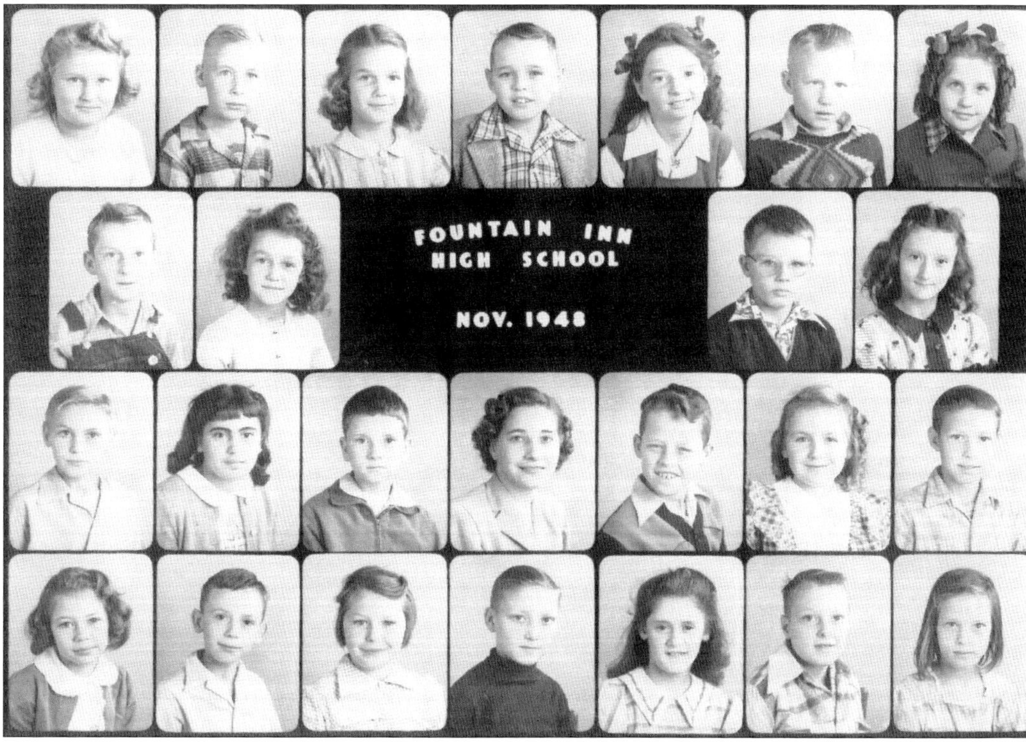

This grammar school photograph from November 1948 shows, from left to right, (first row) Patricia Armstrong, Benjamin Gault, Doris Bonds, Don Hudson, Frances Shelton, Henry ?, and unidentified; (second row) two unidentified, Jackie Parsons, unidentified teacher, Richard Abercrombie, Ann Eibs Hughes, and unidentified; (third row) unidentified, Peggy Willis, Bobby Putman, and unidentified; (fourth row) unidentified, Bruce Cooper, Mary Ellen Spoone, John Richard Vaughn, Helen Armstrong, and Elaine Jones. (Courtesy of Elaine Jones Carver.)

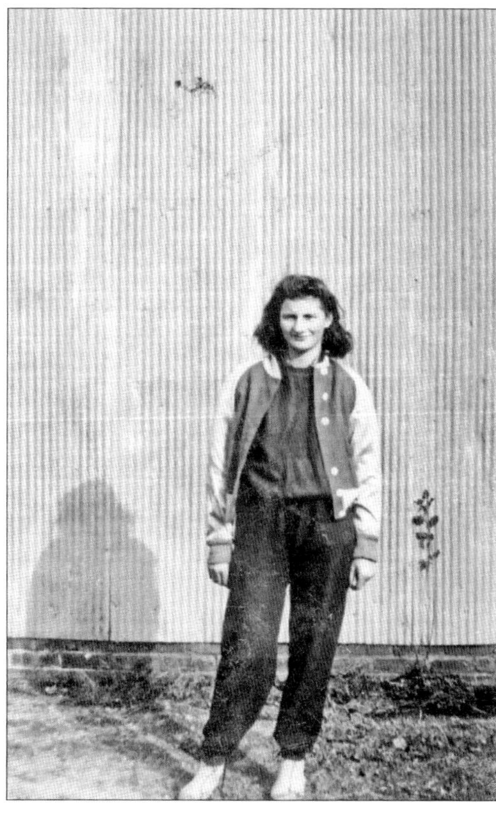

Many a good time was had in the gymnasium watching basketball games and going to dances. This was the "activity center" for the community. The outside was corrugated tin. The gym was located behind the 1919 school. Both are gone now. The lunch room and ball field are still there. Annie Mae Fowler was head of the lunch room for many years. Sarah Margaret Nash, in her athletic jacket, is standing out front. (Courtesy of Sarah Margaret Nash Thackston.)

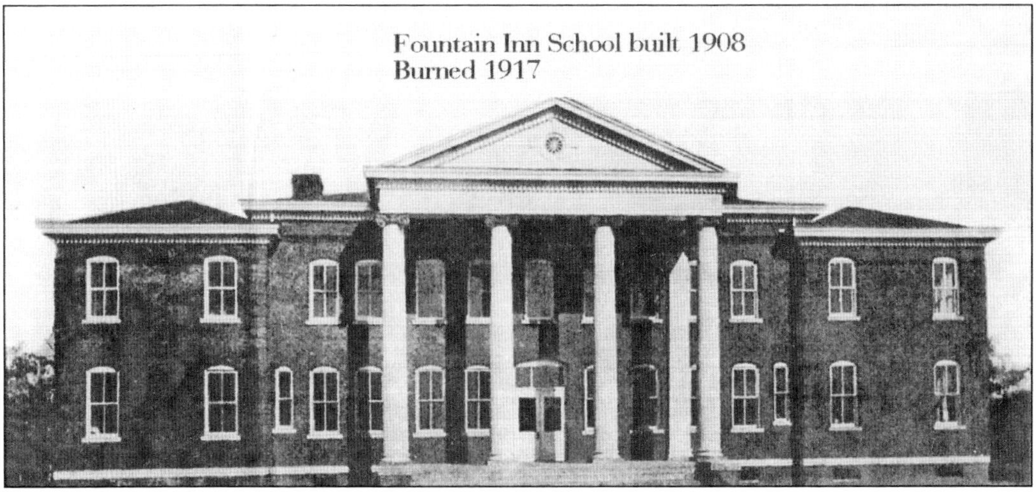

Fountain Inn School was built 1908. This beautiful building burned down in 1917. There were many other schools before it, as early as 1880. It contained grades 1 through 11. There was no 12th grade many years ago.

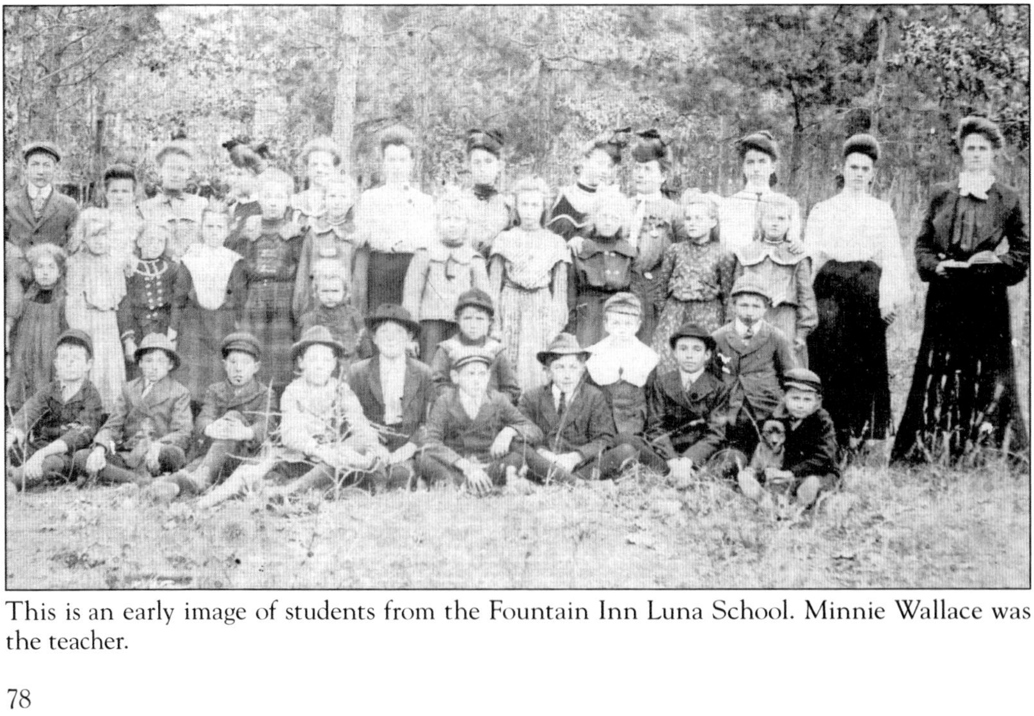

This is an early image of students from the Fountain Inn Luna School. Minnie Wallace was the teacher.

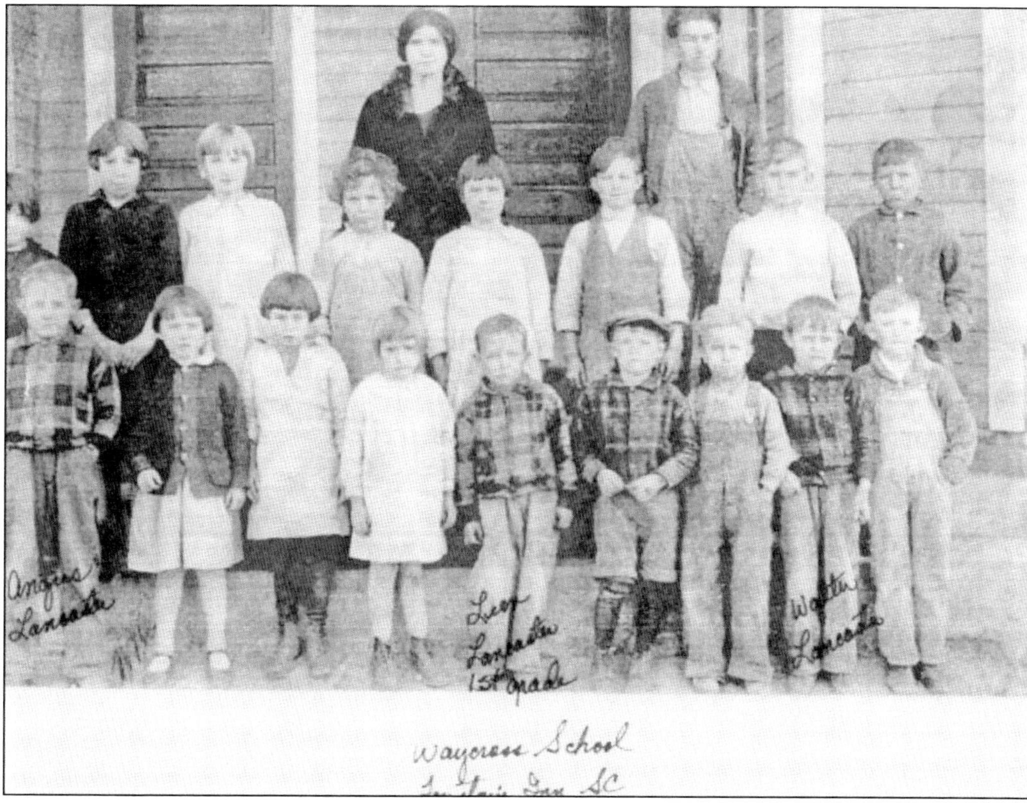

Waycross School was located on Jones Mill Road, past the old mill. The school is no longer standing.

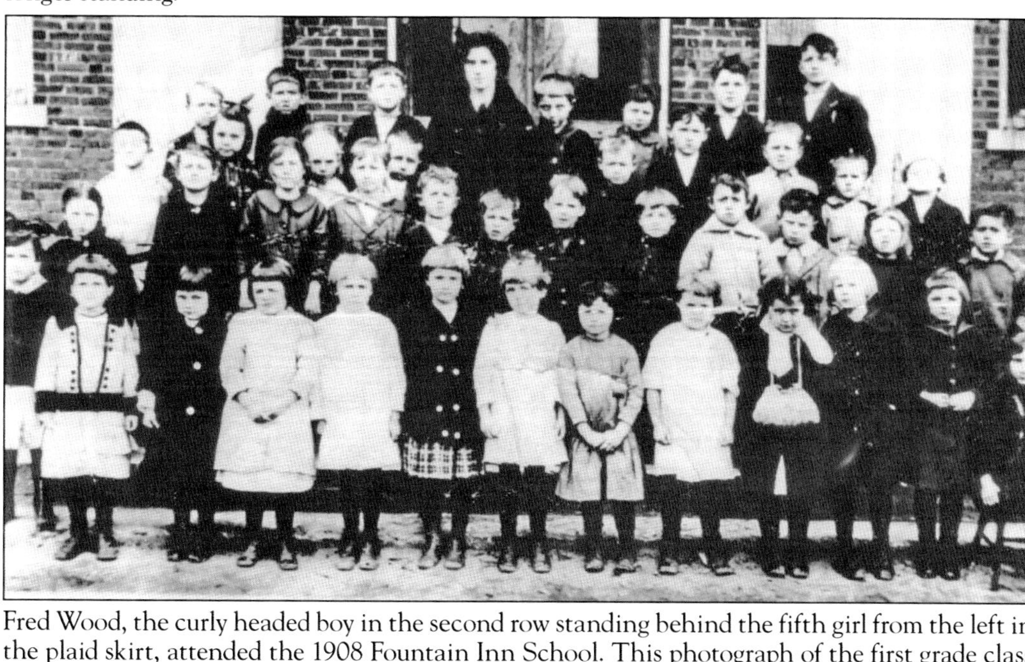

Fred Wood, the curly headed boy in the second row standing behind the fifth girl from the left in the plaid skirt, attended the 1908 Fountain Inn School. This photograph of the first grade class was taken in 1914. (Courtesy of Boroff family.)

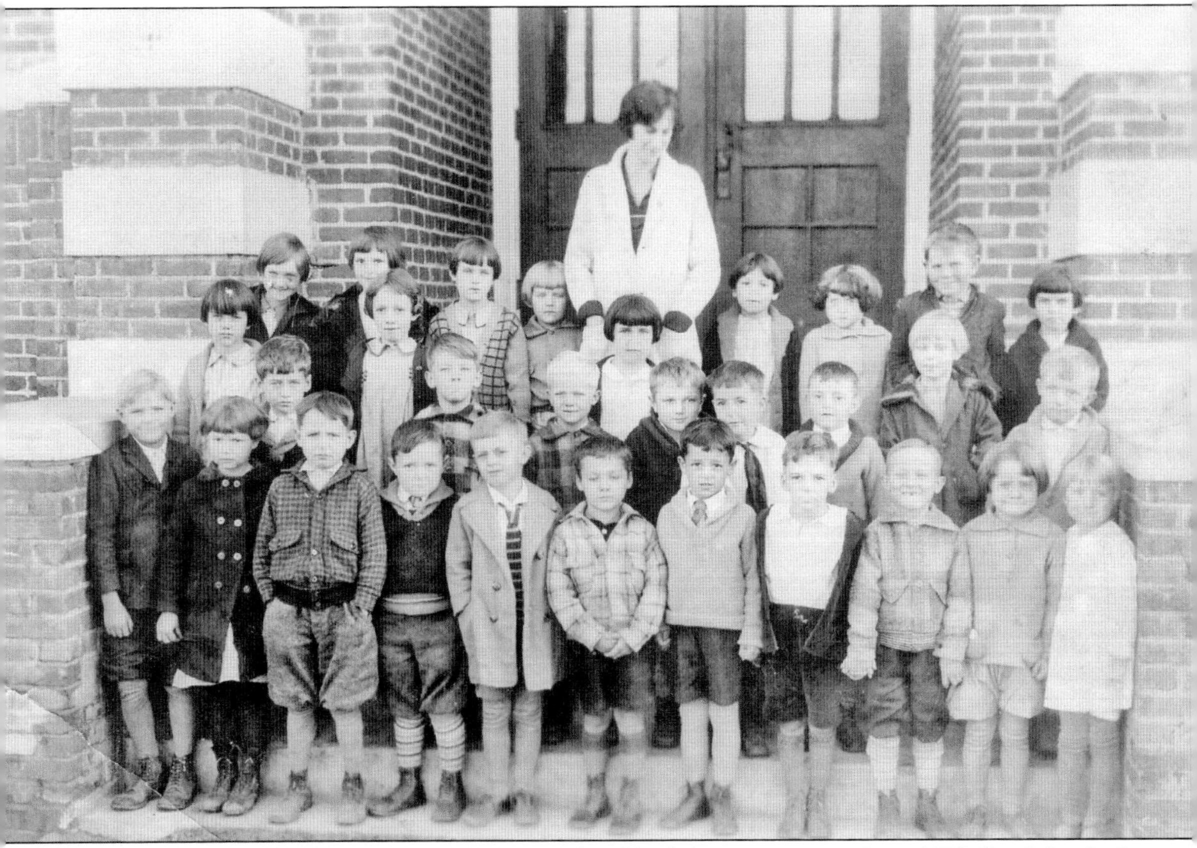

The first grade of the 1919 Fountain Inn School had their picture made in 1927. Frank Leake Jr. grew up and took over Leake's Dairy, started by his father. Frank Jr. is fourth from left in the first row. (Courtesy of the Mike and Carol Leake family.)

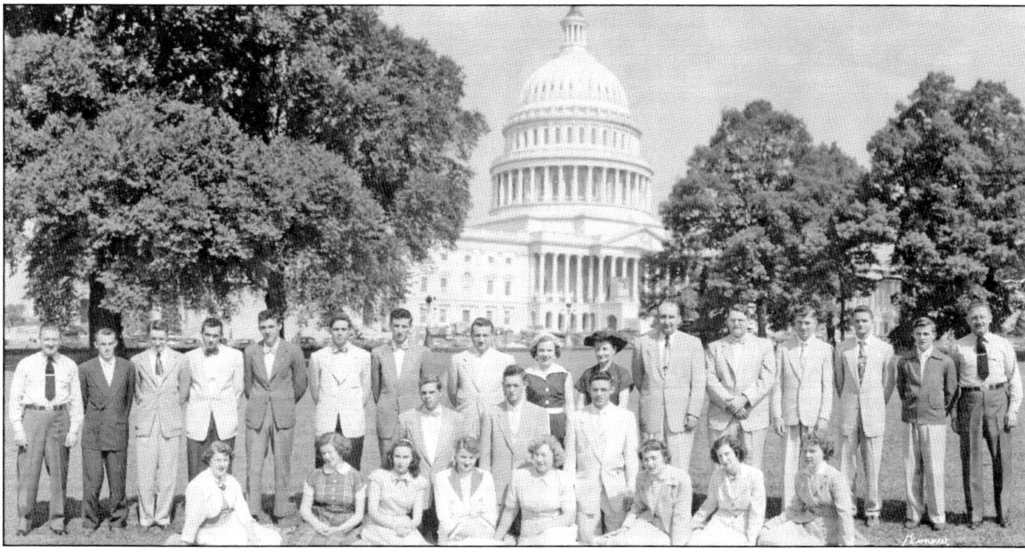

Imagine the thrill of the senior class of 1952 going to the nation's capital. Some of the kids had never been out of the state of South Carolina. They must have been in awe of the beautiful city. Fundraisers were held so seniors could go on their trip.

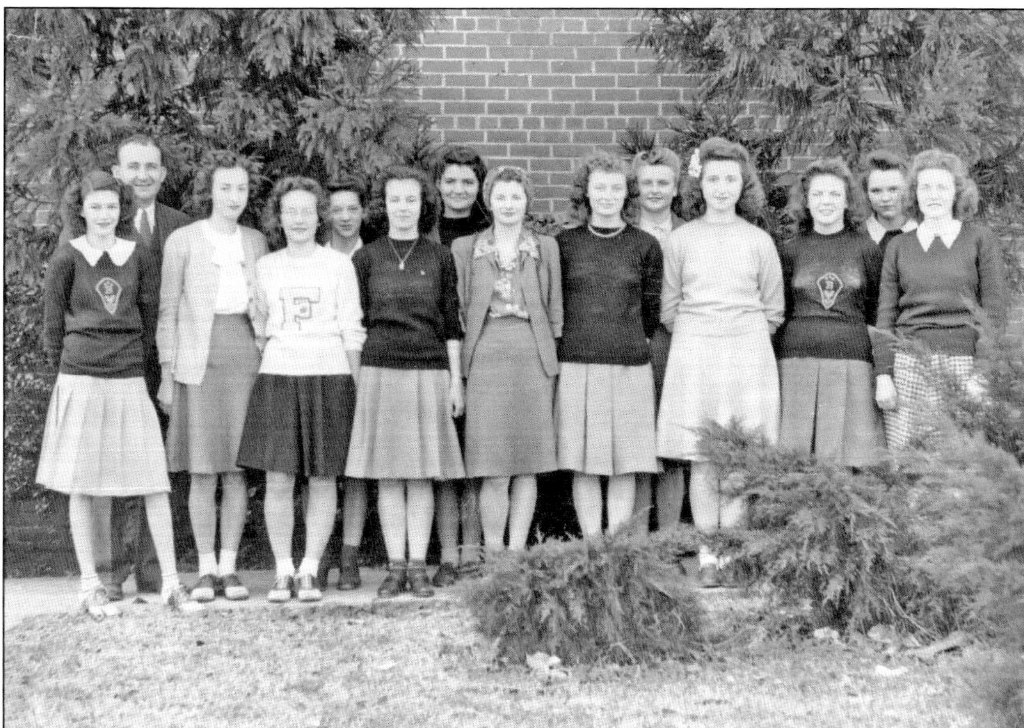

This picture shows the girls basketball team in 1944–1945. From left to right are Patricia Culbertson, coach M.D. Putman, Nancy Mahon, Betty Jo Phillips (Stoddard), Evelyn Balcombe, Alice Jane Gault, ? Owens, S.M. Thackston, Lois Lancaster, Betty Jane Dodson, Kathryn Marlar, Louise Mahon, Betty Jane Willis, and Olive Templeton.

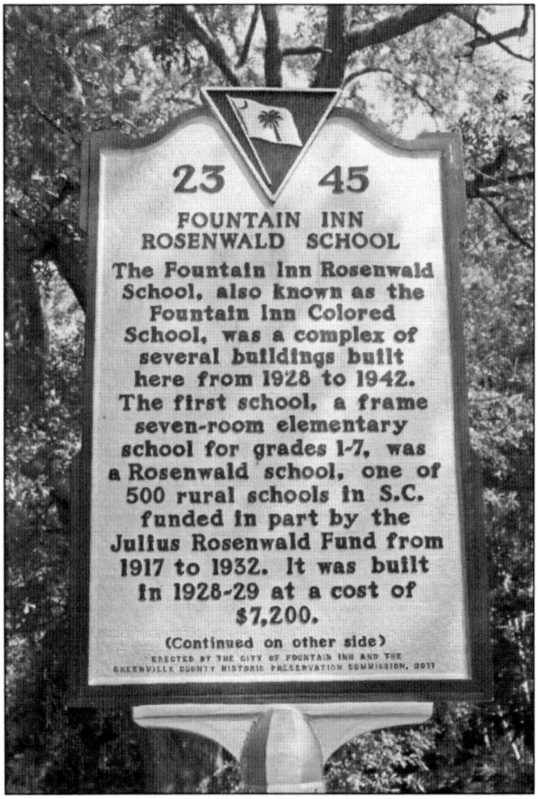

The Rosenwald school complex was located on Mount Zion Drive near Mount Zion Baptist Church. According to the South Carolina Department of Archives and History, "The principal's house and Teacherage, built in1935, is significant with the Fountain Inn Negro School and the African-American history in the town. The house is the only remaining building of the complex, comprised of a grade school built in 1928, high school 1930, a library and the Clayton 'Peg Leg' Bates gymnasium. These buildings were designed to offer comfortable domestic amenities like front corner porches and modern indoor bathrooms, but they were also meant to serve as instructional facilities." (Courtesy of Ron Urso.)

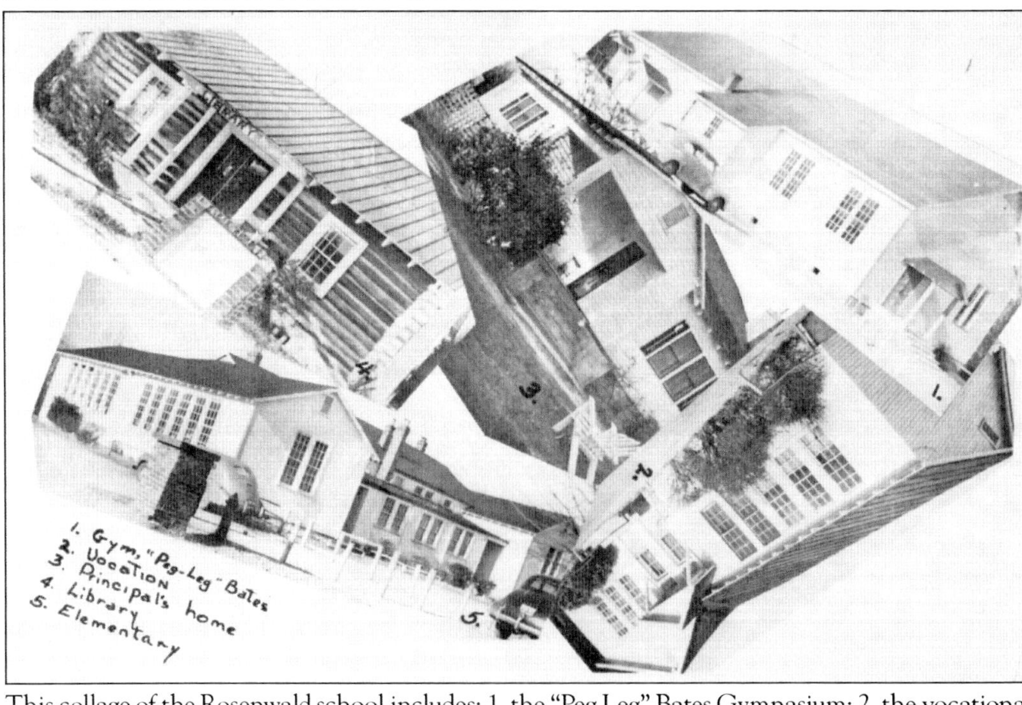

This collage of the Rosenwald school includes: 1. the "Peg Leg" Bates Gymnasium; 2. the vocational building; 3. the principal's home; 4. the library; and 5. the elementary school.

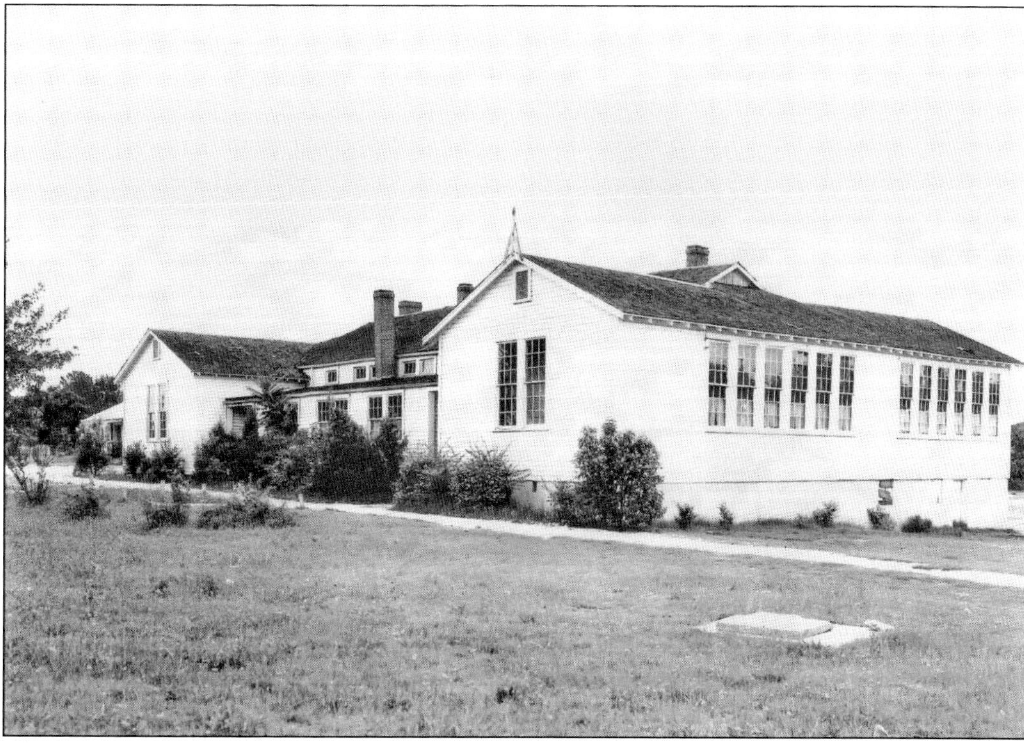

The Fountain Inn Rosenwald School pictured above is no longer standing. (Courtesy of Emmanuel Sullivan.)

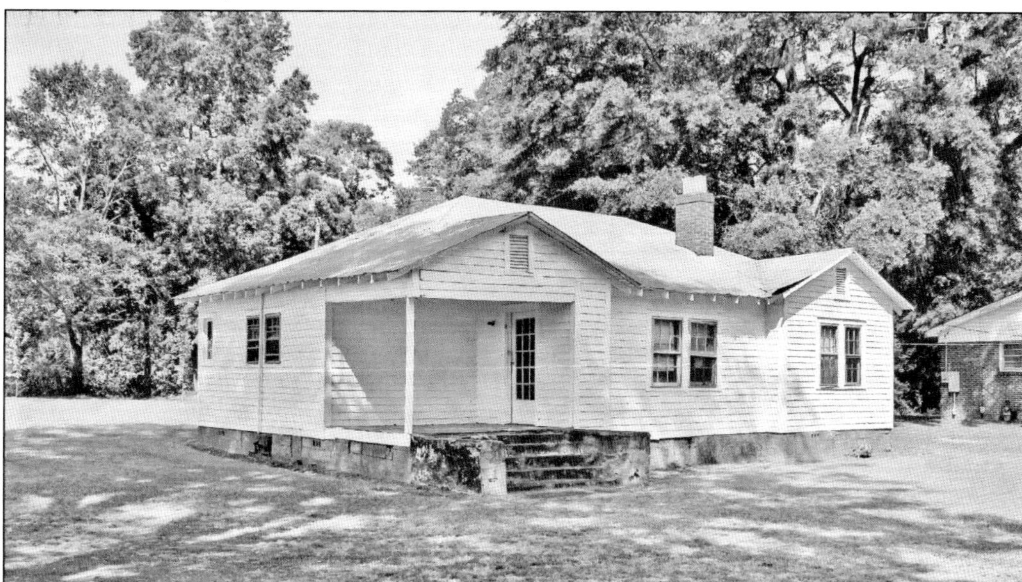

The teacherage for the Fountain Inn Rosenwald School was constructed originally as a home for teachers who provided educational instruction for African Americans. By the 1940s, it housed teachers, the principal, and his family. A separate entrance at the building's southwest corner accessed the kitchen and accommodated home economics classes. It is still standing. (Courtesy of Ron Urso.)

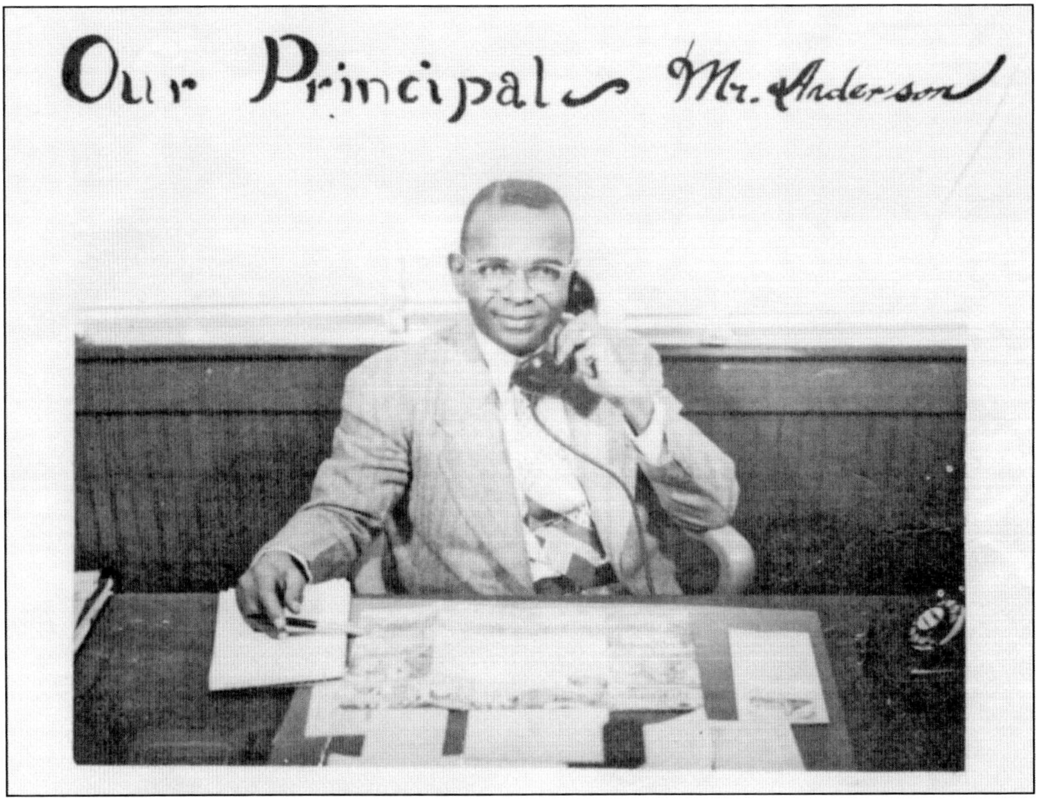

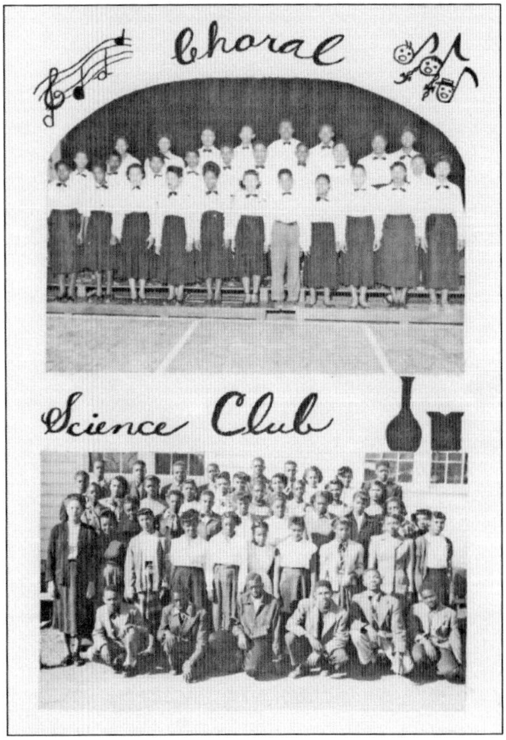

Dr. A.M. Anderson was principal of the Rosenwald School and then the first principal at Bryson High School when it was built in 1954 as a segregated high school for African American students in Greenville County. The school encouraged student participation in clubs and sports activities. To the right is a photograph of students in the choral and science clubs. Dr. Anderson remained principal when the school was integrated. (Both, courtesy of Emmanuel Sullivan.)

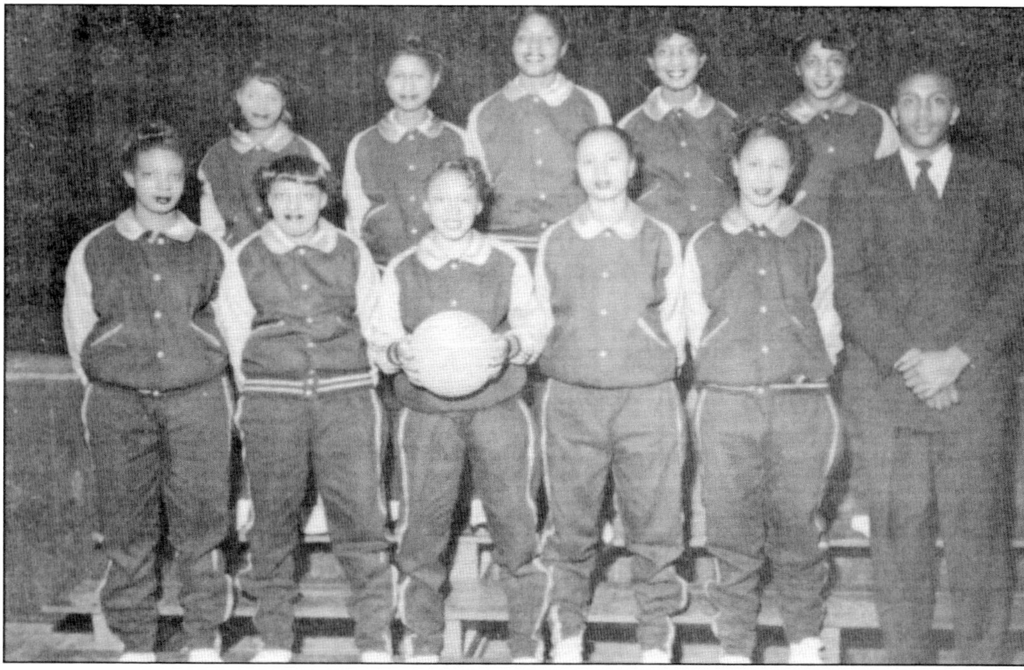

The Bryson High School had basketball teams for girls and boys. (Both, courtesy of Emmanuel Sullivan.)

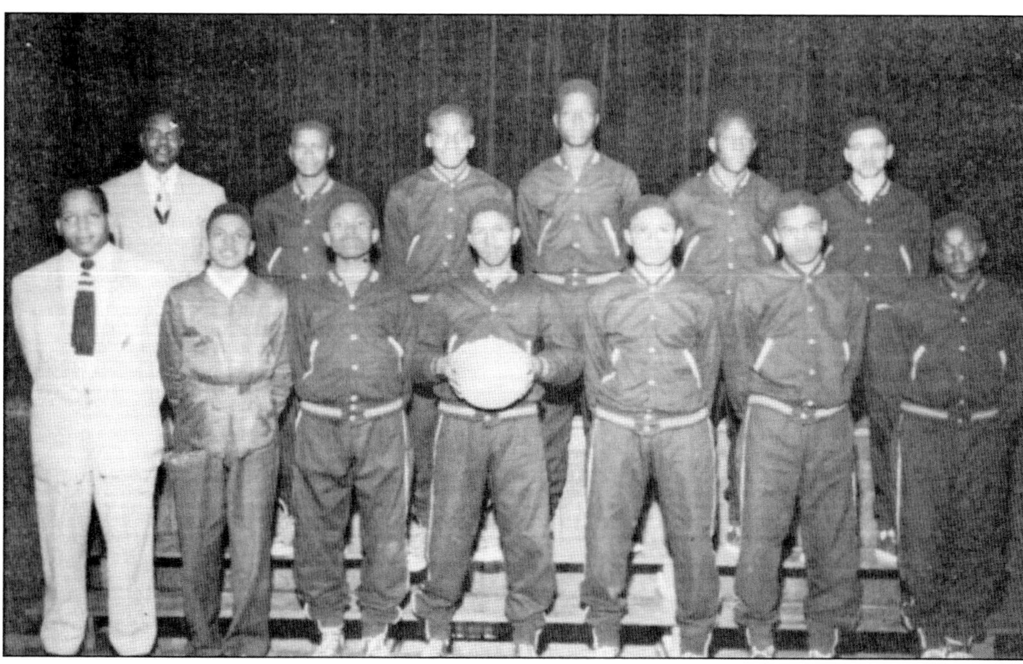

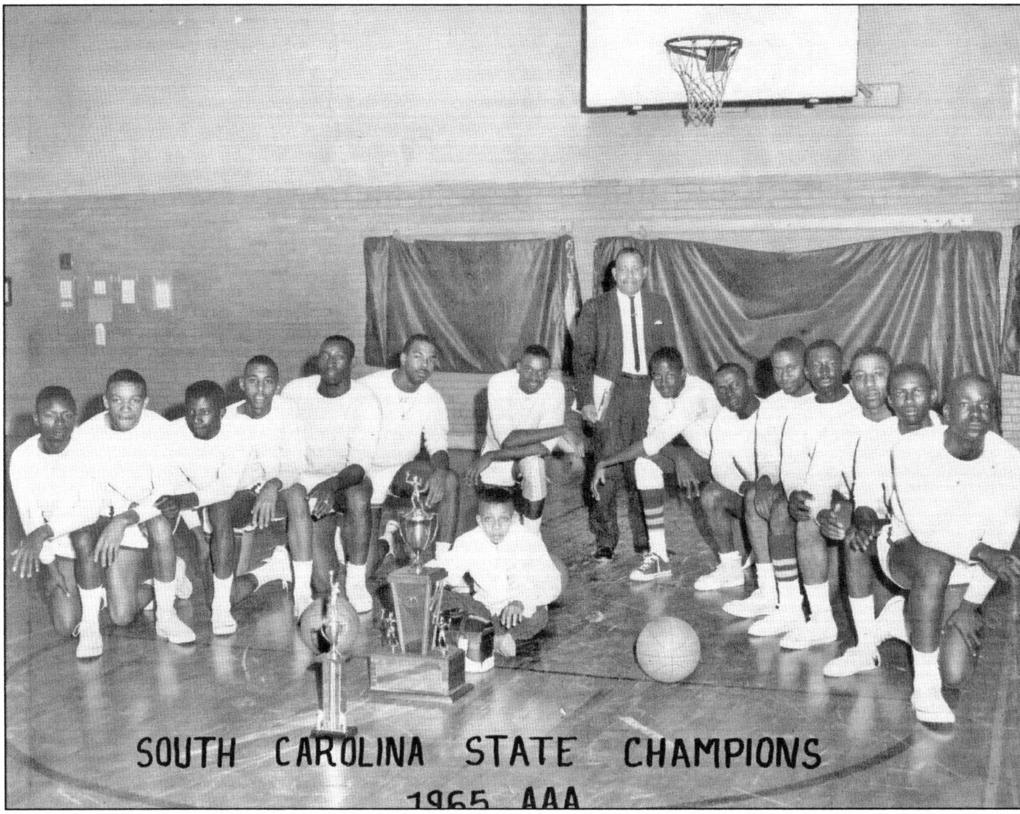

The 1965 boys' basketball team at Bryson High School were South Carolina state champions. (Courtesy of Emmanuel Sullivan.)

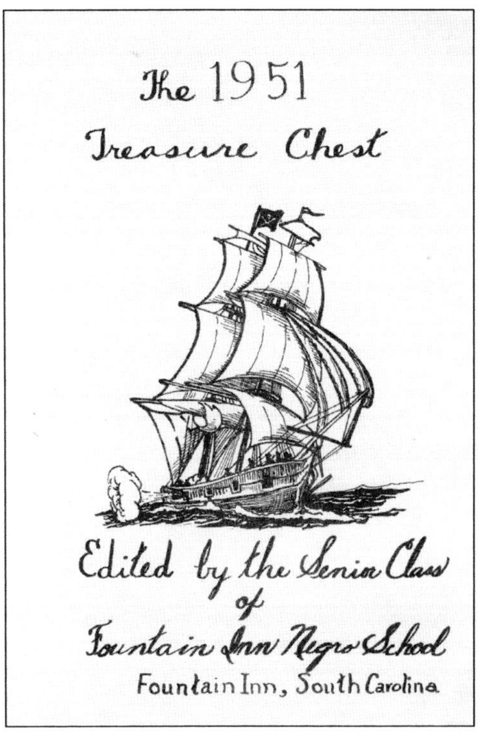

Other white and black schools were located in farming communities on the outskirts of Fountain Inn. A number of Rosenwald-funded schools were located nearby. Rural communities made up the majority of lower Greenville County, and most black families lived and worked on the farms.

Seven

Civic and Social Places

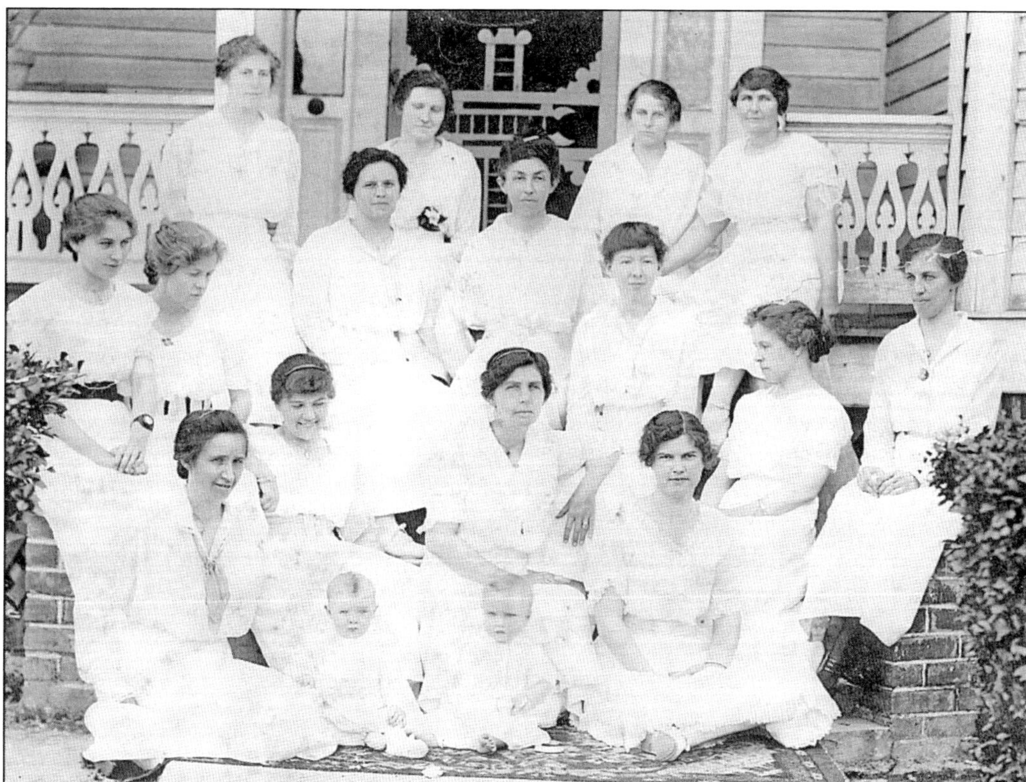

The Sewing Club is seated on the steps of the McKnight Hotel on South Main and Jones Streets. From left to right are (first row) unidentified, Minnie McDowell Walton, unidentified, Mary McDowell, Lula McDowell, unidentified, and unidentified children; (second row) Ella Nash, Belle Peden, and three unidentified; (third row) Pearl McCarter Armstrong, Lillian Armstrong McCarter, Jennie McDowell, and Eva McDowell Smith. Nettie Peden, Helen Martin, and Lillie Harrison are known to be in the picture but have not been identified. (Courtesy of Ann Vaughan.)

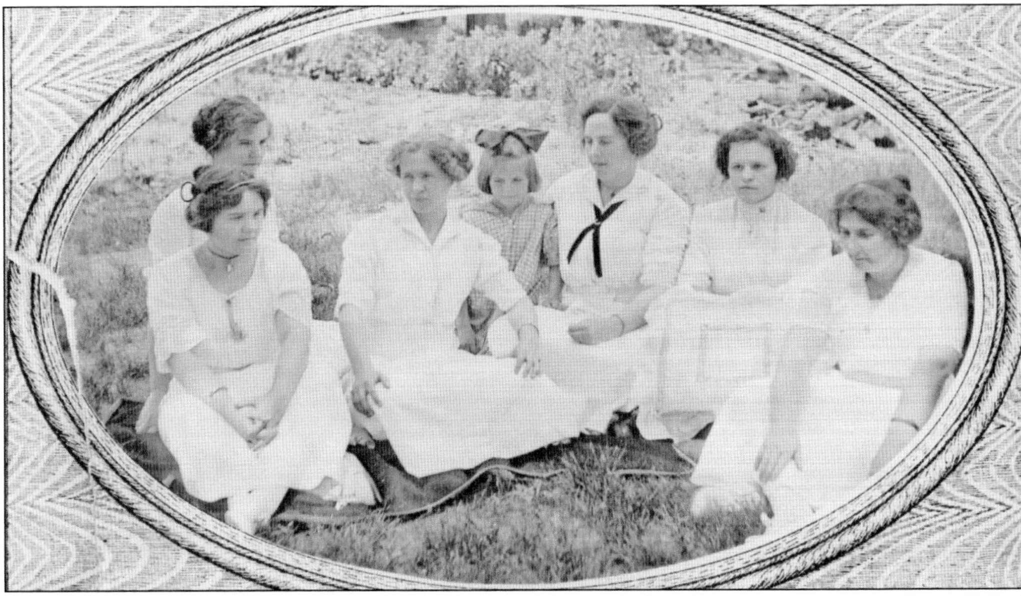

The Embroidery Club is pictured about 1911. From left to right are cousins "Min" McDowell (18), "Net" Peden, Willie McDowell, Annabelle McDowell, Jennie Armstrong, Mary McDowell, and Eva McDowell. (Courtesy of Ann Vaughan.)

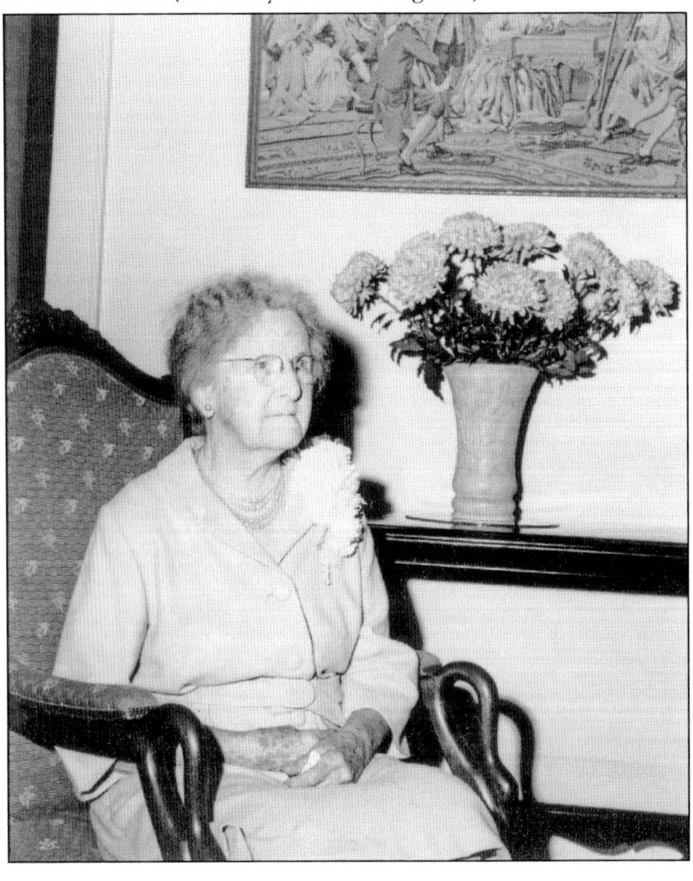

The Garden Club was established in 1954. It became a federated club in 1962. Charter members included Lila Cannon, Emmie Fulmer, Fern Garrett, Mabel Knight, Mrs. A.S. Peden, Mrs. R.L. Pettit, Susie Sloan, and Lois Woods. This organization has worked tirelessly over the decades to create beauty in the lives of its members and the community. The Garden Club maintains the Memorial Garden, located at the police department on Main Street, and has beautified many other areas of the town. It has won numerous awards from the National Garden Club and the Garden Club of South Carolina. In 1981, Emmie Fulmer (1878–1989, left) was honored as the nation's oldest active Garden Club member.

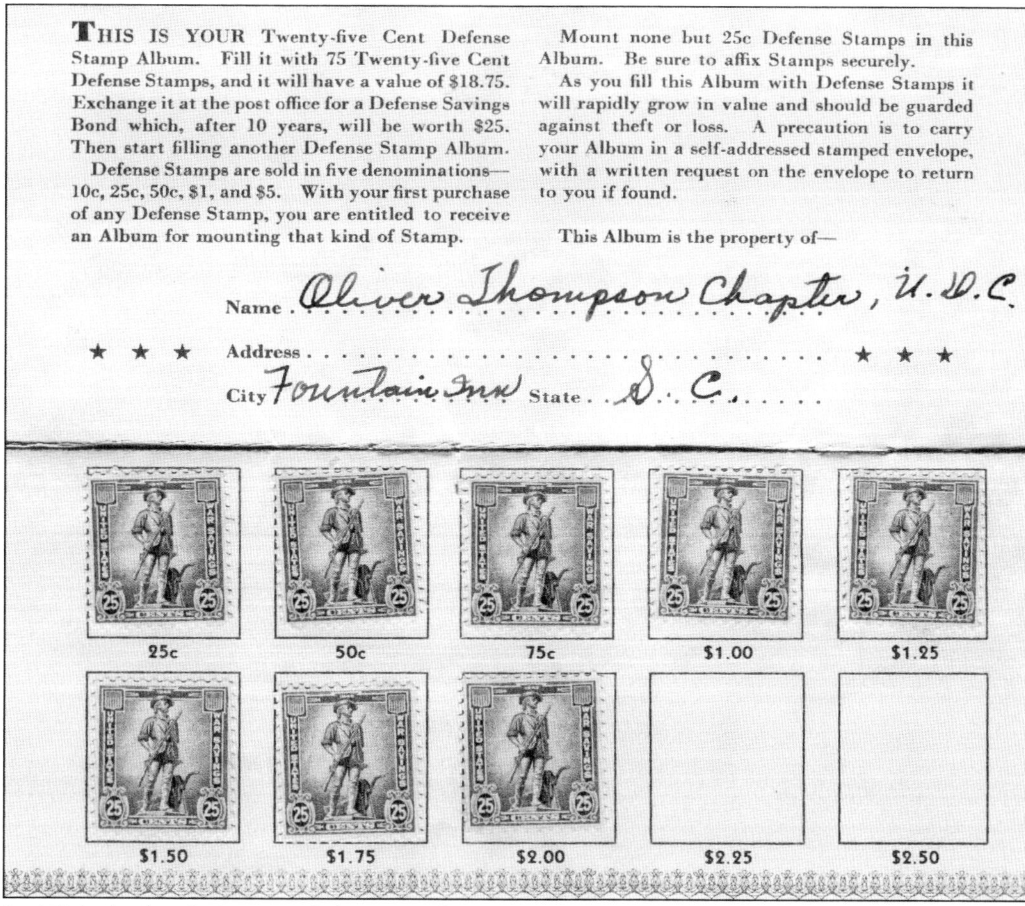
THIS IS YOUR Twenty-five Cent Defense Stamp Album. Fill it with 75 Twenty-five Cent Defense Stamps, and it will have a value of $18.75. Exchange it at the post office for a Defense Savings Bond which, after 10 years, will be worth $25. Then start filling another Defense Stamp Album.

Defense Stamps are sold in five denominations—10c, 25c, 50c, $1, and $5. With your first purchase of any Defense Stamp, you are entitled to receive an Album for mounting that kind of Stamp.

Mount none but 25c Defense Stamps in this Album. Be sure to affix Stamps securely.

As you fill this Album with Defense Stamps it will rapidly grow in value and should be guarded against theft or loss. A precaution is to carry your Album in a self-addressed stamped envelope, with a written request on the envelope to return to you if found.

This Album is the property of—

Name Oliver Thompson Chapter, U.D.C

★ ★ ★ Address ★ ★ ★

City Fountain Inn State S. C.

In 1924, the local chapter of the United Daughters of the Confederacy (UDC) was organized with 44 charter members. The national organization grew out of ladies' hospital societies and knitting circles that worked throughout the South during the War Between the States to supply the needs of the soldiers. After the war, these organizations evolved into cemetery, memorial, monument, and Confederate Home Associations. During World War II, the ladies in Fountain Inn used their refreshment money to purchase Defense Stamps that could be converted into US Defense Savings Bonds. The Sons of Confederate Veterans preserve the legacy of Confederate soldiers. It is a historical, patriotic, and nonpolitical organization. (Courtesy of Carol Leake.)

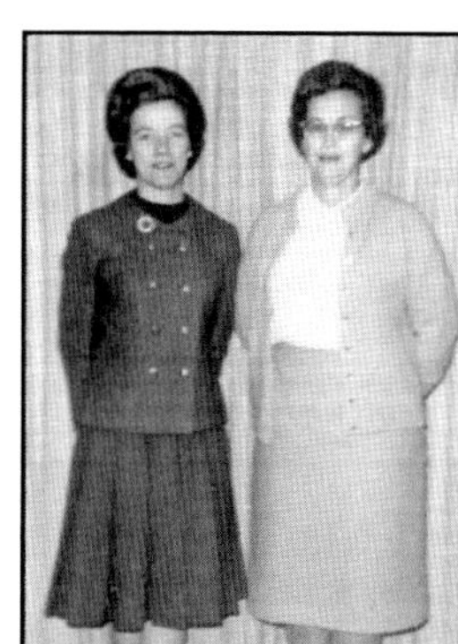

The Caroline S. Coleman Chapter of the Children of the Confederacy 537 was named for a local historian, charter member of the Oliver Thompson Chapter of the UDC, and honorary president of the South Carolina UDC. The Children of the Confederacy chapter was chartered in April 1959. Pictured in 1967, June Leake (left) was president general of the National UDC, and Bonnie Thackston (right) was the original director of the local chapter of the C of C. The Children of the Confederacy have historical programs and honors all patriotic holidays; they serve society through contributions to civic organizations such as Wounded Warriors, the Ronald McDonald House, and St. Jude. Two chapter members, Gordon Garrett and Henry Fulmer, became South Carolina division presidents, and Gordon became president general. (Courtesy of Carol Leake.)

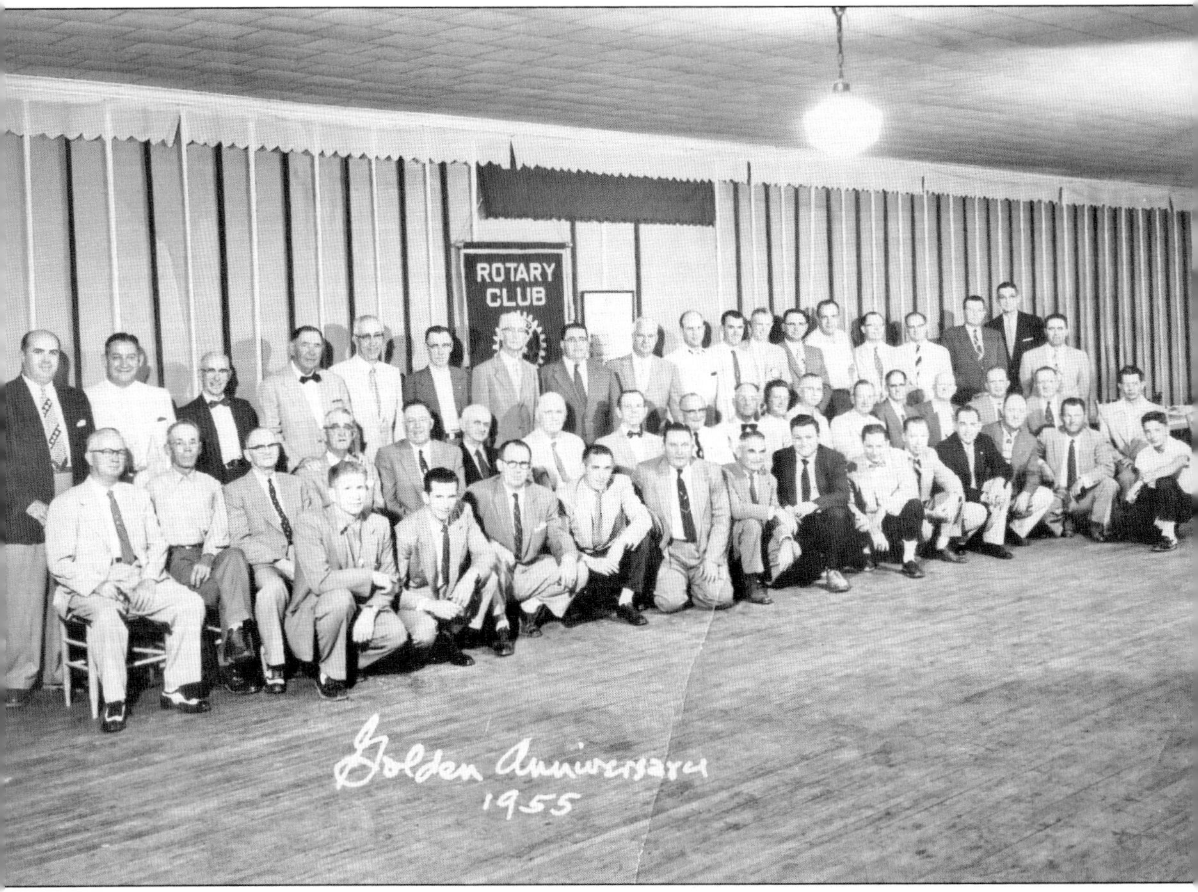

The local Rotary chapter was formed in 1937 with 18 charter members. The first president of the club was A.D. Cannon, who took the lead in organizing it. From left to right are (first row) Dr. E.A. "Gene" Thomason, Shell Thackston Jr., unidentified, Mike Erwin (Woodside Mills), Lloyd Garrett (agriculture service), J.E. Herndon (school superintendent), Jake League (Woodside Mills), Dr. Calhoun Epps (pharmacist), George Edwards (insurance), Dick Rabb, Bob West (dairy), S.B. Rouse (frozen food plant), and Hayne Shumate Jr. (visitor); (second row) Mentone McGee (post office), John Armstrong, Claude Parsons (Ford dealer), West Kellett (farmer), B.C. Givens (hardware), Henry Curry (cotton buyer), J.A. Barry (retired), Dick Cannon (mortuary), Conway Jones (furniture), George Wenck (banker), B.L. Holland (grocery), George Saye (agriculture teacher), Clint Smith (shoe repair), Warren Curry (grocery), Earl White (plumbing), V.M. Babb (insurance), and "Buck" Babb (V.M.'s son, insurance); (third row) two unidentified Woodside Mill executives, Stuart Rabb (retired), Shell Thackston Sr. (farmer), Clyde Brooks (insurance), Forrest Younts (insurance), Rufus Shumate (farmer), Walter Smith (cotton gin, fertilizer, and ice plant), unidentified, Sam Gault (clothier), Leland Stoddard (banker), Melvin Younts (lawyer), unidentified, Blake Garrett Sr. (Garrett and Garrett), Dr. James Fulmer (dentist), Henry Hudson (shoe shop), Charlie Case (lumber company), Mark Nelson (Fountain Inn Tribune), and J.E. White (White's Men's Shop).

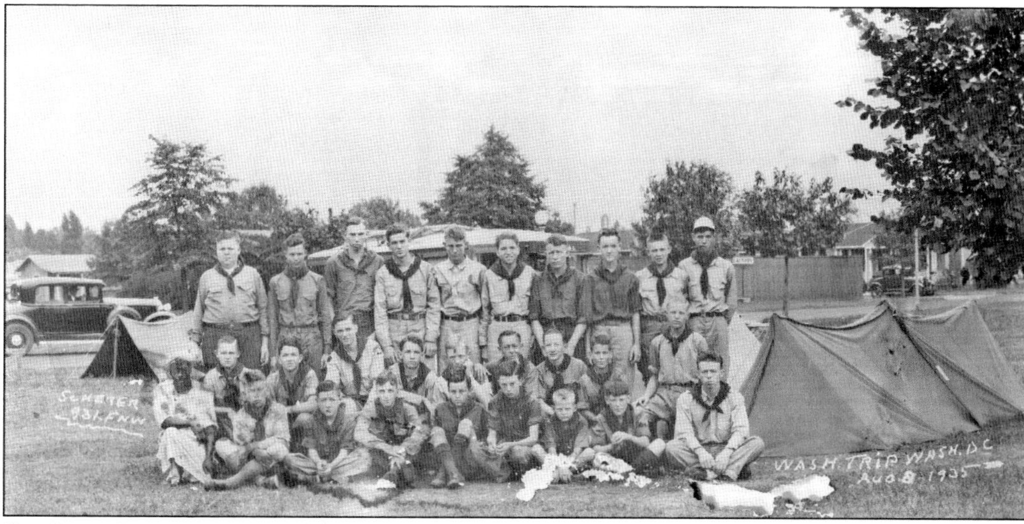

Boy Scout Troop 48 is one of the oldest in South Carolina. It was organized in 1937 by the Rotary Club. It meets at the "Scout Hut" on Woodvale Avenue. (Courtesy of Jayne Smith Thompson.)

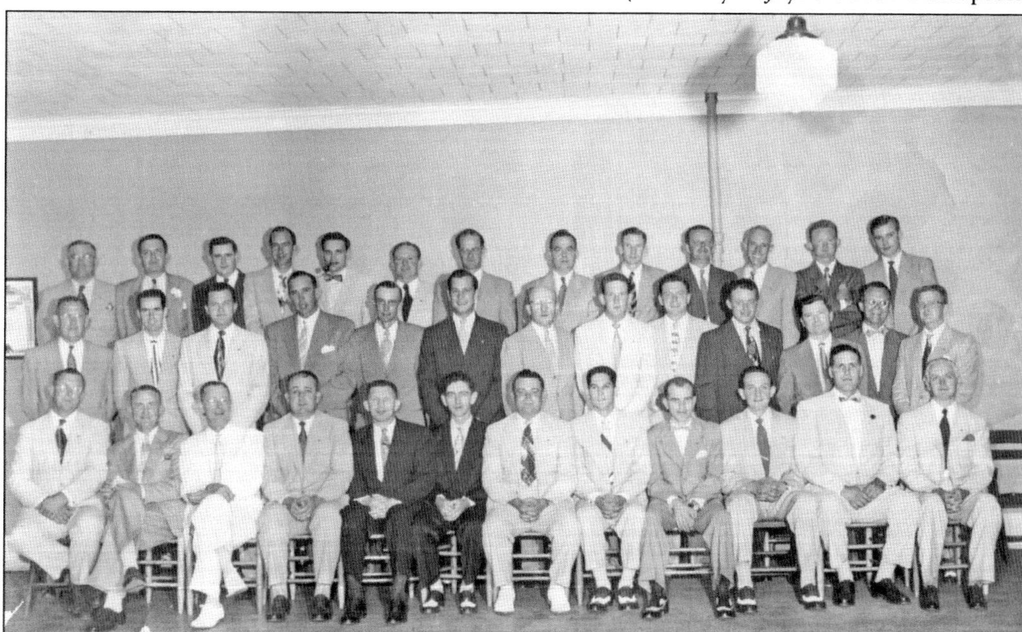

The local Lions Club was organized in 1952 with 37 charter members. From left to right are (first row) unidentified, Ed Whitmire (builder), Reverend Jones (First Presbyterian Church), M.D. Putman (educator), Max Karelitz (dry goods), Boyne Givens (hardware), coach Bill Turnley, James Cannon (mortuary), Paul Gault (clothier), Buddy Jones (T.E. Jones), Dr. Walter McLawhorn (McLawhorn Clinic), and Rev. Sam Glenn (Trinity Methodist Church); (second row) unidentified, Rudy Jones (Home Comforts), unidentified, David Garrett (Garrett and Garrett), Charlie Bell (Fountain Inn Gin), Harry Lee Tate, Dr. James Fulmer (dentist), Richard Edwards (service station), Jack Patton, two unidentified, Fred Wood (Fred Wood Fuel Oil), and Bob Holland (insurance); (third row) unidentified, Ben Holland (grocery), Carrol Garrett (farmer), two unidentified, Murk Gault (dry cleaner), Jete Garrett (barbershop), Joe Thomason (grocer), Bill Parsons (banker), Dick Vaughn (service station), unidentified, and Alvin Nelson.

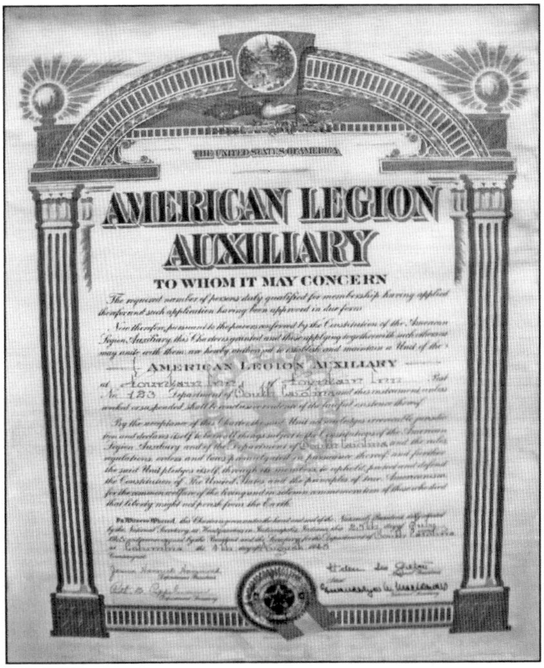

The American Legion Auxiliary was organized in 1919 and is the world's largest women's patriotic organization. Poppies are sold on Memorial Day to benefit disabled veterans. The American Legion was chartered and incorporated by Congress in 1919 as a patriotic veteran's organization. In 1965, this was the largest organization in town. It mentors youth and advocates patriotism. Each year, the American Legion and the Auxiliary send local high school boys and girls to Boys State and Girls State to learn about the government. (Courtesy of Peggy White Nickson and Carolyn White.)

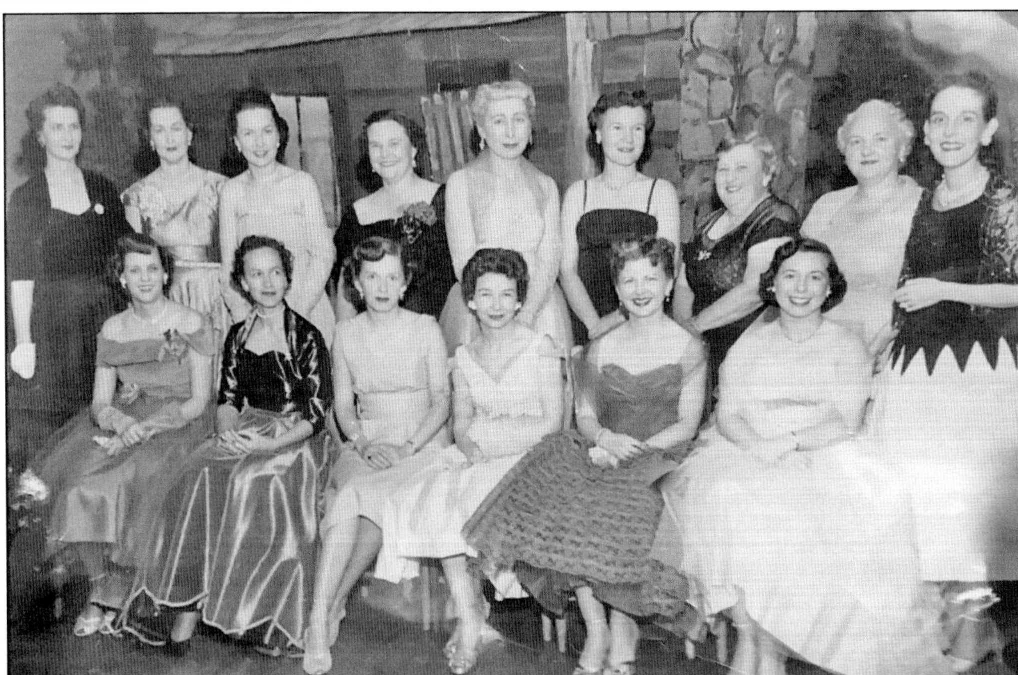

These pretty ladies of the Music Club, organized in 1939, are all dressed up for their annual banquet. The banquets and meetings were always held in upstairs in the Rotary Hall on South Main Street. From left to right are (first row) Nelle Holland, Barbara Rabb, Yvonne Smith, Jean Kellett, Joyce Kellett Cook, and Sara Cannon; (second row) "Dot" McLawhorn, Bonnie Green Thackston, Mildred Givens, Mabel Thackston Knight, Gladys Hudson, Louise Garrett, Rene Kellett, Carolyn Childress McGee, and Rebecca Kellett Jones. (Courtesy of Francelle Kellett.)

Eight

Old Home Places and Ancestors

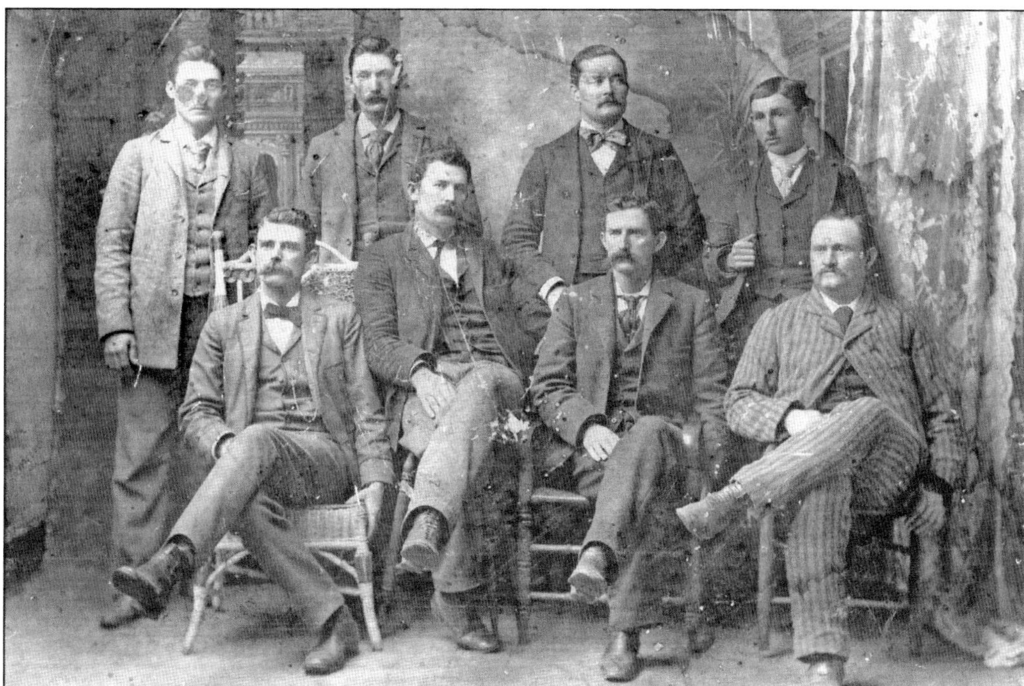

From left to right are Stewart Boyd, R. Boyd, C. Boyd, G. James Culbertson, Charleton Boyd, John Boyd, Howard Y. Boyd, and Walter Fowler. The Boyd and Culbertson families lived near what is now Jenkins Bridge Road. Allene Leake (Mrs. Frank Sr.) and her sister Kate Rodgers (Mrs. Alex) were Culbertsons. They lived next door to each other north of town. The Culbertson history was reported by Kate Rodgers in a series of articles for the *Tribune*. The Culbertsons were Scotch-Irish Covenenters, coming from Scotland, via Londonderry, Ireland, to Chester County, South Carolina. James Culbertson married Delia Boyd of Boyds Mill, Laurens, and was a founding member of Unity Baptist Church near Simpsonville. (Courtesy of Mike and Carol Leake.)

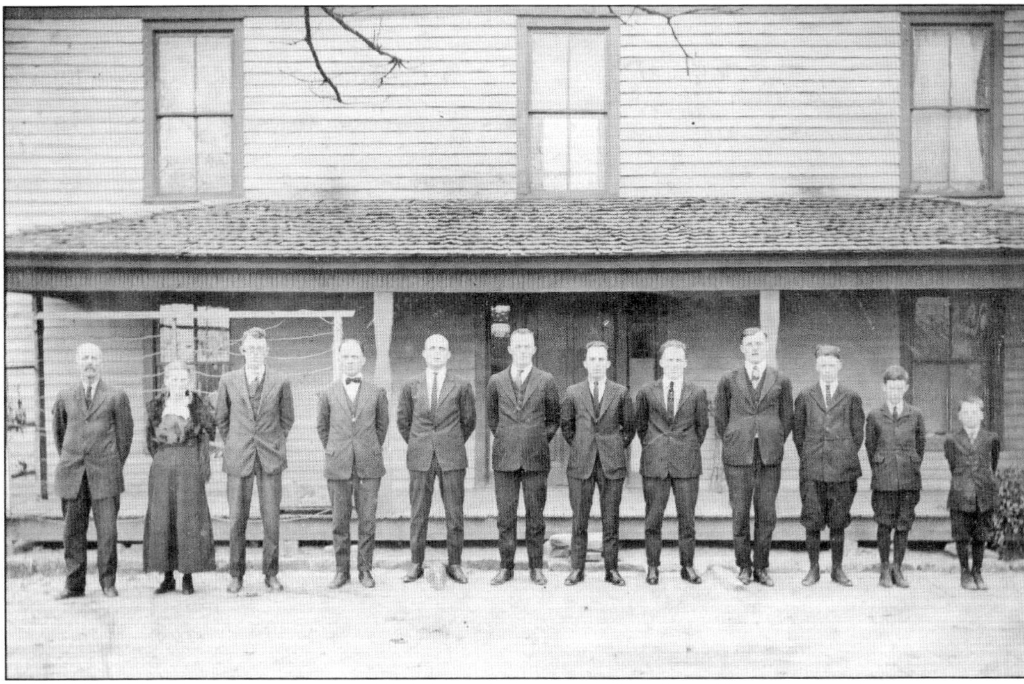

From left to right are parents Newton and Lillian Gault and sons Ernest, Lester, Hovie, Austin, Marvin, Felton, Guy, Horace, Lloyd, and Bernard "Bud." The c. 1850 Newton Gault house, on North Main Street, is one of the oldest homes in town. It was an I-house plan, popular in the South during the 19th and early 20th centuries among moderately wealthy rural families, according to the Historical Survey of Fountain Inn. The home remains today in the Hovie Gault family. Guy Gault was coauthor Dianne's grandfather. (Courtesy of Richard Gault.)

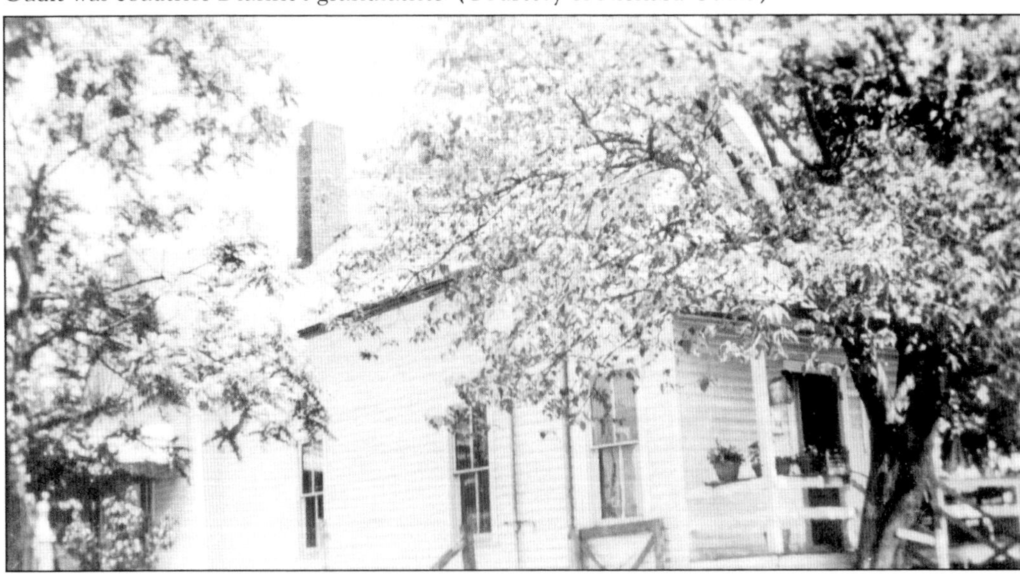

It is unknown if this home is still standing. The Jay "J.C." Drummond home was on the corner of North Main Street and Georgia Street in 1938. Jay Drummond and Nita Drummond Nelson were brother and sister. Nita was Juanita Moorman's grandmother and mother to Marjorie Adamson, a well-known educator. (Courtesy of Juanita Adamson Moorman.)

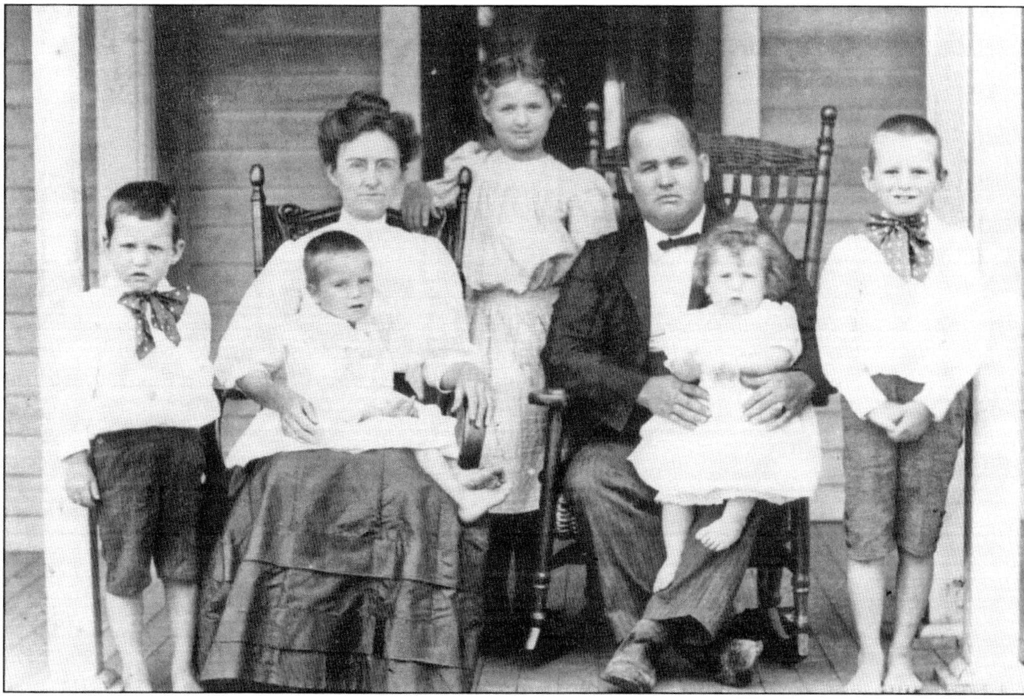

The Drummond family is, from left to right, Fred, Eugene, mother Mary Owings Drummond, Nita (Mrs. Paul Nelson), father James H., Larry, and J.C. J.H. Drummond was a member of the South Carolina Legislature. When he died, there were 12 pallbearers at his funeral, six white and six black, all his friends. (Courtesy of Juanita Adamson Moorman.)

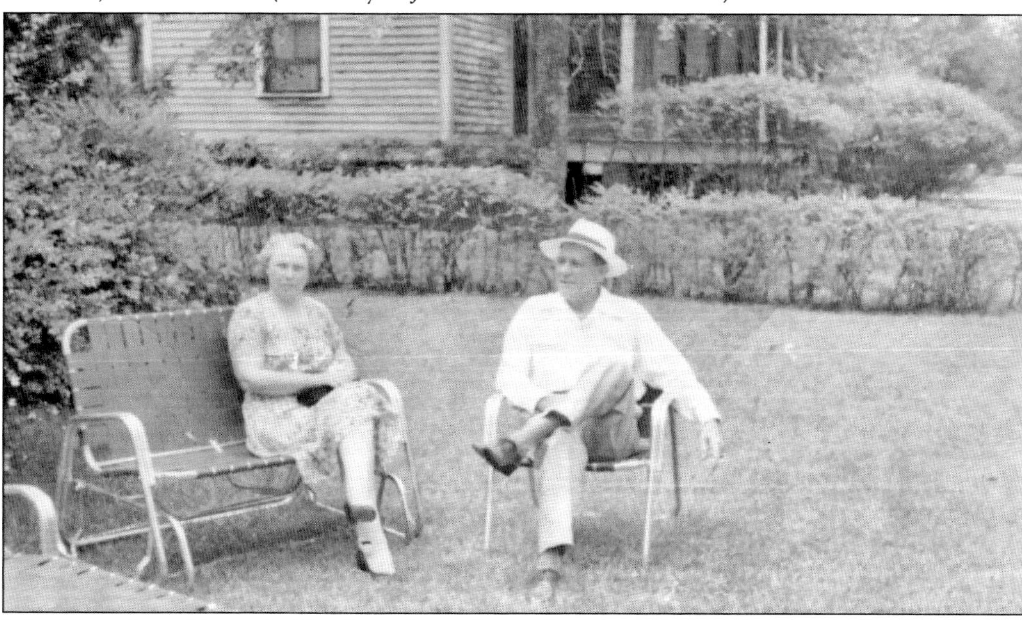

John Mims Sr. and his wife, Hazel, are shown here relaxing in their yard in 1954. In the background is the Fletcher Abercrombie home, which was sold and torn down. A small office building is there now on the corner of North Main and Craig Streets. The Mims home has been remodeled, and a member of the family is living there.

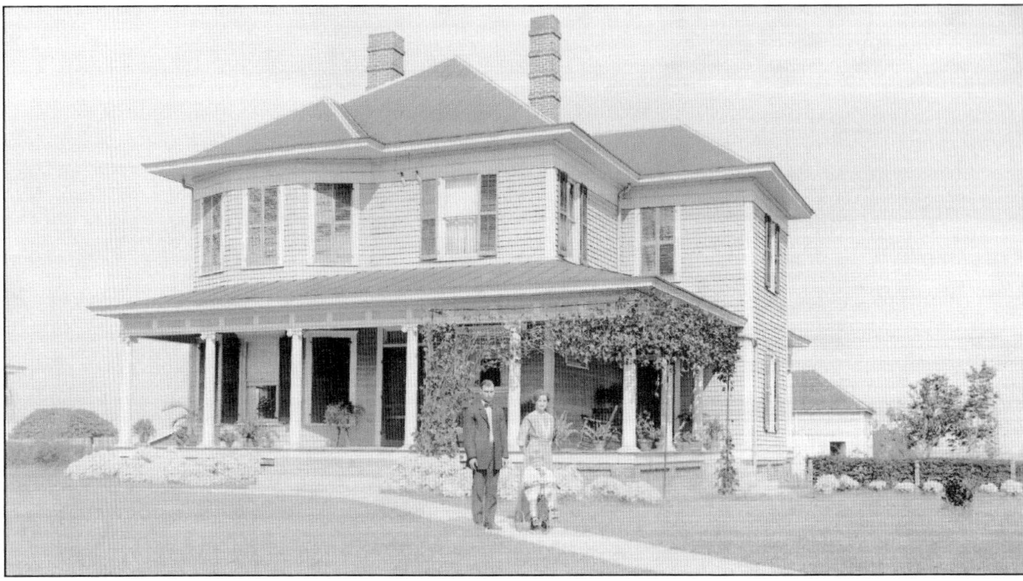

Dr. James Ambrose Fulmer Sr. and his wife, Emmie Belle Stewart Fulmer, pose with their son, James Jr., in front of their first residence around 1916. Constructed in 1912 by Fountain Inn contractor Richard Abner "Dick" Jones at the northeast corner of North Main Street and present-day Quillen Avenue, this dwelling was demolished in 1965 so that the Fountain Inn branch of the Greenville County Library could be constructed. The Fulmer house was patterned loosely upon the W.W. Kellett house on South Weston Street. Dr. Fulmer married Emmie Belle Stewart in 1912. This house was later purchased by William Butler Garrett Sr. (Courtesy of Henry Fulmer.)

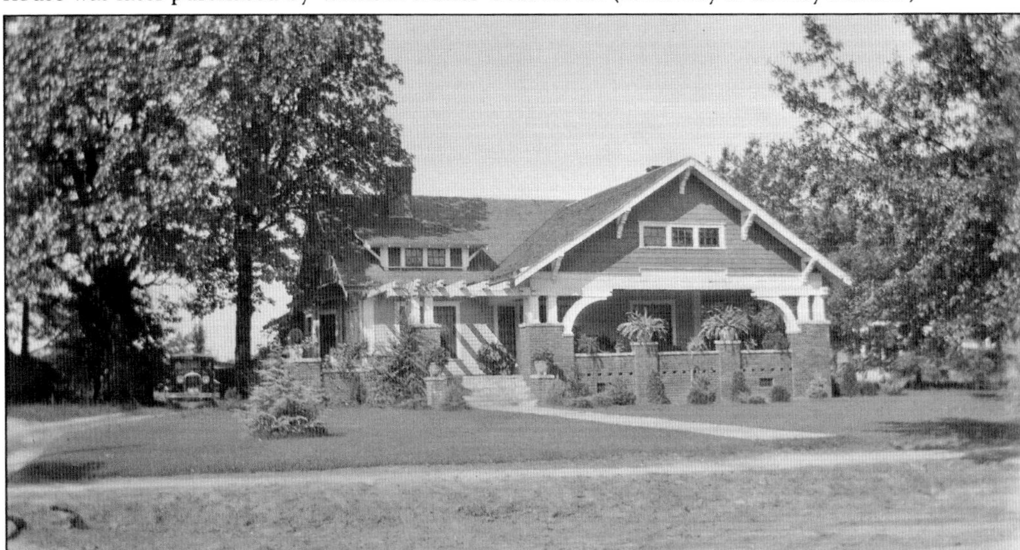

The Anderson house was on North Main Street between the Fulmer home and the First Presbyterian Church. It was built at the cost of $17,000 but in 1928 was for sale by John Hughes for $12,000. In the 1940s, it was owned by J.B. Wasson of Fairview Road and rented to the Walter Smith family. In the early 1950s, Avery Patton purchased the house. The Patton family lives there now. It was built in the Craftsman style, as was the McDowell house on 500 North Main Street. (Courtesy of Henry Fulmer.)

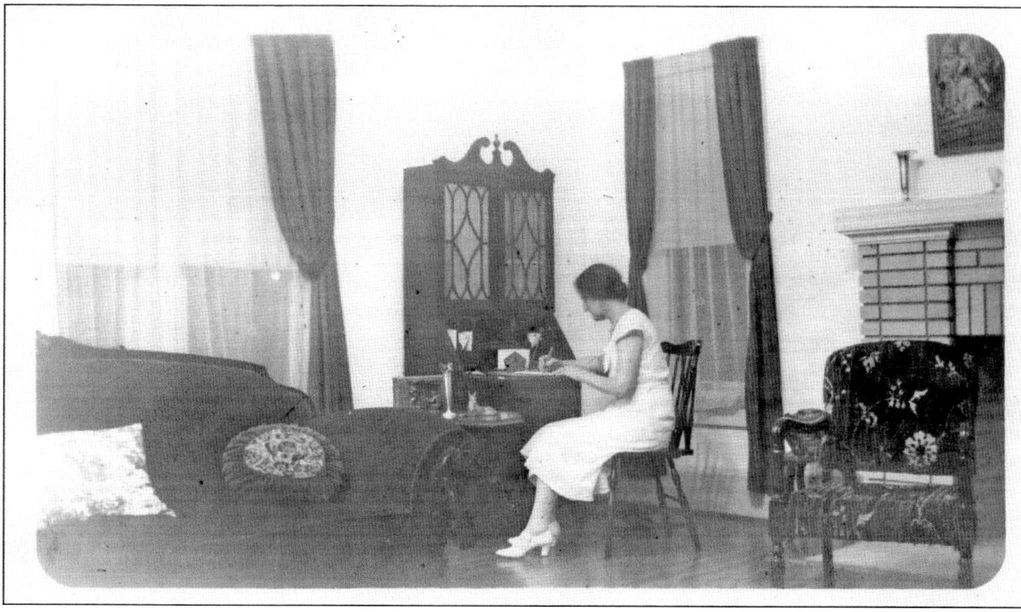

Emmie Belle Stewart Fulmer, wife of Dr. James Ambrose Fulmer Sr., is seated in the living room of her home at 303 North Main Street in 1933. This last home built by the Fulmers was constructed in 1932 by local contractor Richard Abner "Dick" Jones. Based on house book plans by Atlanta architect Leila Ross Wilburn, the floor plan of the Fulmers' house, which was listed in the National Register of Historic Places in 2015, was drawn by the couple's high school–age son, who followed in his father's footsteps and practiced dentistry in Fountain Inn for more than four decades. (Both, courtesy of Henry Fulmer.)

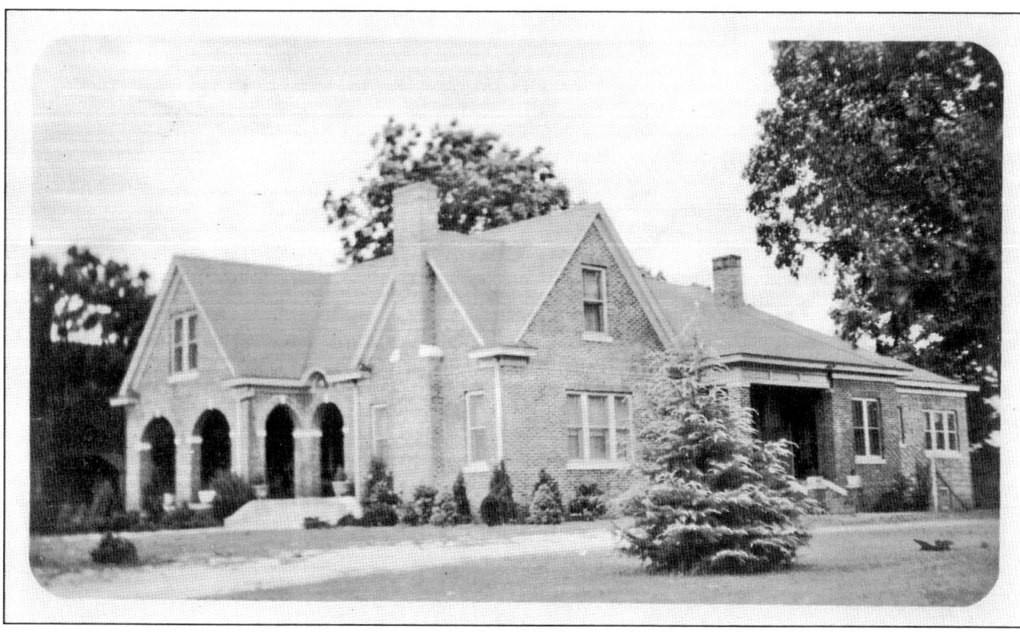

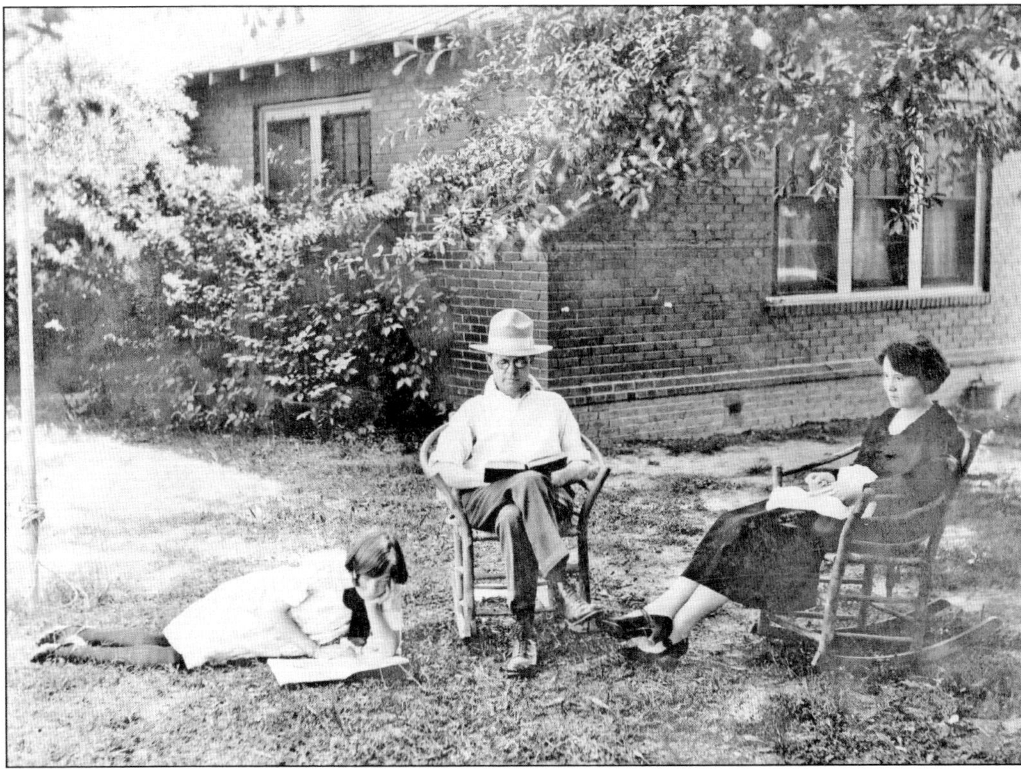

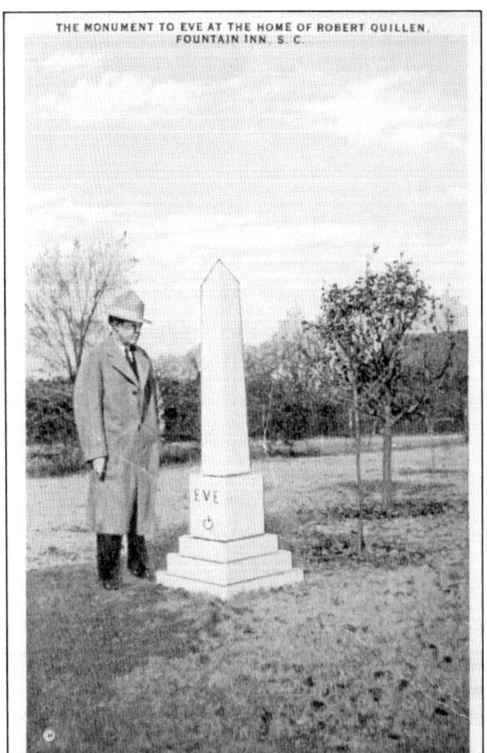

Robert Quillen; his second wife, Marcelle Babb; and Louise, their adopted redhead daughter, are shown in 1925 in front of their brick home on North Main Street where city hall now stands. At 16 years old, young Bob decided that school was not for him. He had grown up with his father in the printing business. Bob left his town of Syracuse, Kansas, and traveled. Still in his teens, he arrived in Fountain Inn, answering a newspaper ad. He was 19 when he married Donnie Cox. After the death of Donnie, he married Marcelle Babb and raised Louise. Bob became a syndicated columnist and cartoonist with letters to his daughter and cartoons of Aunt Het and Wee Willie Willis. During his last years, he wrote a daily editorial syndicated in 400 newspapers. Bob was a one-man relief agency. He took care of sick and poor, regardless of color. When it was known that he had erected a statue to "Mother Eve," he was criticized by some as being sacrilegious and was asked why. He replied, "She was a relative on my mother's side." The monument still stands near the reflecting pool.

The Greek temple Bob Quillen erected for an office still stands on city hall grounds and was never used. He wrote in his living room. Quillen's office and reflection pool are shown to the right. (Courtesy of Henry Fulmer.)

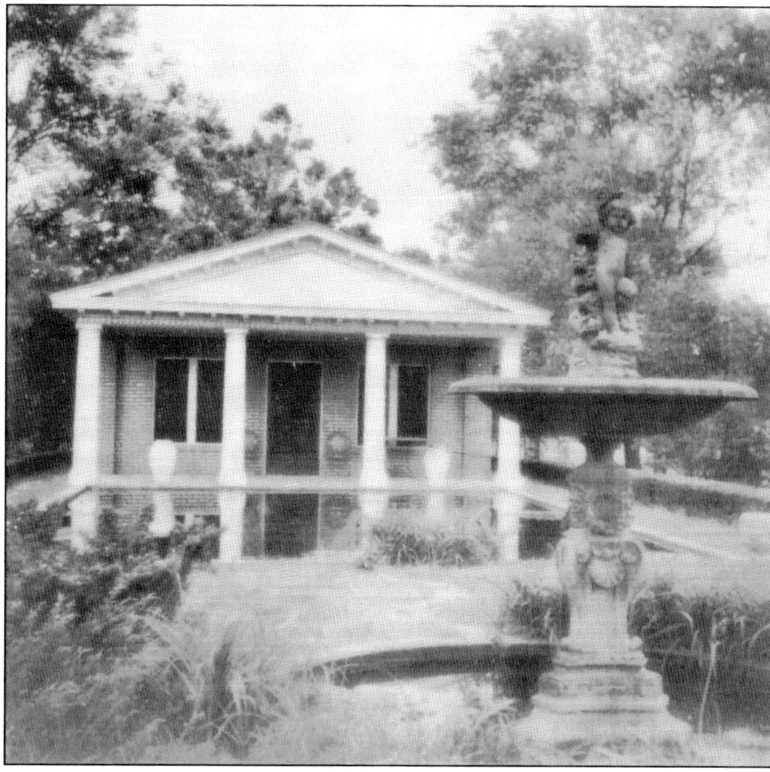

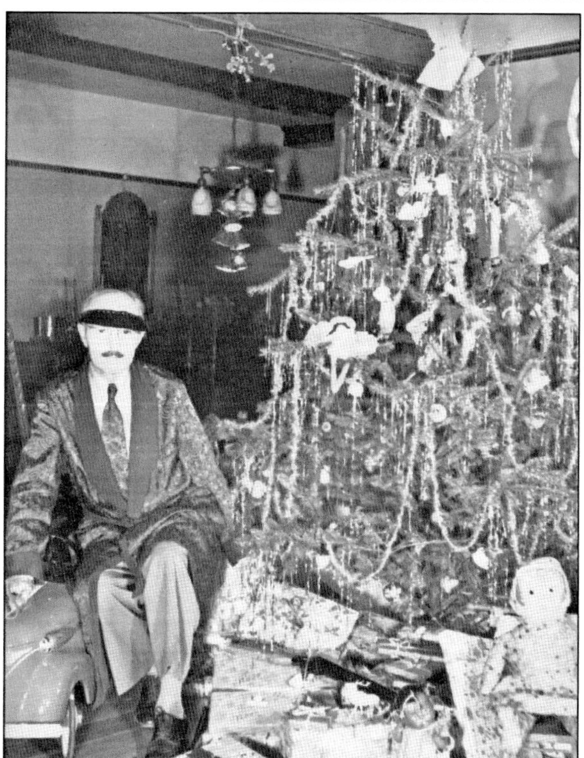

Young James Fulmer, who was an amateur photographer, captured this image of Quillen at Christmas. Quillen has on his green visor that he wore when writing. (Courtesy of Henry Fulmer.)

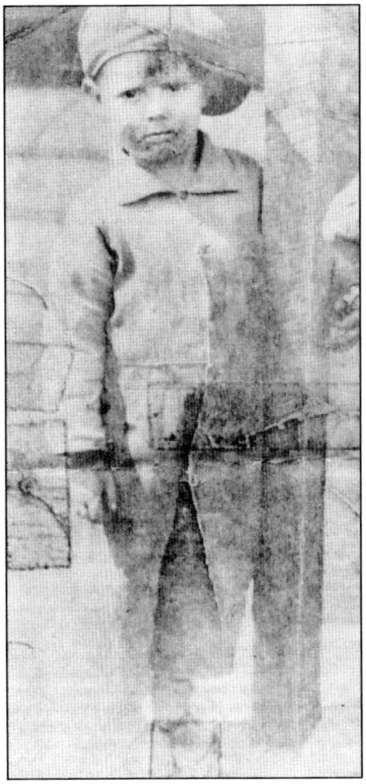

One day young "Junior" Smith, oldest son of Clint and Lula Smith, was out walking. Marcelle Quillen summoned him over and asked to take his picture. Bob Quillen was inspired by the photograph, and Willie Willis was born as one of Quillen's syndicated cartoons. Lula Smith was very embarrassed—Junior was dressed in too-short overalls and covered in chocolate that he had just eaten, and his cap was cocked to one side. Robert Quillen made him famous! When Junior Smith was grown, he became an assistant radio operator–waist gunner in World War II, flying over 50 missions. He married Marion Jones. (Courtesy of Jayne Smith Thompson.)

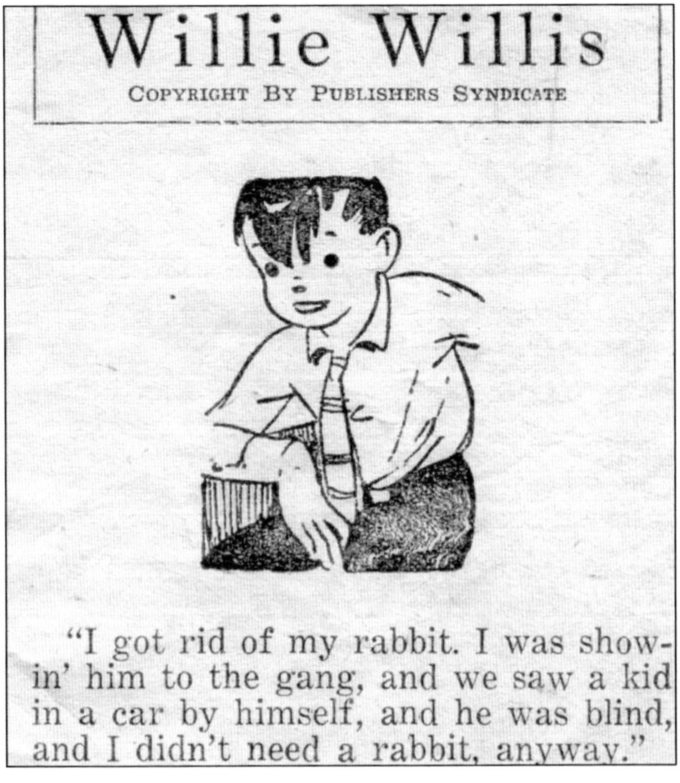

Elizabeth Massey Nelson was known throughout the community as "Grandma Nelson." She grew up in the old inn. One of her sisters was "Pretty Polly Massey," depicted in the Art Frahm painting. Her father, Zion Massey, was the innkeeper. Zion Massey, Pretty Polly, and her husband, William Darnell, are buried in the family plot. Granddaughters of "Grandma" and Thomas B. Nelson were Harriet Nelson Winn and Buena Nelson Farrow. (Courtesy of Juanita Adamson Moorman.)

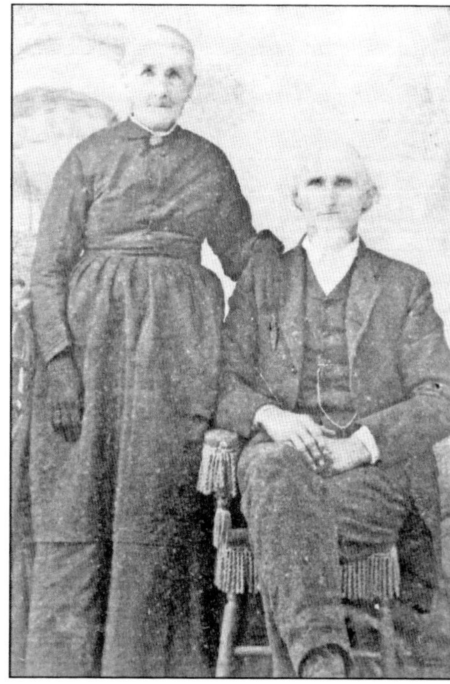

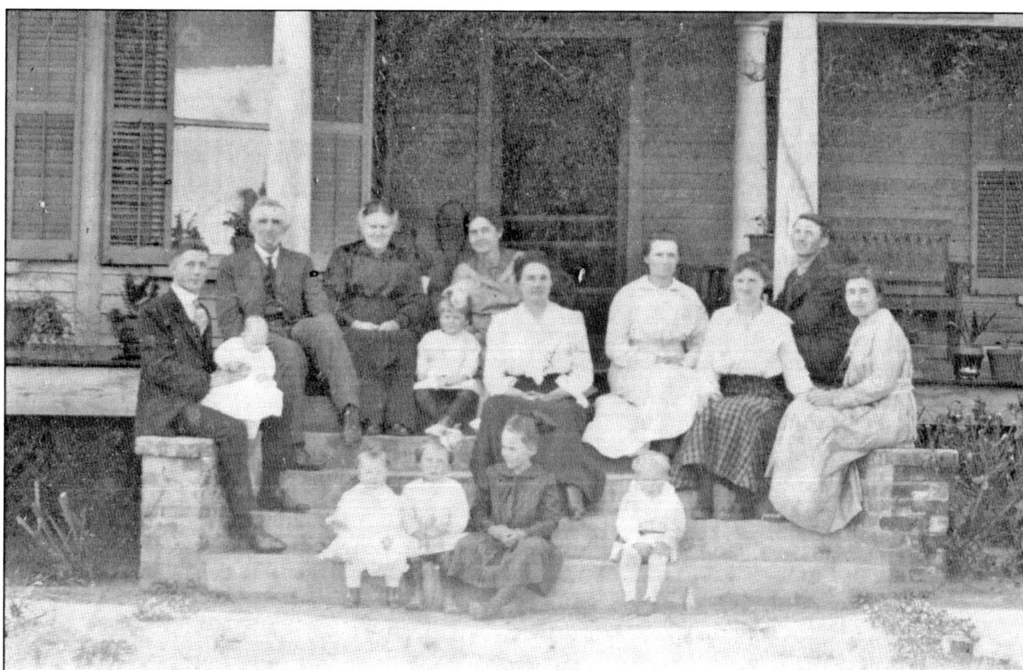

Family pictures were often taken on front porches, and this photograph shows the Nelson family in front of a home on Fairview Street. From left to right are (first row) Lala Templeton, Virginia Templeton, Nell Taylor, and Ralph Taylor; (second row) Guy Nelson holding Joe Drummond Nelson, John Henry Nelson, Julia Nelson, Julia McGee (child), Flora Templeton Nelson, Roxie Taylor, Maggie Nelson McGee, Nita Drummond Nelson, Paul Nelson, and Goldie Nelson Marlar. (Courtesy of Juanita Adamson Moorman.)

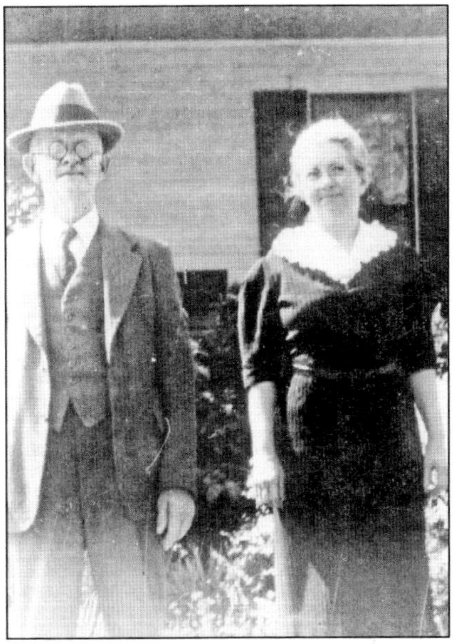

Sam Coleman was the son of Robert Coleman. A lifelong Baptist, he became a deacon in the First Baptist Church. He attended Clemson College and was a farmer and part-time veterinarian in the area, doctoring farm animals. Sam's wife, Caroline "Carrie," a graduate of Asheville Normal College, was a homemaker and writer. She had taught in a one-room school in Pelzer. This photograph was taken in the 1930s. (Courtesy of the Coleman family.)

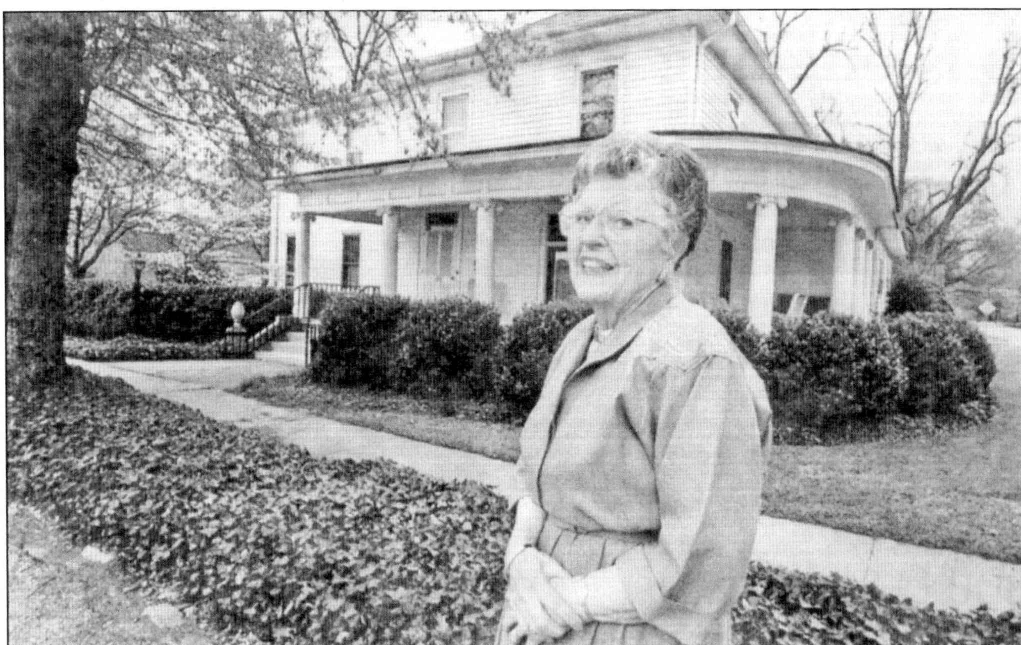

Mr. and Mrs. John Joseph Hitch, who lived in the Harmony community, moved to town because they wanted their children to attend the school held in the Masonic Hall. Hitch bought two lots from Cannon and West and built a home about 1885. In 1909, Hitch sold the property to his cousin Frank F. Edwards, who lived there with his family for almost 10 years. In 1920, Frank sold the lots and buildings, equaling over two acres on what is now Weston Street, to Arthur Guy and Nivia Cook Edwards, who moved with their daughters, Nell and Mary Frances Edwards Garrett (1916–2015), from the Edwards home place in Laurens County. The original two-story frame structure, built on a brick foundation and with white oak sills, remains intact today. The porch with its Ionic columns was added in 1914 and another wing in 1954.

The J.P. Kellett home, erected in 1909 on Weston Street, was listed in the *Tribune* as the most costly in Fountain Inn. Built for $8,000, it includes a large reception hall furnished in white with a huge fireplace and mission-style mantle. It also contains a living room, bedroom, and bath, a parlor furnished with mahogany, a dining room, a butler's pantry, and a kitchen downstairs. On the second floor are three bedrooms, a dressing room, and a trunk room. Both floors have long halls, and there are front and back stairways. J.P. was born in the Greenpond community and came to town in 1888. He was the son of Abner Babb and Betsy Babb Kellett. His wife was Mary Ellen West Kellett. J.P.'s son James "Bub" and Rene Kellett lived on one side in a brick home built around 1925; West and Mattie Kellett lived on the other side, built around 1920. The J.P. Kellett home is now occupied by great-grandson Ward and his wife, Starr Kellett. Ward has renovated many old Fountain Inn buildings.

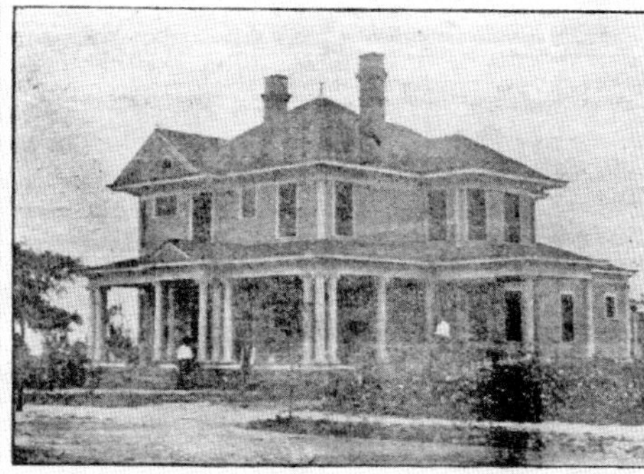

Fountain Inn Beautiful Homes, No. 1

J. P. Kellett's beautiful home is the most costly residence property in Fountain Inn. The house was erected in the summer of 1909, and the original cost was about $8,000.

It has thirteen rooms; a reception hall, living room, bed and bath room, parlor, dining room, butler's pantry and kitchen down stairs, and on the second floor three bed rooms, a dressing room and trunk room. A long hall runs through the house on both floors, and there is a front and back stairway.

The reception hall is finished in white, with a huge fireplace and Mission mantle. The furniture in this room is also Mission, and lends an air of substantial hospitality and comfort to the room.

The parlor is white throughout, mantle and all, and is furnished in mahogany, a combination of tones that contrasts sharply and yet seems fittingly harmonious.

A four horse power gasoline engine and dynamo, in a small building at the rear of the house, furnishes an excellent electric light service, and also pumps water to the 1500-gallon copper tank in the garret.

Mr. Kellett is a fancier of no mean reputation, and keeps four breeds of thoroughbred fowls, besides a kennel of Scotch Collies. He has the Kellerstraus strain of Crystal White Orpingtons, Rhode Island Reds, Black Orpingtons and War Horse Pit Games.

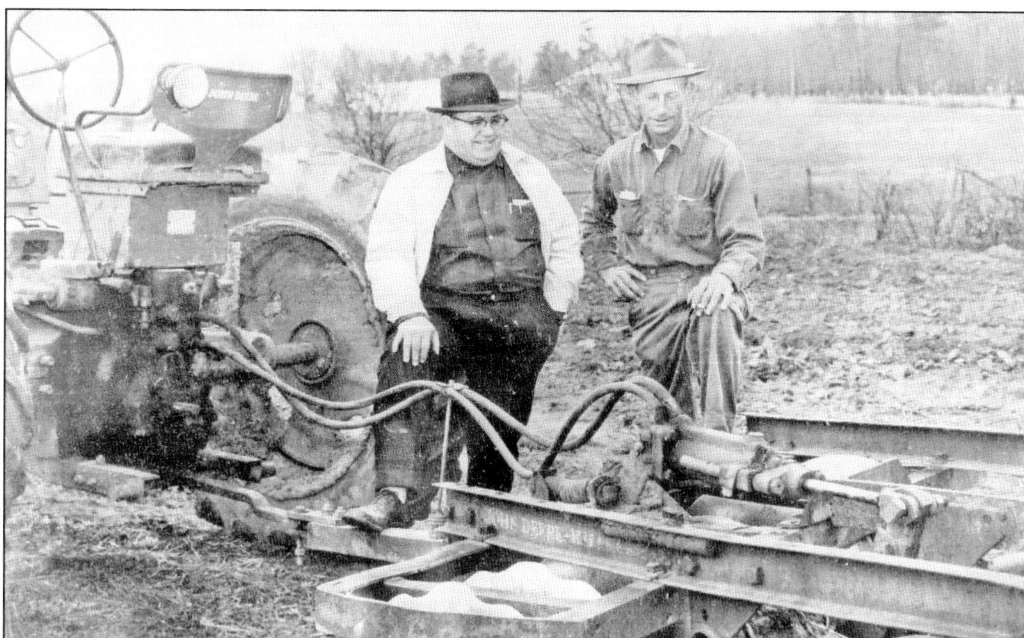

Walter Smith (left) and J.P. Kellett (right), first- and second-place winners in a county cotton growing contest, are shown discussing equipment to be used in preparing land for cotton. (Courtesy of Buzzy Smith.)

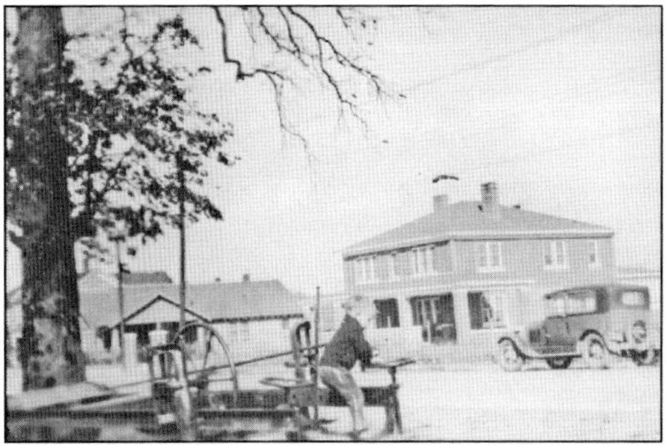

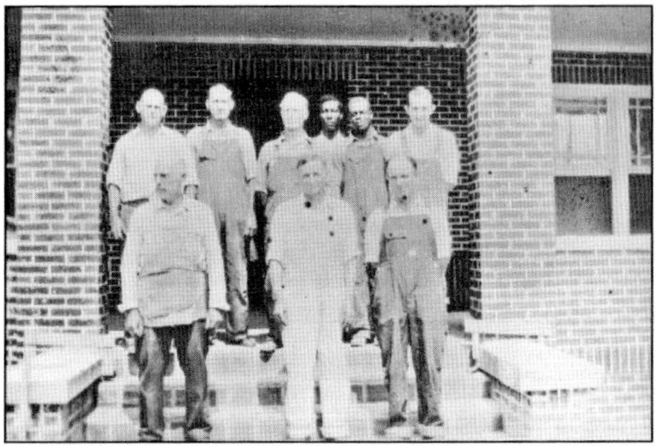

The V.M. Babb Jr. home was erected in 1930 by Dick Jones on the former property of the McNeeley family. The McNeeleys lived on what is now South Main Street and Highway 418. Their store on this property was one of the first in the area. In 1838, the post office was located here. William McNeeley was postmaster. They were one of the wealthiest families in the area. Harriet Nelson Winn and Beuna Nelson remembered them driving in a large carriage to one of the first Baptist churches in the area, New Prospect. The church was on what is now Highway 418 behind the old Arthur Fowler home on land owned at one time by Sam Coleman. After the Civil War, the McNeeley family lost their money and opened an inn in their home. Above left is the V.M. Babb home. Dick Jones and his workmen are pictured above right on the steps. (Courtesy of Donna Brown.)

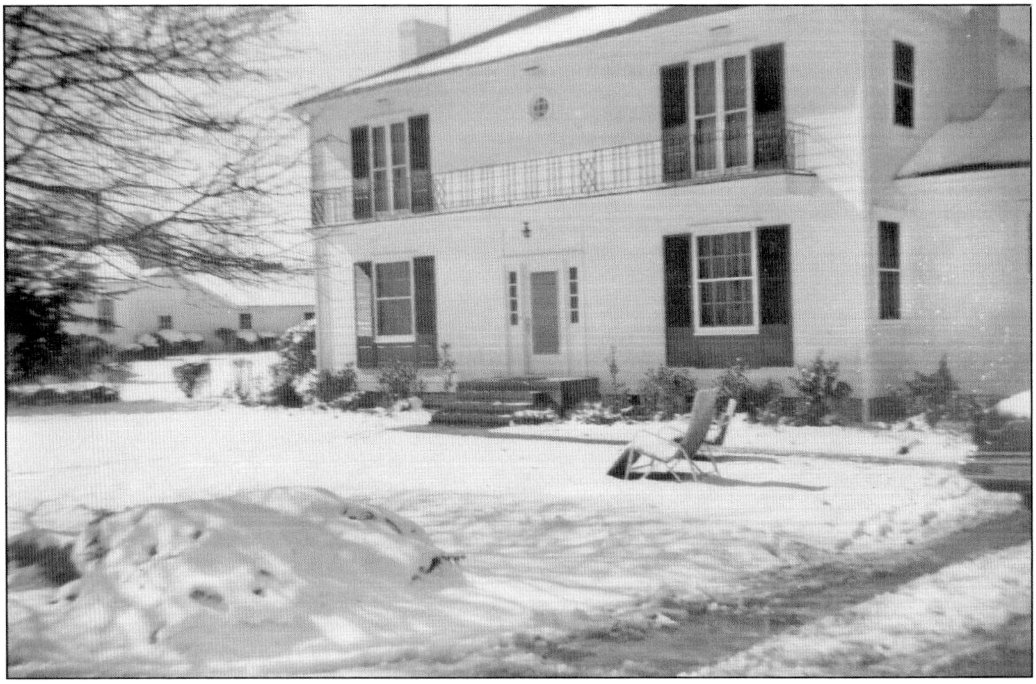

The George Wenck home was built in 1941. At that time it was considered the most modern home in Fountain Inn. George came from Piedmont and was a businessman and banker. He married Ann Woods White. Ann was the daughter of Hugh Dolphus and Mamie Wham Woods. Her first husband was Oscar Earnest "Pete" White, not to be confused with his cousin "Pete" White, the businessman in Fountain Inn. Ann's granddaughter Nancy and husband, John Yennie, reside there now. (Courtesy of Nancy Yennie.)

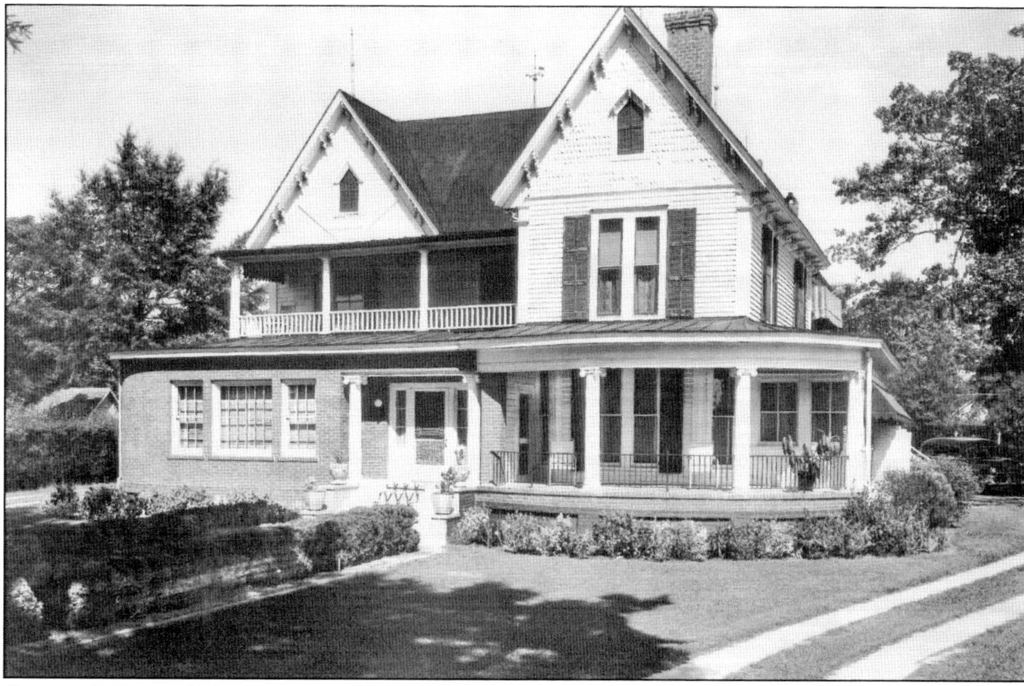

Cannon's Funeral Home on South Main Street was originally the home of the Cannon family. In 1936, Dick and Lila Cannon built a beautiful brick home on South Weston Street and converted their original home into an elegant funeral home for their business. Dick and Lila had three children: James, who continued the business, "Dickie," and Caroline. James and his wife, Sara Frances, started their married life across the street from James's parents. Sara Frances operated a kindergarten for Fountain Inn children and was very active in the Music Club and all civic organizations. She was the chair of the 1963 Clean-Up, Paint-Up and Fix-Up Day, which received national publicity and a large trophy.

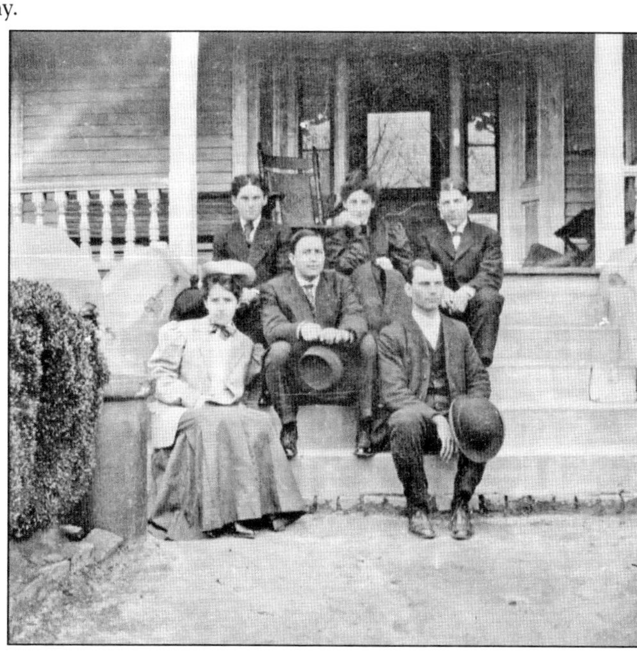

In 1907, friends gather on the back steps of the old Cannon home. From left to right are Annie Peden (Kellett), "Doc" Fulmer, ? Touchstone, Dick Cannon, and John McGee. (Courtesy of Henry Fulmer.)

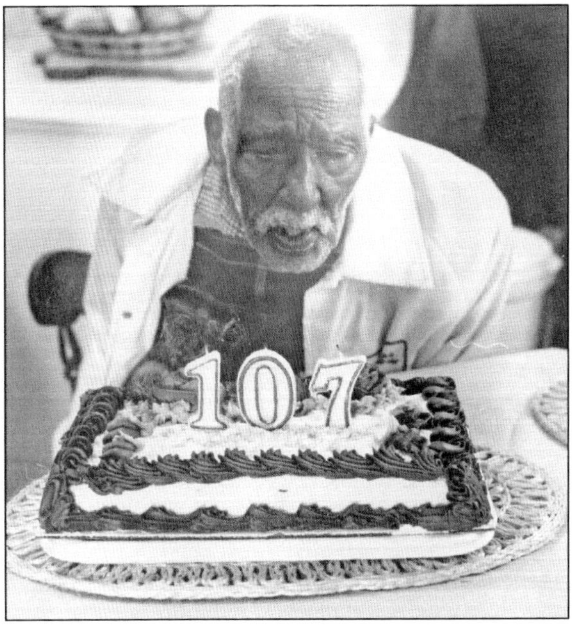

Sam Smith, born 1839, is shown here at his birthday party on June 20, 1946, when he was one of the oldest people in town. His memory was unfailing, and his reminiscences of Southern plantations and slavery times were so interesting that they were written down and filed with the historical department of the South Carolina United Daughters of the Confederacy. He remembered talking with John C. Calhoun on the plantation neighboring that of his master, Billy Bull, where he was born near the present Calhoun Falls. He saw the prosperity of the South and then devastation after the war, when whites and blacks alike had no homes and lived in poverty.

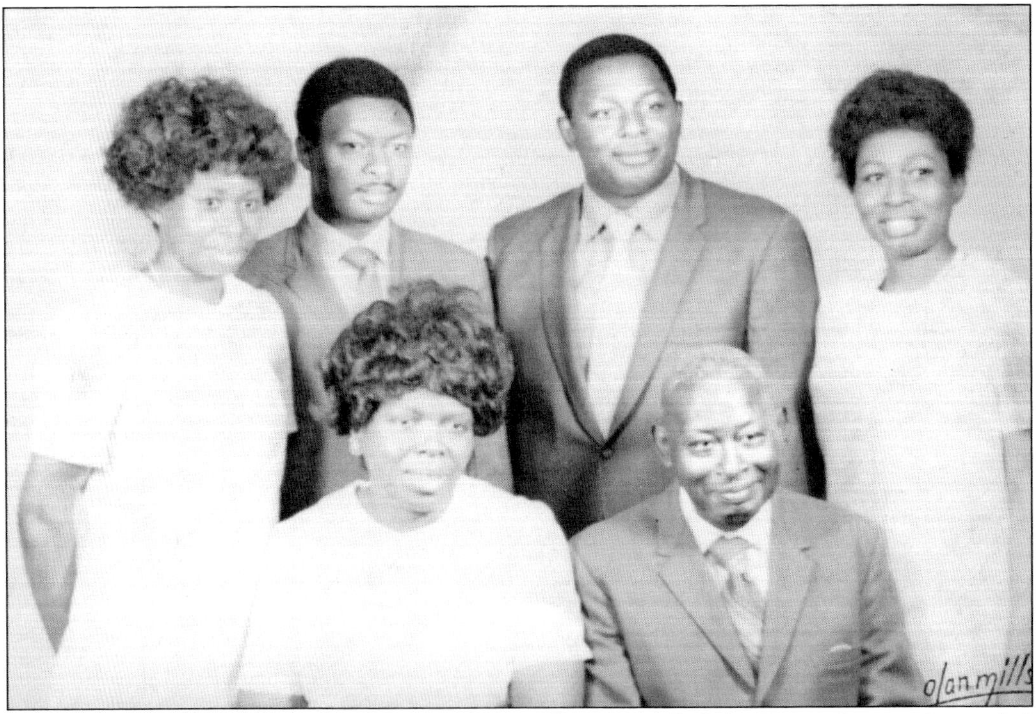

Emmanuel Sullivan grew up in Fountain Inn on what was called the Brown Line at Sanctified Hill. His wife is the former Lillie Moore. He was coach for the Recreation Association for 30 years and influenced many young lives. He was chairman of the Zoning Board, a member of the Rotary Club, and currently serves on the Museum Board. His father, John, was a carpenter and worked at Woodside Mill and the flour mill. The Sullivan family, pictured from left to right, are (seated) mother Terather and father John; (standing) Betty, Ezell, Emmanuel, and Sadie. (Courtesy of Emmanuel Sullivan.)

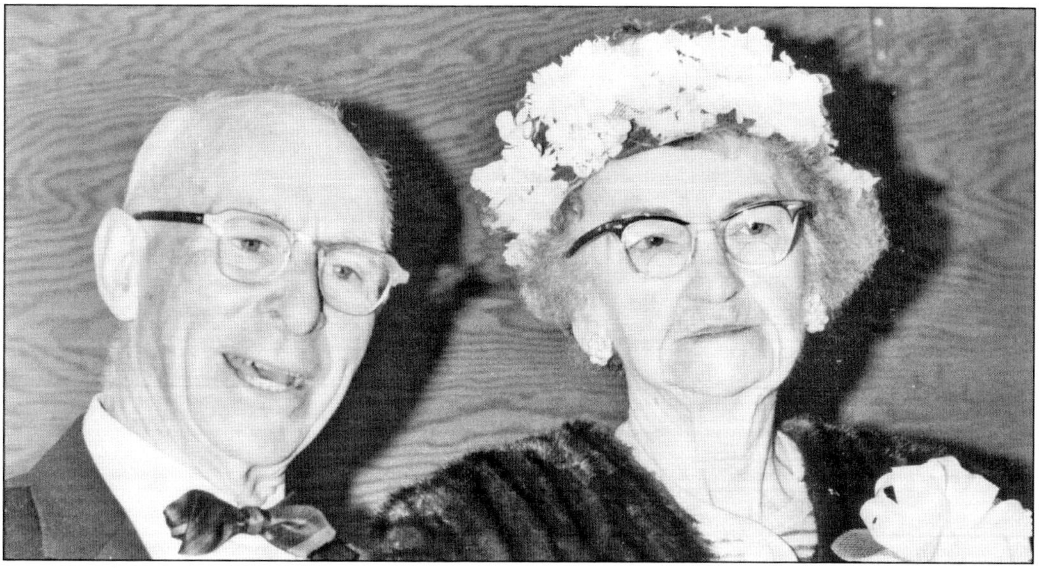

Stuart and Susie Rabb came to Fountain Inn from Lexington, North Carolina, and Washington, DC, in the 1940s. They became an integral part of the community, living on Thackston Street and then Weston Street, next to their son Dick and his wife, Barbara. Susie, known for her poetry, was a member of the American Pen Women, as was her friend Caroline S. Coleman. Rabbit Hollow was their summer home in Cedar Mountain, North Carolina. It was always open to friends and neighbors. The Rabbs were instrumental in organizing Holy Cross Episcopal church, which met in homes, the Rotary Hall, and a small chapel on Harrison Bridge Road before moving to Simpsonville.

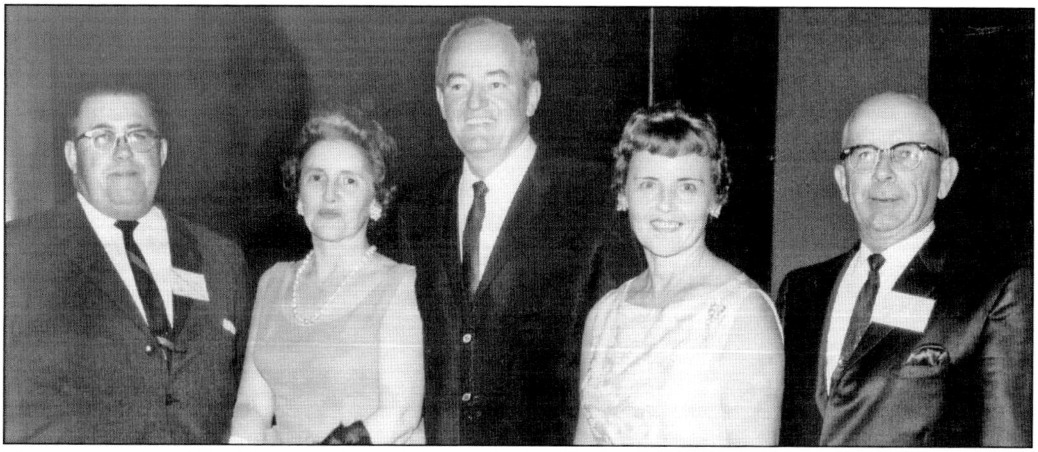

Walter Smith (1908–1981) graduated from North Carolina State with a degree in textiles and received a master's degree from American University. He retired from the Army Reserves as a lieutenant colonel after serving in France and Germany at the end of World War II helping renovate bombed mills. He was active in all civic organizations and was a charter member of Fountain Inn–Simpsonville Country Club, chairman of Greenville County Board of Commissioners, vice-chairman of Western Carolina Sewer Authority, and a member of the Masons, Shrine, Farm Bureau, and First Baptist Church. He married Marjorie Coleman (1912–2004), a Winthrop graduate and teacher. She was assistant librarian at Hillcrest High School for many years. They are shown here meeting with Vice Pres. Hubert Humphrey. Walter and Marjorie are on the left. (Courtesy of Buzzy Smith.)

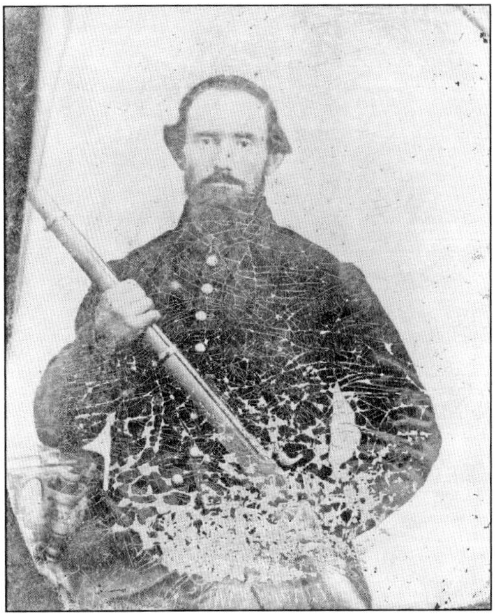

Pvt. Young H.E. Hitch (1825–1864) was in Company I, 16th South Carolina Volunteer Infantry. Young, born in Laurens, married Mary Ann Edwards in 1847. Two sons were born to them, John Joseph and Augustus Lucian. Young was killed while on picket duty at Kennesaw Mountain near Marietta, Georgia, on June 19, 1864. His body was not recovered. Absalom White, from Durbin, was in this regiment. Two other neighbors, Samuel McKittrick and James Scipio Peden, both in Company I, were wounded in the Battle of Atlanta and died in the hospital in Decatur within days of each other—McKittrick on July 22, 1864, and Peden on July 28. Their bodies were brought home to Fairview by a neighbor. (Courtesy of Elinor Holland Mowbray.)

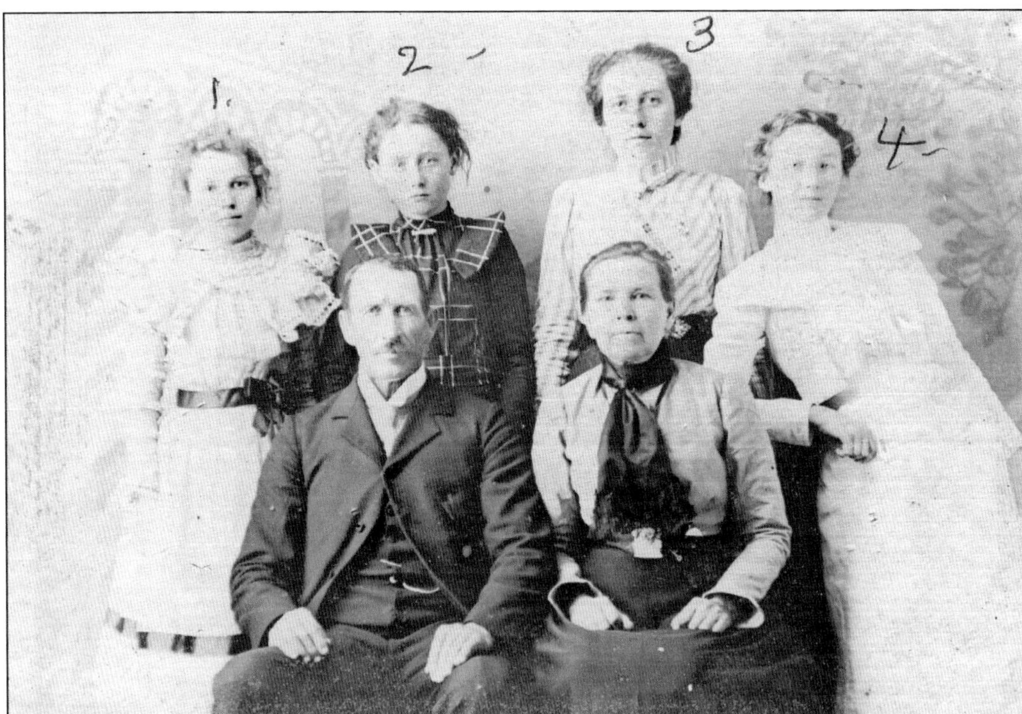

Augustus Lucian Hitch (great-grandfather); Sarah Elizabeth Bryson Hitch (great-grandmother); Nancy Mary Elizabeth "Bessie" Hitch (grandmother); Bessie's best friend, Grace Franks; cousin Mamie Cox; and cousin Zula Hitch West are shown above. According to the book *Oh, Lordy*, by Michael Givens Hitch and Elinor H. Mowbray, the family history in America began in Maryland in the 1700s, then moved to Laurens County around 1798. Some members of the family went to Georgia, Alabama, and Arkansas before the Civil War. (Courtesy of great-granddaughter Elinor Holland Mowbray.)

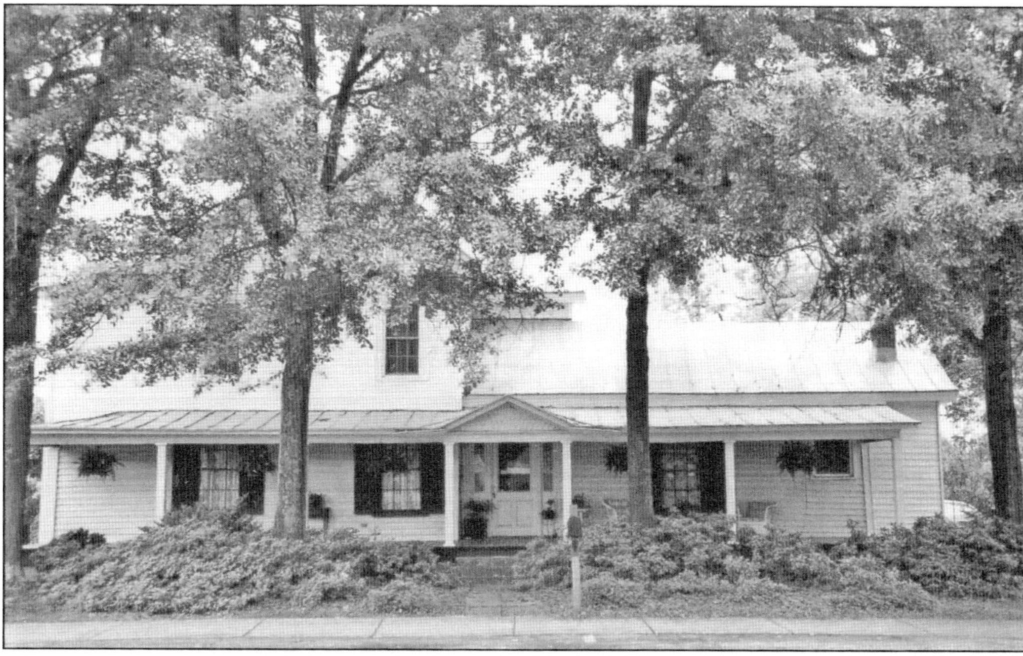

The property at 201 Hellams Street was purchased in 1893 by Augustus Lucian Hitch. Fred Bascomb Holland married his cousin Nancy Mary Elizabeth "Bessie" Hitch on November 24, 1910, at the home of her parents, Augustus Lucian and Sarah E. Bryson Hitch, built by J.R. Hellams. Fred and Nancy's daughter was educator Azilee Holland Mowbray. In the 1950s, there was a pasture where the bank building is now on the corner of Weston and Hellams Streets. The home is still in the family. Hellams Street was originally named Townville Street. (Courtesy of Elinor Holland Mowbray.)

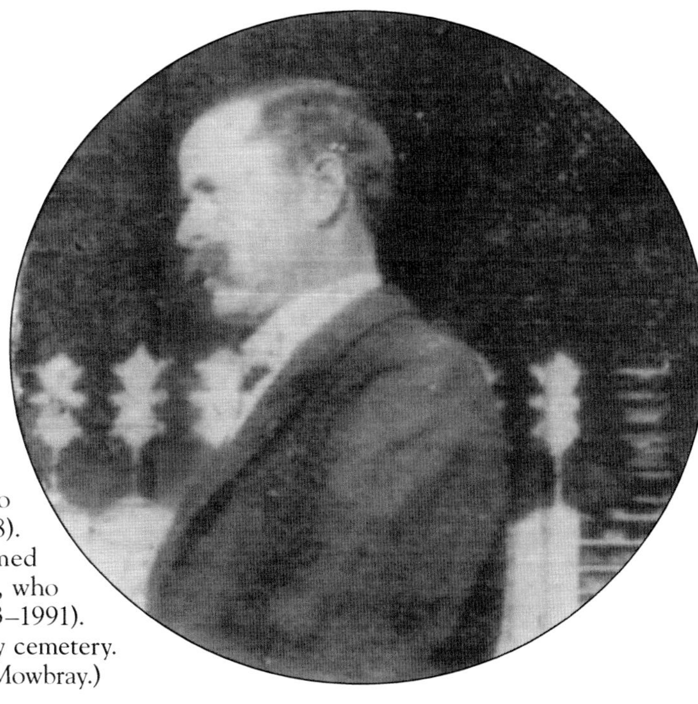

Nannie Hitch was married to John W. Givens (1857–1918). They had one son, also named John W. Givens (1901–1977), who married Nannie Jones (1903–1991). All four graves are in the city cemetery. (Courtesy of Elinor Holland Mowbray.)

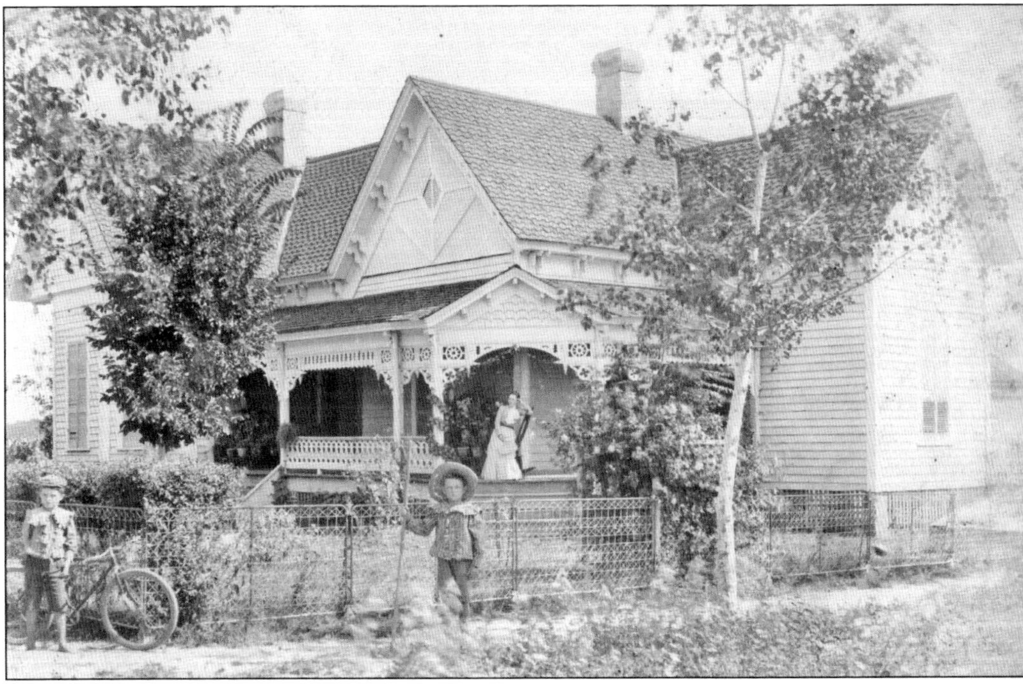

The Nannie Hitch Givens house was on the corner of Main Street and Hellams. Nannie Hitch Givens lived next door to her sister Zula Hitch West. The police station is located where both of these homes stood. (Courtesy of Elinor Holland Mowbray.)

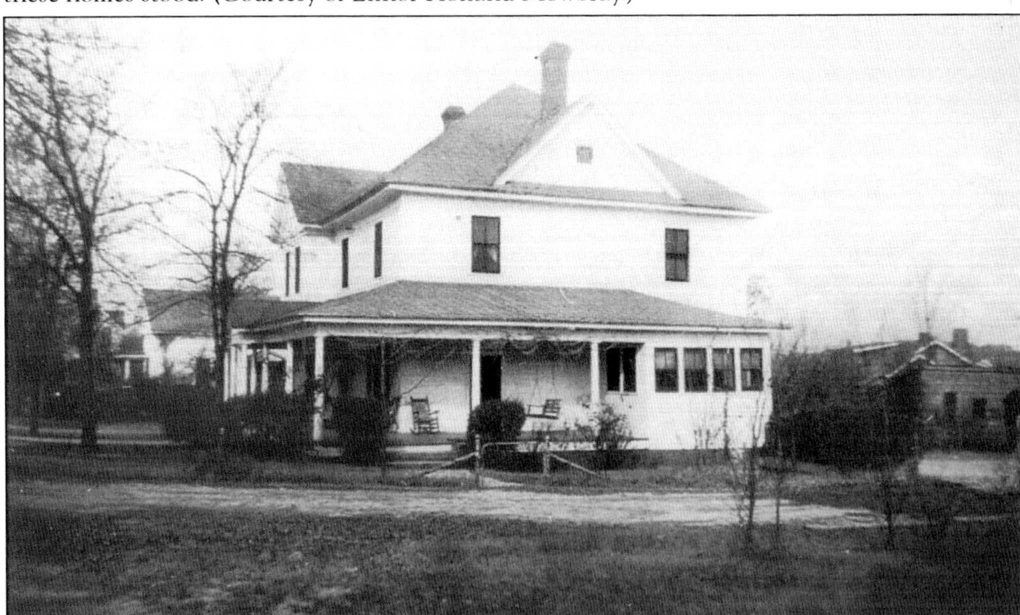

The Dolph and Mamie Woods children were Lula, Ann, Eleanor, and Roy. Ann was married first to Oscar "Pete" White, who died at the age of 50. Then she married George Wenck. This Woods home burned in the 1960s. It was located across from the First Presbyterian Church and is now a parking lot for the church. Another Woods home was located on the right, and the Charleton and Annie Lee Armstrong home was on the left. (Courtesy of Nancy Yennie.)

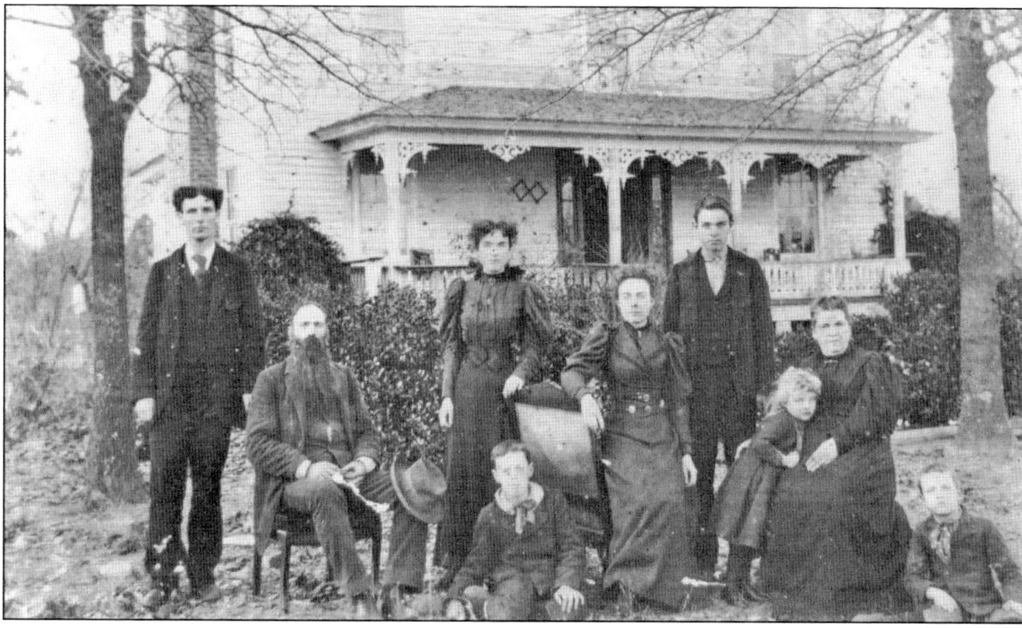

Traveling photographers would contact families in the late 1800s and offer to make a family photograph, for a fee of course. This picture of Butler Garrett's family was taken near Fountain Inn in 1895.This home, which burned down, was on the property where the Blake Garrett Jr. family lives. The mother in this photograph, Isabella, was one of Gideon Yeargin's daughters. She had two more children after this photograph was taken. (Courtesy of Blake Garrett Jr.)

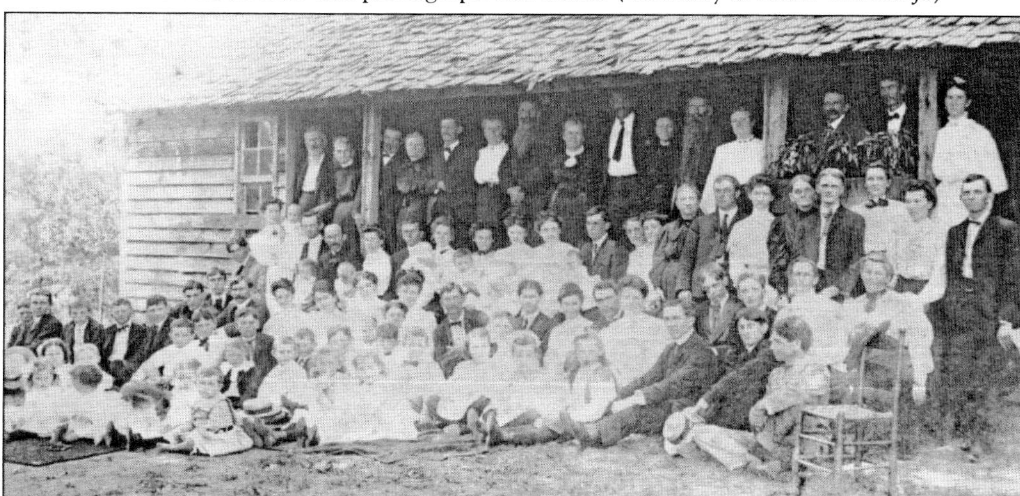

Butler Garrett is the tall man with the long beard seventh from left in the back row. Eighth from left in the back row is Isabella Yeargin Garrett; Butler and Isabella were great-grandparents of Blake Garrett Jr. Charles G.Y. Garrett, grandfather of Blake, is sixth from the right on the second row. Large families tended to be the norm in the 1800s. This is a picture of the family reunion of Gideon Yeargin taken in the Green Pond area of Fountain Inn in 1904. Yeargin had four sons and 10 daughters. The younger folks shown in this picture were said to have over 100 first cousins each. Gideon's daughters were the matriarchs of numerous families still living in Fountain Inn, including the Abercrombies, Garretts, Taylors, Hughes, Hellams, and Currys. (Courtesy of Blake Garrett Jr.)

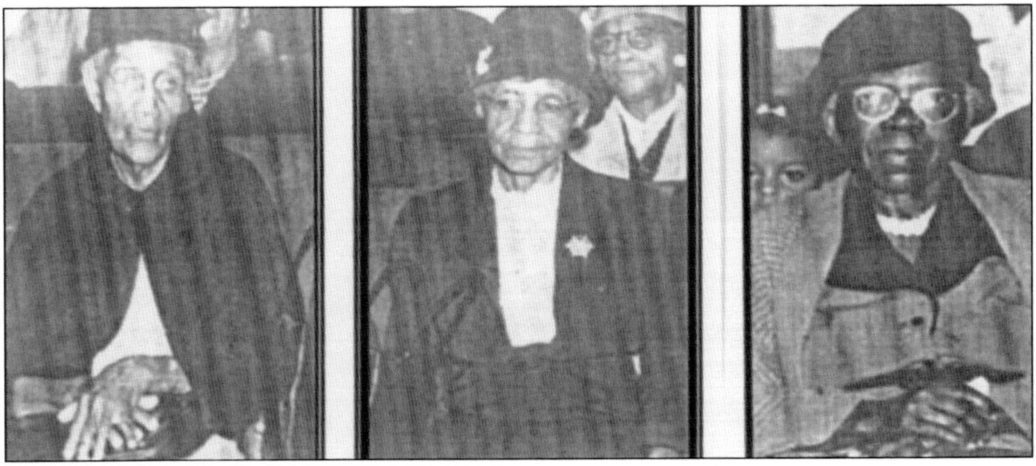

The women of Mount Zion Baptist Church always wore hats on Sunday as a sign of reverence, respect, and confidence. These hats could be passed down from one generation to another. Most of the hats were pull downs. Some would be brightly colored and embellished with flowers, ribbons, or feathers to look more formal. (Courtesy of the Putnam, Young, and Jones families.)

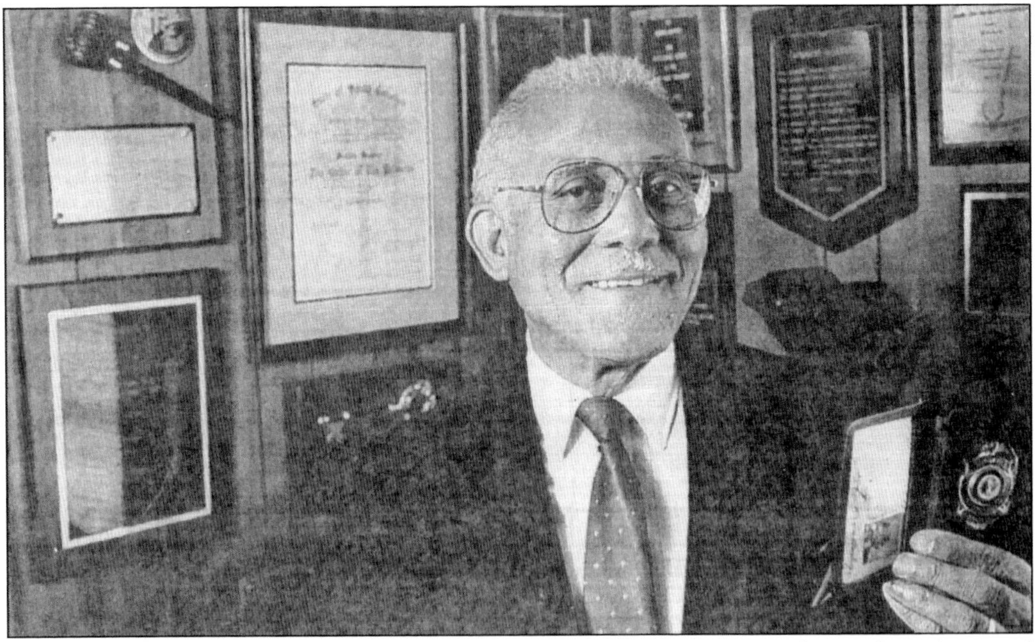

The Beasley Funeral Home, Inc., was established in 1947 in Laurens, South Carolina. A second location was established in Fountain Inn in 1961. Marion Beasley and his wife, the former Sarah Cunningham, now a retired librarian from Greenville County Schools, raised their three children in Fountain Inn. According to the funeral home's website, Mr. Beasley was the "first black in history to be appointed to the South Carolina Probation, Parole and Pardon Board in 1969 by Governor Robert McNair [and] first black chairman of the board in 1985." He has been presented with the Order of the Palmetto twice. (Courtesy of the Young and Jones families.)

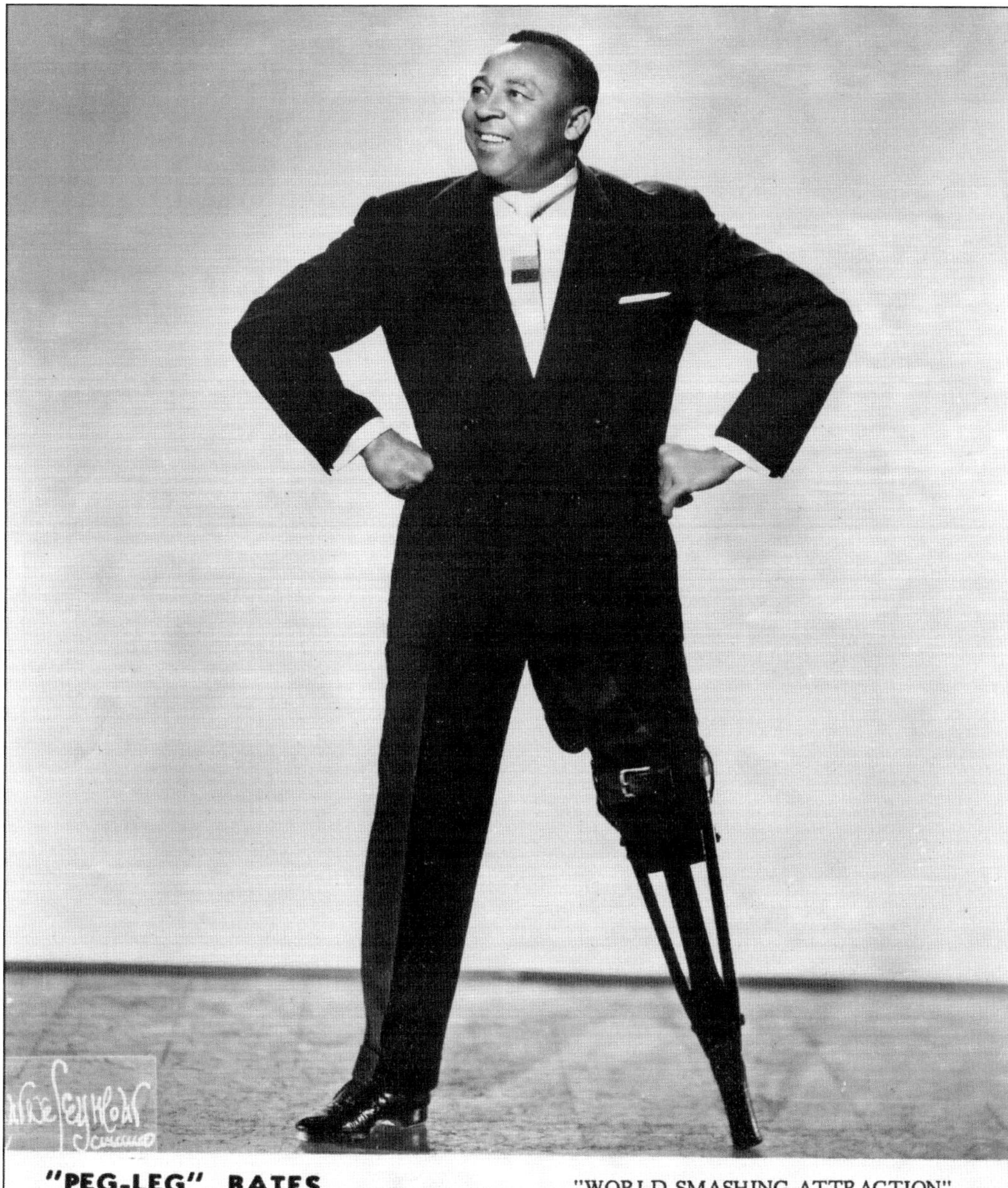

"Peg Leg Bates: Hero of Handicap" was written by Caroline S. Coleman and published in 1952 in the SC *Magazine*. She states that he was rated third in the nation for heroism in overcoming handicaps. Only Helen Keller and Franklin Roosevelt exceeded him. Peg Leg was born Clayton Bates in Fountain Inn to Emma Bates. His mother was a hard-working single parent, cooking and washing for families to support herself and her son. Clayton's mother taught him to mind and have good manners. One day, while at the oil mill plant in town, his leg became entangled in the machinery. It could not be saved. The town doctors operated and amputated his leg. The town families helped Emma and brought supplies and food until Clayton was better. They said he would never dance again. He had entertained in town and there had always been a crowd wherever he danced. But this young man did not let it get him down. His uncle made a wooden leg for him, such as was used by amputees in that day.

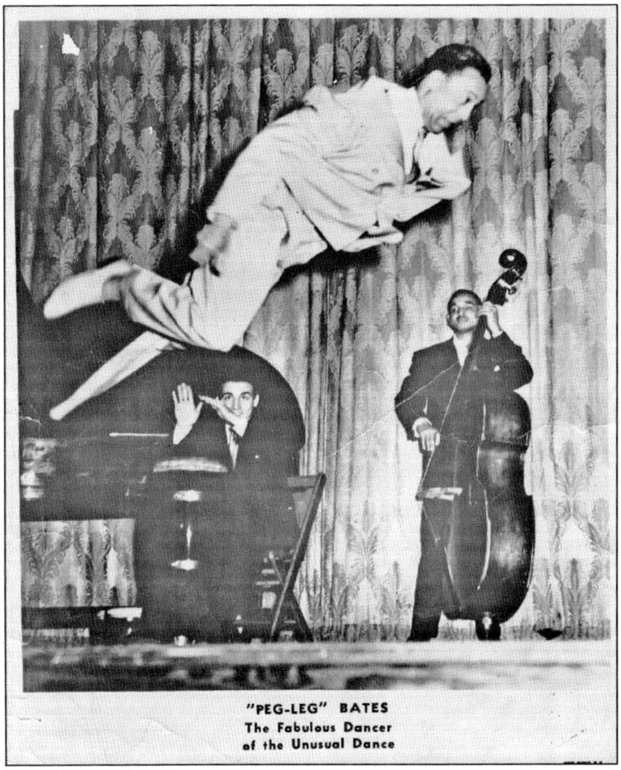

Peg Leg Bates and his mother, Emma Bates, moved to the larger town of Greenville, and many times he ran away to be in shows. Eventually a showman gave him a chance, and he went overseas to dance before great audiences. He danced a command performance before King George VI, Queen Mary, and the Prince of Wales. His mother was called to the stage to take a bow. Clayton danced more than anyone on the *Ed Sullivan Show*. He returned many times to Fountain Inn and was honored by civic organizations. He contributed largely to the Rosenwald school, and an addition was named after him. He never forgot his hometown and the folks who had supported him and his mother. Fountain Inn is proud to claim him as a citizen, and a monument was erected in his honor on the Robert Quillen and city hall grounds. (Courtesy of the Coleman family.)

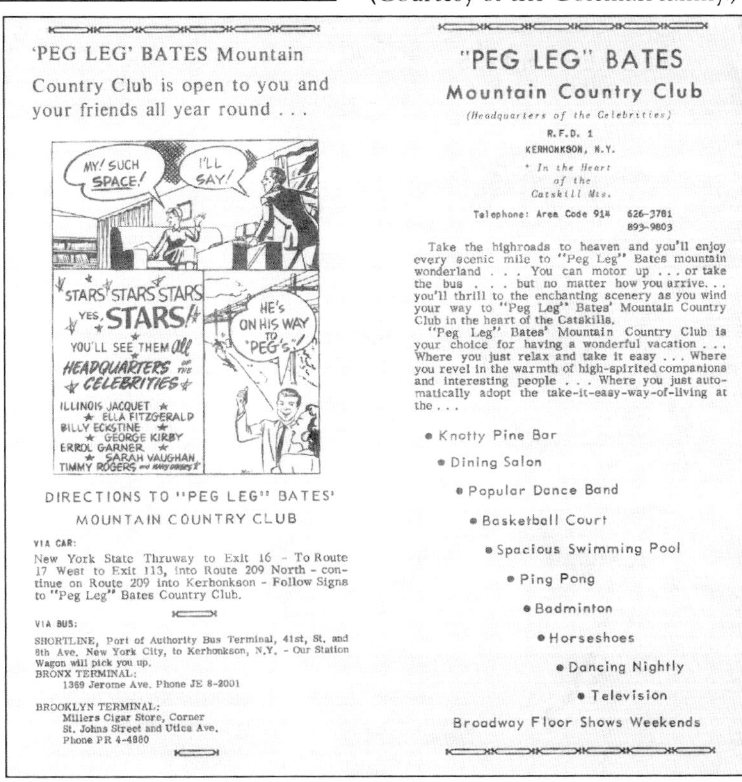

'PEG LEG' BATES Mountain Country Club is open to you and your friends all year round . . .

DIRECTIONS TO "PEG LEG" BATES' MOUNTAIN COUNTRY CLUB

VIA CAR:

New York State Thruway to Exit 16 - To Route 17 West to Exit 113, into Route 209 North - continue on Route 209 into Kerhonkson - Follow Signs to "Peg Leg" Bates Country Club.

VIA BUS:

SHORTLINE, Port of Authority Bus Terminal, 41st, St. and 8th Ave. New York City, to Kerhonkson, N.Y. - Our Station Wagon will pick you up.

BRONX TERMINAL:
1369 Jerome Ave. Phone JE 8-2001

BROOKLYN TERMINAL:
Millers Cigar Store, Corner
St. Johns Street and Utica Ave.
Phone PR 4-4880

"PEG LEG" BATES

Mountain Country Club

(Headquarters of the Celebrities)

R.F.D. 1
KERHONKSON, N.Y.

In the Heart of the Catskill Mts.

Telephone: Area Code 914 626-3781
893-9803

Take the highroads to heaven and you'll enjoy every scenic mile to "Peg Leg" Bates mountain wonderland . . . You can motor up . . . or take the bus . . . but no matter how you arrive. . . you'll thrill to the enchanting scenery as you wind your way to "Peg Leg" Bates' Mountain Country Club in the heart of the Catskills.

"Peg Leg" Bates' Mountain Country Club is your choice for having a wonderful vacation . . . Where you just relax and take it easy . . . Where you revel in the warmth of high-spirited companions and interesting people . . . Where you just automatically adopt the take-it-easy-way-of-living at the . . .

- Knotty Pine Bar
- Dining Salon
- Popular Dance Band
- Basketball Court
- Spacious Swimming Pool
- Ping Pong
- Badminton
- Horseshoes
- Dancing Nightly
- Television

Broadway Floor Shows Weekends

Joe, son of Nita and Paul Nelson, was stationed at Hickam Field, Pearl Harbor. When he saw bombs dropping, he decided to become a pilot. He was a member of 857th Bombing Squad. He was shot down and is buried in England. (Courtesy of Juanita Adamson Moorman.)

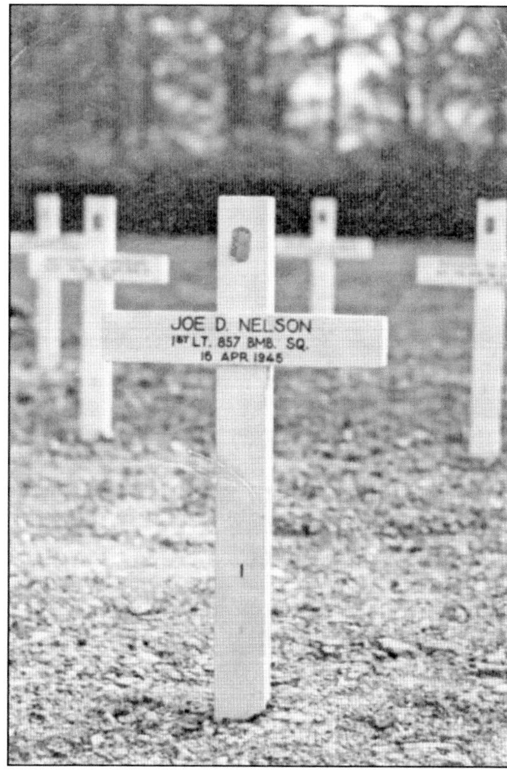

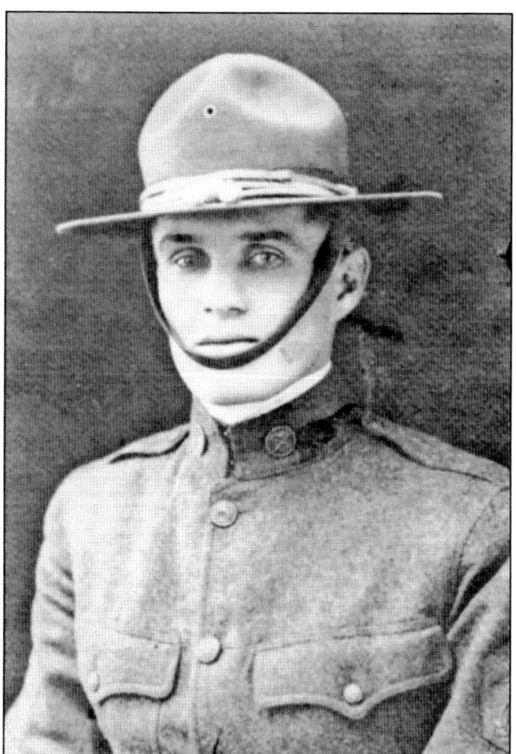

Oscar Earnest "Pete" White's (1892–1912) parents were Virgil and Ella Martin White. They lived between the New Harmony Church and Mount Carmel. His wife was Ann Woods. (Courtesy of Nancy Yennie.)

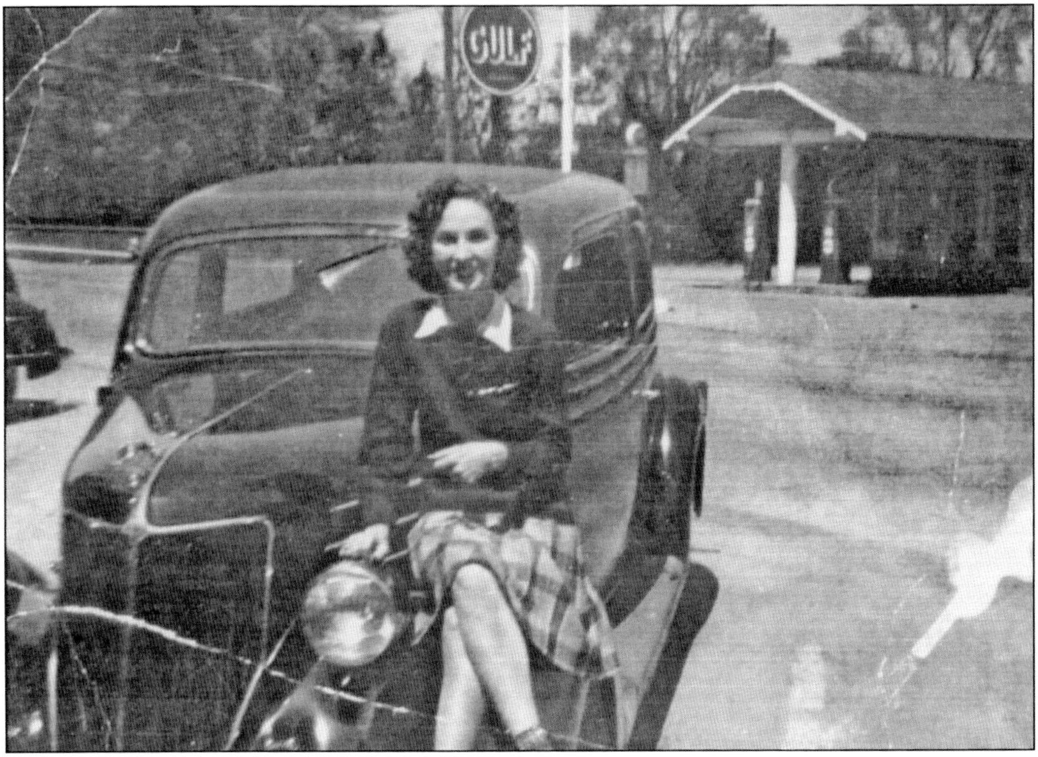

May Willis Gray is pictured in the early 1940s. She was a high school student working at Ben Franklin Five and Dime Store at 111 North Main Street. It was across from Horton's Gulf Station, seen in the background. (Courtesy of Buddy Gray.)

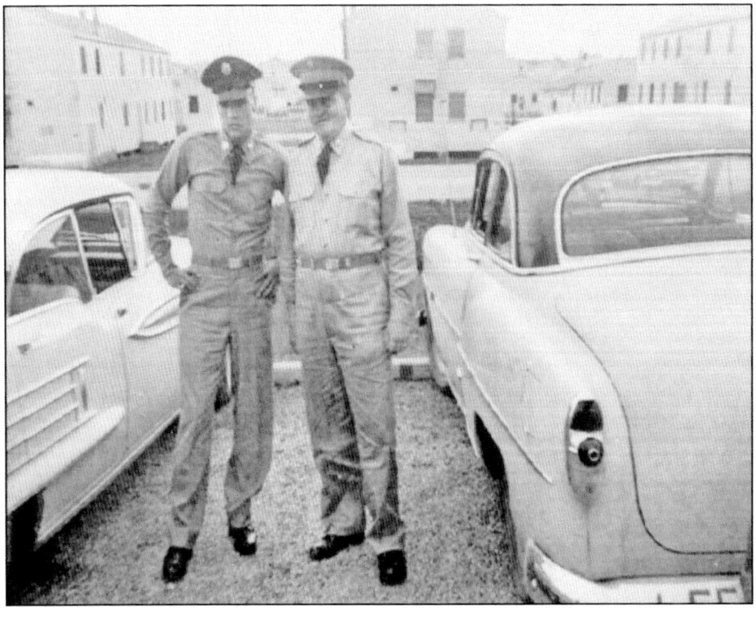

Elvis Presley (left) and Jim Willis (right) became acquainted while serving in the Army together. In 1958, there was an Elvis Presley fan club in Fountain Inn. One day it was rumored that Elvis was coming to visit Jim. Teenage girls ran up and down Main Street trying to find out if the rumor was true. Much to their disappointment, it was not. (Courtesy of Martha Owens Harrison and Candace Willis.)

Nine

Family Fun

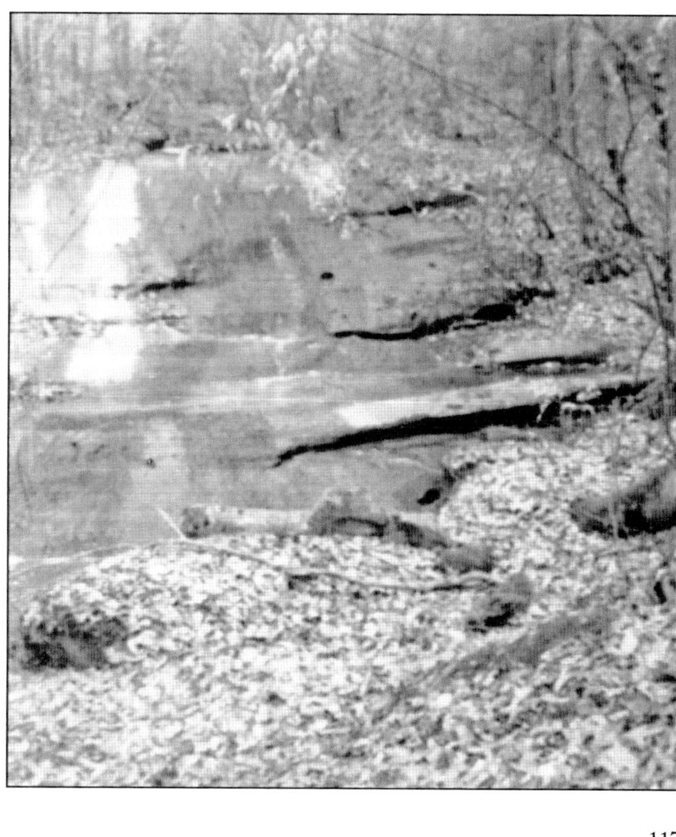

Who remembers the joy of slipping away on a hot summer afternoon up to the pasture to wade in a creek, or the fun of a Sunday afternoon picnic by the shoals? Even for those who lived in town, these pleasures were available nearby. Before there were home swimming pools or the Fountain Inn Simpsonville Country Club (opened 1956), there was the creek with its swimming hole, usually at the end of a big rock for sliding down. The boys would dam up one end to make the deep hole. There were no bought bathing suits; swimmers might wear a flour sack fashioned by their mother. This rock was behind the Terry home. (Courtesy of Edwin Terry.)

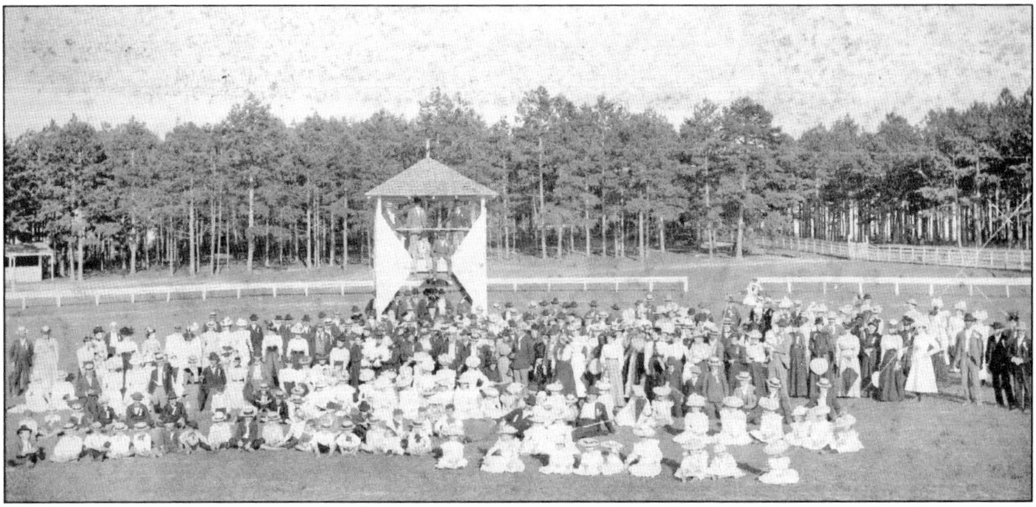

In 1886, Confederate veterans and their sons gathered at Fairview and organized the Fairview Agricultural Society. It later became known as the Fairview Stock and Agricultural Association. Rev. C.B. Stewart was elected president, and the society had 30 members. The first stock show was held on the lawn of Hugh Britt, a Fairview Sunday school teacher. The stock show was such a success that it was held annually and moved to a site on Fairview Church Road going towards Beulah. Always held on the first Friday of October, it was never rained out. The photograph above was taken at the first stock show held on that new site. (Courtesy of Fairview Museum.)

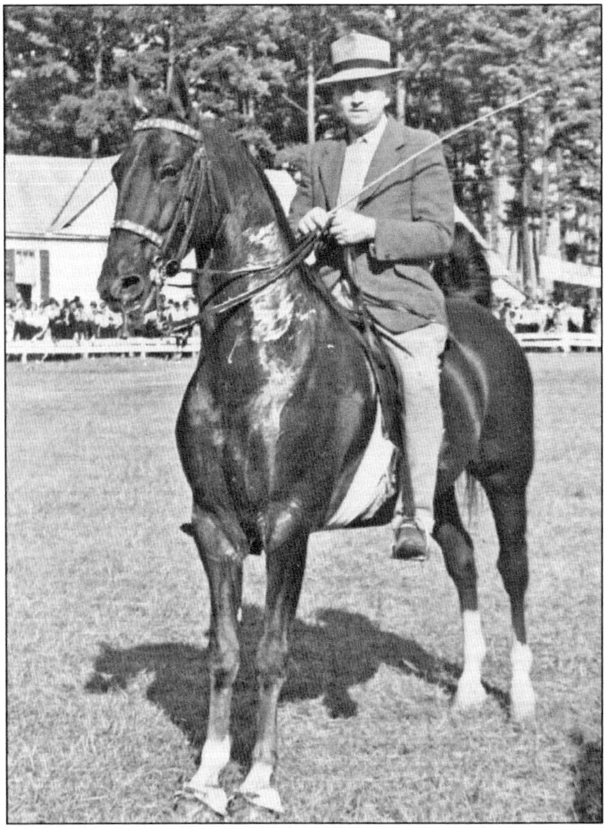

Jack Boyd was a well-known area horseman. He specialized in Tennessee walking horses and traveled to horse shows as far away as Georgia and Tennessee. These horses were shown, not raced, and required a special farrier. "Red" New was a farrier from Atlanta, married to Agnes Coleman of Fountain Inn. Red and Agnes and Jack and his wife, Lucia, became good friends who traveled together to horse shows. The Boyds lived north of Fountain Inn. (Courtesy of Henry Fulmer.)

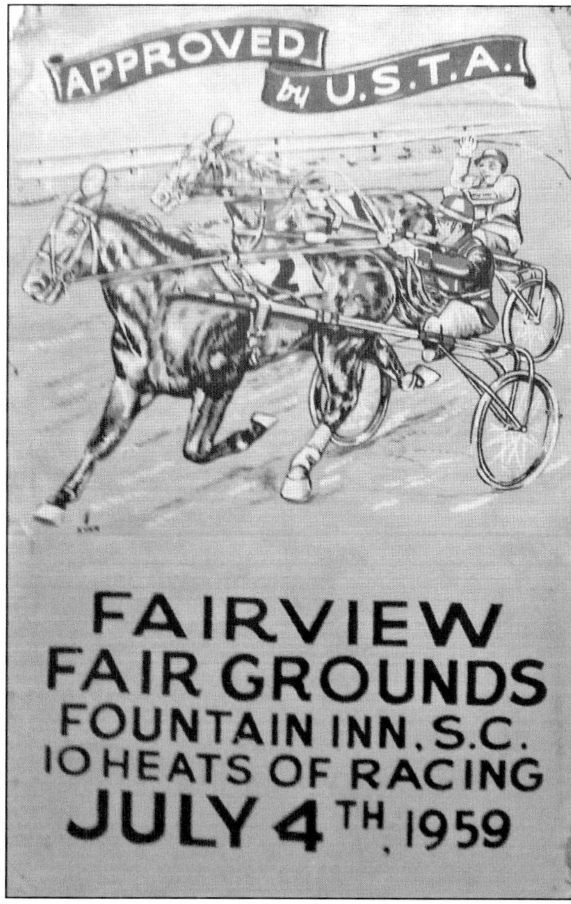

While the band played music, crowds stood around the ring about six layers deep—it was not a good view, unless one paid a quarter to sit in the grandstand. Fine horses pranced around the arena and then the harness races started. Everyone had favorites, and the cheering was loud. One local favorite, Luther Martin, is shown in the poster and the photograph. (Right, courtesy of Jackie Peden and Dale Knox; below, courtesy of Edwin Terry.)

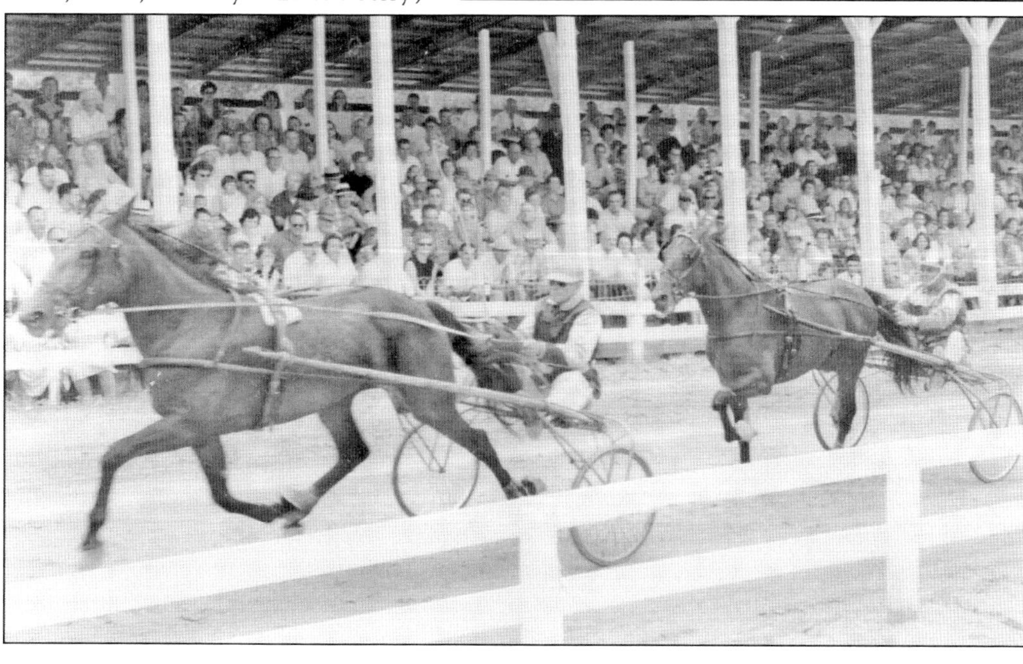

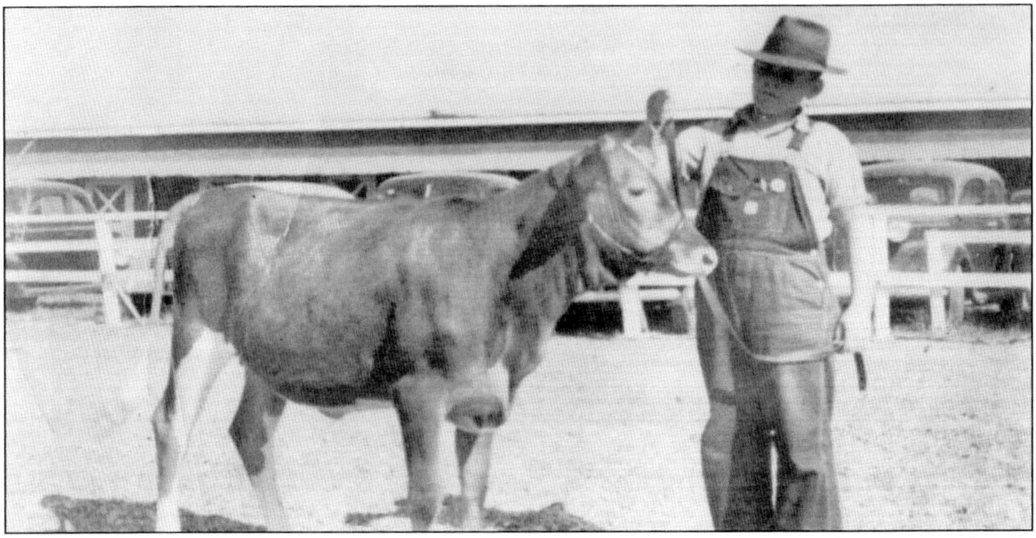

Ray Phillips is pictured above with his cow. The stock show had its heyday in the 1890s and early 1900s. People came from miles around in their buggies and on horses and mules. Before daybreak, the aroma of coffee would fill the air; it was made in big iron pots by the Ladies Aid Society and was 5¢ a cup. They sold plates of food for 25¢: fried chicken, country ham, biscuits, sweet potato pies, and homemade cakes. Lemonade, ice cream, and boiled custard did a booming business. Some families brought their own picnics. Farmers showed their best cows, pigs, and poultry. The Ladies Hall exhibited needlework, lace, and quilts. There was a culinary display of cakes, biscuits, pies, jams, jellies, preserves, and canned goods. Everyone coveted prizes—there was no cash, but blue, red, and white ribbons for first, second, and third place. Even the youngsters had their categories for best biscuits and cakes. (Courtesy of Edwin Terry.)

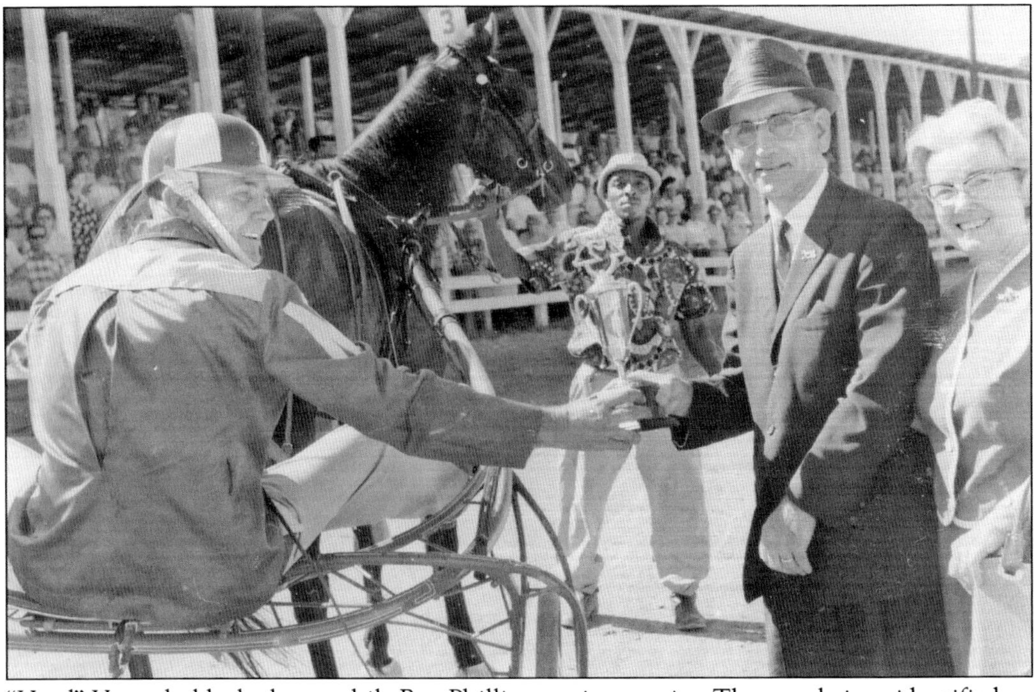

"Head" Henry holds the horse while Ray Phillips receives a prize. The couple is unidentified.

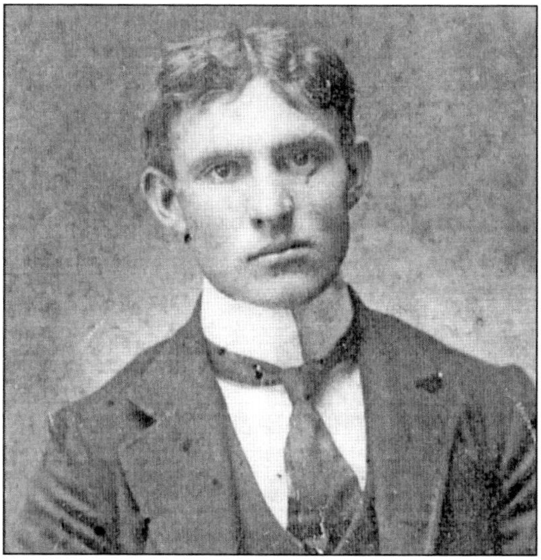

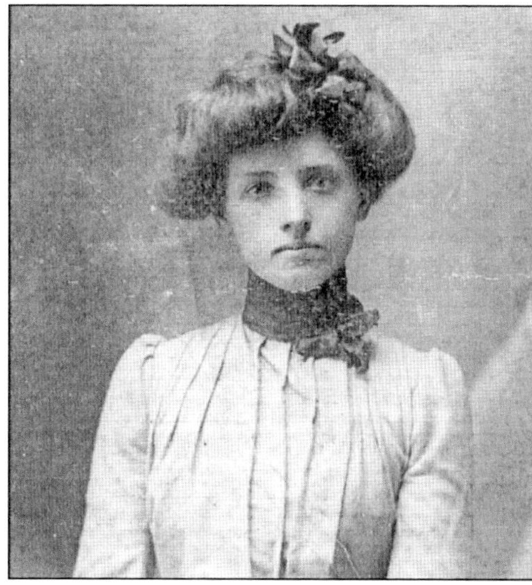

Flaud Curry (1882–1963) was a gentleman who was ahead of his time in recreation. He and Maida Gray (1881–1967) were married in 1907. They had two children, Gray Rapley and Sarah Alice. The family lived on the original Curry plantation, which Nathan Curry had purchased before 1800 from the Owings family. Peachline Branch was on his farm, so he built his family a swimming pool. Later, he hosted fish fries and swimming for his family, church, and community. (Both, courtesy of Sarah Jane Armstrong.)

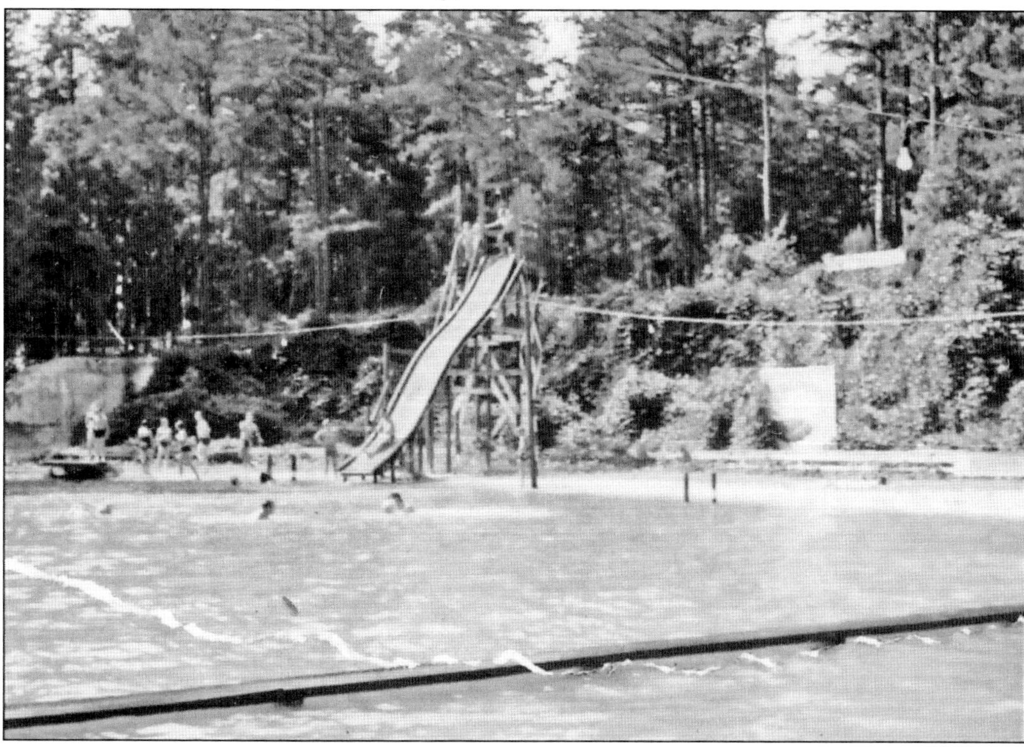

Flaud kept enlarging the pool until it became a lake with a white clay bottom and white sand for the beach and grounds. This was the highest man-made slide in Laurens County. Cool spring water rushed down it all the time. Flaud made the diving boards. (Courtesy of Sarah Jane Armstrong.)

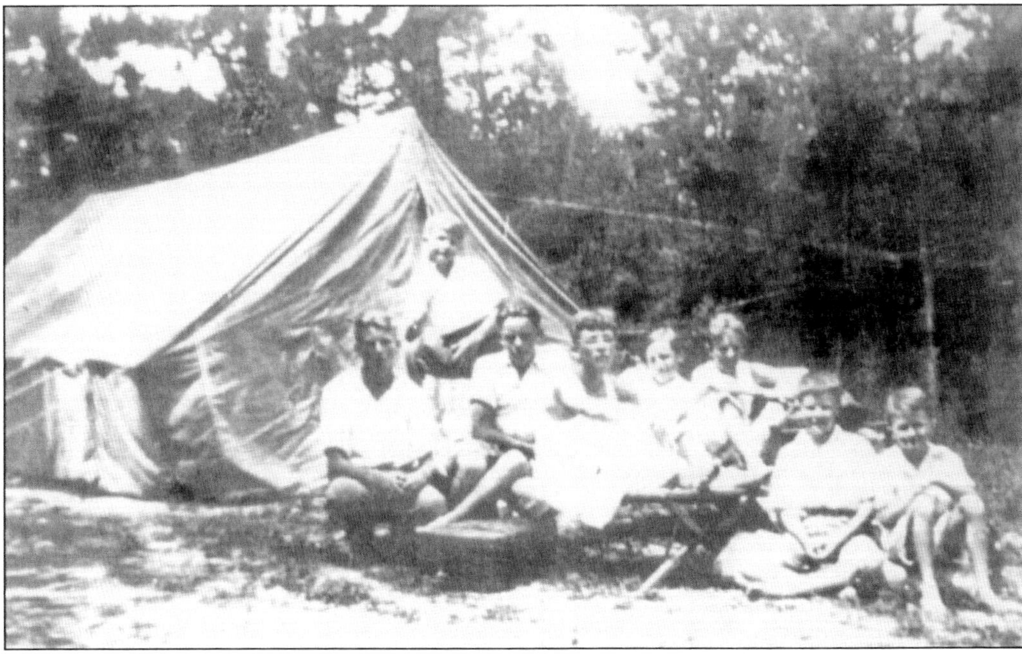

In the early days, Flaud had big canvas tents. Families came for the week with a cast-iron stove, a cow, and a cook. They came to Curry's Lake instead of going to the beach or mountains. There were picnics, family reunions, churches, schools, and companies. There were picnic grounds, white clay tennis courts, a dance hall, bowling, pony and horseback rides, high strike, automatic baseball pitch, miniature golf, go-karts, and concession stands. Red Cross swimming lessons were given, and Boy Scouts from several counties came to earn their swimming badges. (Both, courtesy of Sarah Jane Armstrong.)

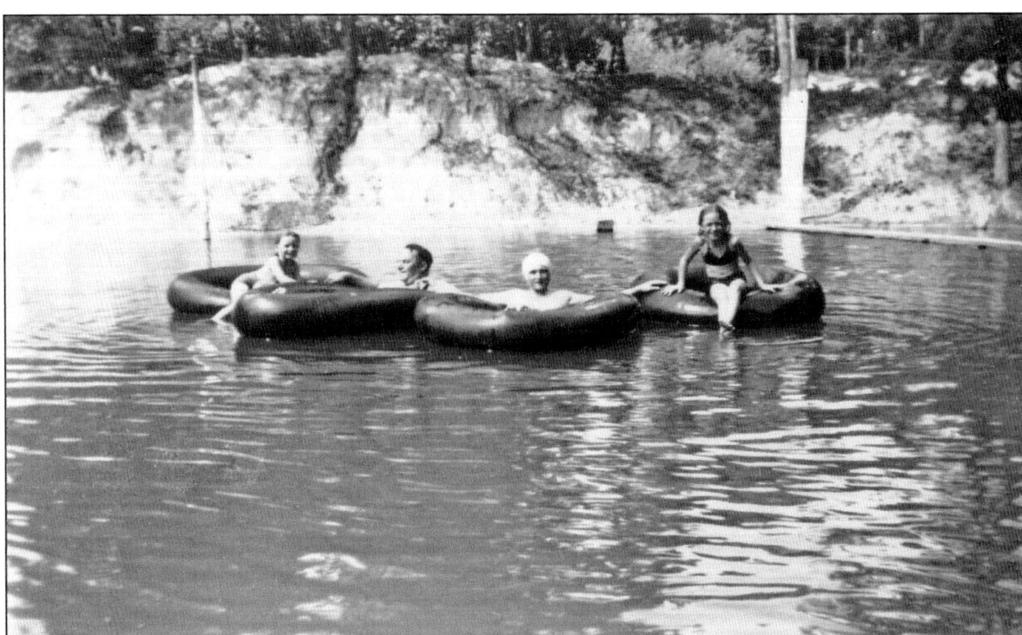

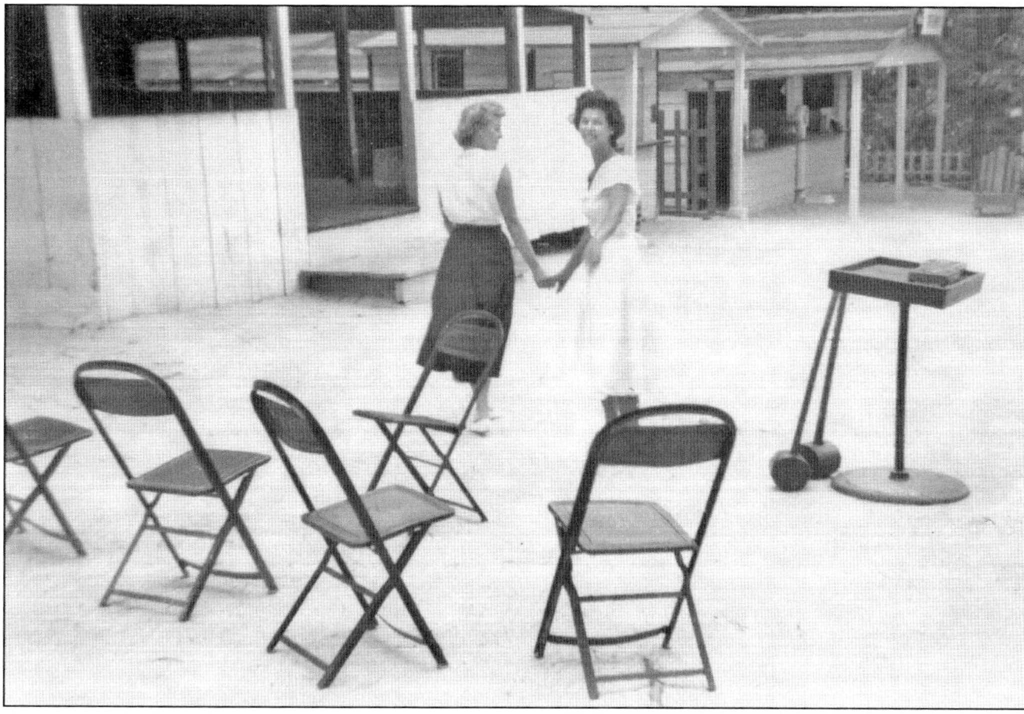

The dance hall had square dances in the early days. Later there was a player piano, jukebox, and live bands with the shag and the twist. Curry's was known for its good dancers. Many teenagers had their first date; several met and got married. Flaud believed that everyone should conduct themselves as ladies and gentlemen. If one's shirttail was not tucked in, he would notice. He did not allow drinking or profanity; violators were asked to leave. He enjoyed seeing folks have fun. Everyone was treated like family. (Courtesy of Sarah Jane Armstrong.)

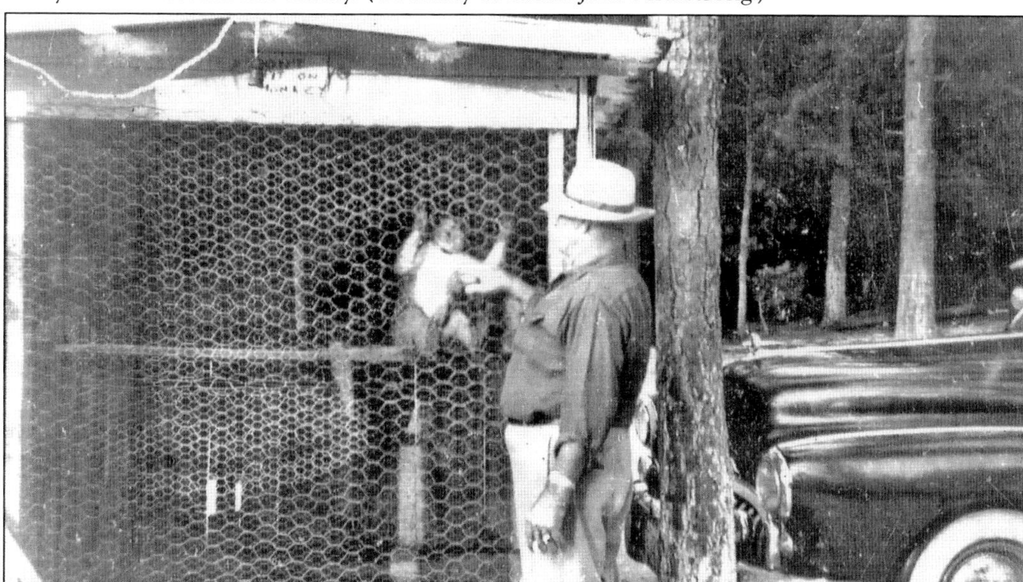

This is a picture of Flaud and his pet monkey, Jip. A variety of animals lived there. (Courtesy of Sarah Jane Armstrong.)

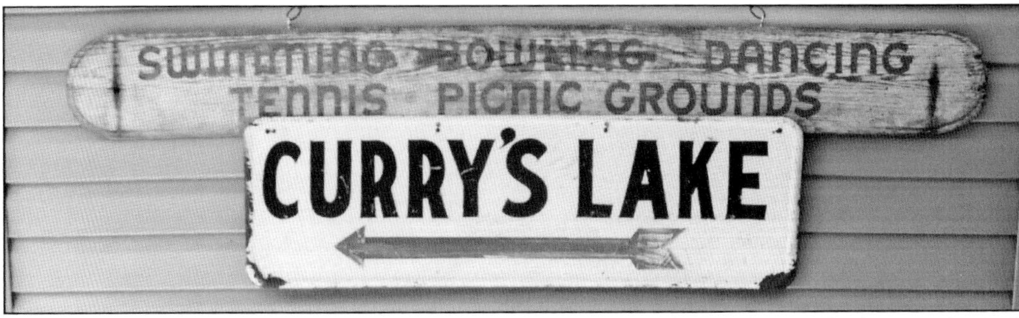

Flaud died in 1963. Gray and the grandchildren ran Curry's Lake until Gray died in 1965. Maida and Flaud's grandchildren, Sarah Jane and Ginger Limehouse and Carolyn and Gray R. Jr., closed the lake in 1967. The last picnic was a Methodist District Youth Fellowship. Sarah Jane reminisces that it started with church groups and closed with church groups. It was one of the most popular places in the Upstate for over 50 years. Curry was a cotton and cattle farmer, but this was his dream. It is a dream today in the minds of those who grew up shagging on the dance floor at Curry's Lake. Curry's was not officially in Fountain Inn, but many Fountain Inn families enjoyed this recreational facility. (Courtesy of Stanley Masters and Ron Urso.)

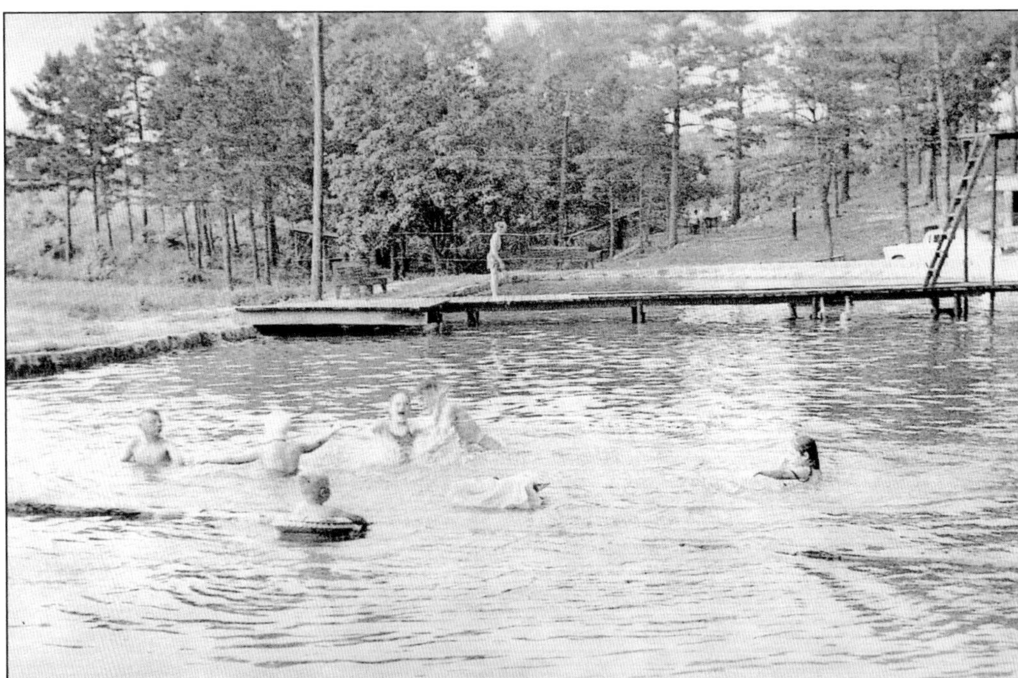

In the 1950s, the American Legion Park opened outside of Fountain Inn on the Fairview Road that led from town to Fairview Church (not to be confused with Fairview Road from Simpsonville). The land was owned by Marvin Curry, commander of the local American Legion. All summer long, family reunions and picnics were held in the available shelters. At least one romance blossomed there. There was a man-made lake fed by underground springs with freezing-cold water and a high tower for diving. At the top of the hill was a big dance hall where square dances were held. (Courtesy of Stanley Masters and Buzzy Smith.)

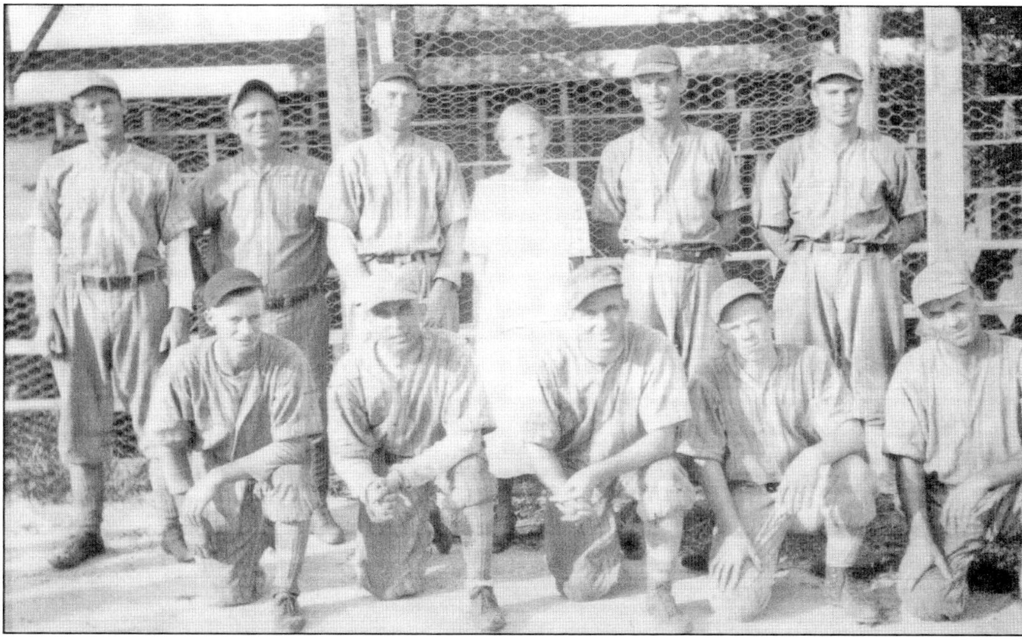

Baseball was the most popular sport in town in the 1900s. It was played in the park in Cannon's pasture. Uptown businesses shut down for a couple of hours. People came from all over to watch the games. Later, ball was played on the field at the old grammar school. This was the Gault family team. The field at Sanctified Hill accommodated the black families. (Courtesy of Richard Gault.)

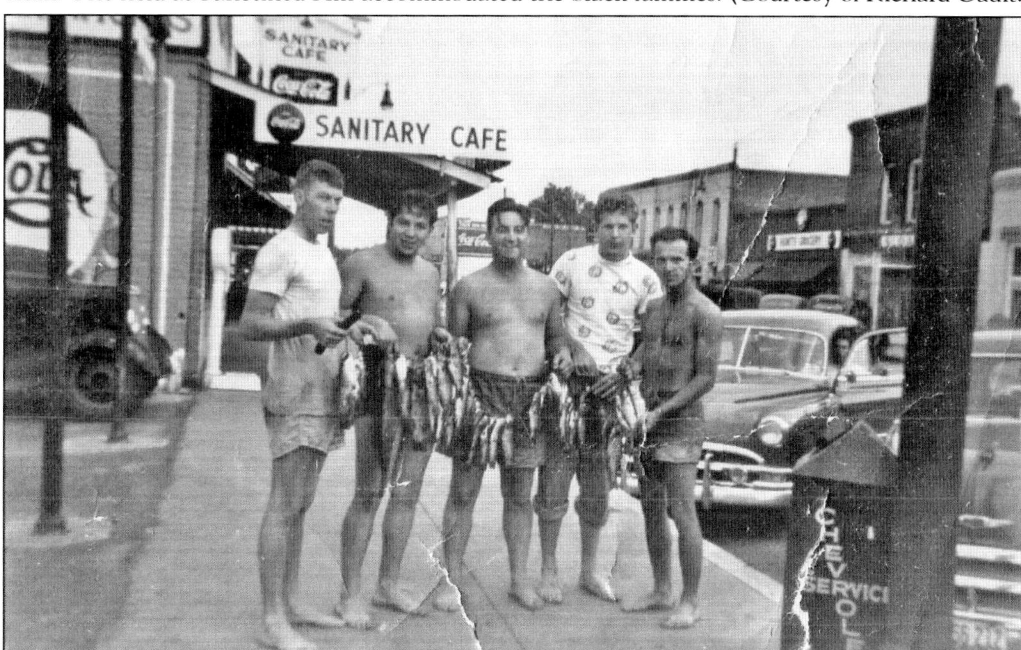

These five young men proudly show off their catch. John Allen Mims recalls with a chuckle that it was seine fishing, which was somewhat frowned upon. But they certainly got a good mess of fish for supper, and after all, the coach was with them. From left to right are John Allen Mims, Jack Casey, coach Bill Turnley, Richard Edwards, and Buddy Gault. (Courtesy of Nancy Yennie.)

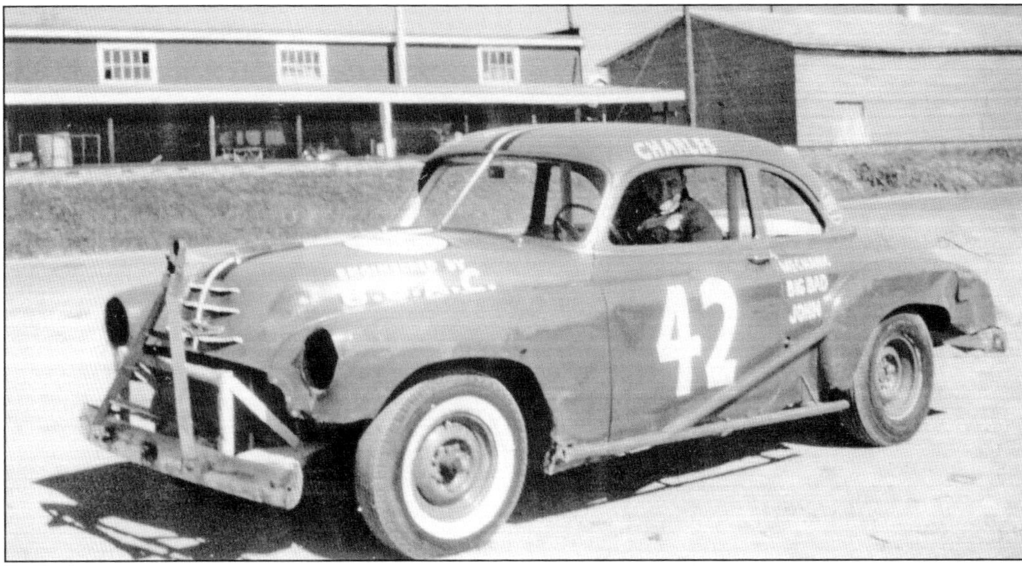

When David Garrett, Blake Garrett Sr., George Wenck, Jimmy Cook, and James Kellett built the Fountain Inn racetrack about 1957, everyone was excited, except for those who lived nearby and complained about the noise on Saturday night. It was located on Jones Mill Road, just outside of town. NASCAR driver David Pearson raced there as a young man. Toby, David's son, had to haul water to wet down the track, and on Monday afternoons, they cleaned up from the weekend before. The largest prize was $100, and there was a $5 tow fee. Jayne Smith Thompson remembers going with her dad and coming home covered in red dust. John Willis Marlar, a Fountain Inn favorite, is pictured in his car. (Courtesy of Jack Marlar.)

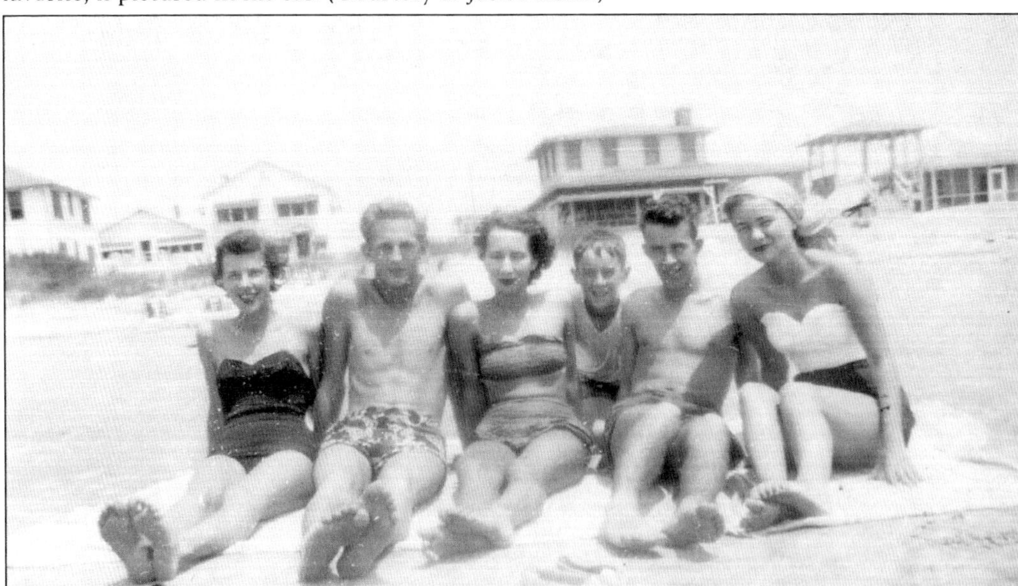

Pictured during a visit to the beach are, from left to right, Jean Martin, Richard Edwards, Petesy White, John Bull, Buddy Wenck, and Betty Epting. Jean Martin was the niece of Sheriff Bob Martin. Richard Edwards and Petesy White were parents of Nancy Yennie. John Bull was a member of the Woods family, and Buddy Wenck was George's son. Betty Epting was a Coker College roommate of Petesy White. (Courtesy of Nancy Yennie.)

About the Fountain Inn Museum

The Fountain Inn Museum began as the dream of many local residents. A number of groups joined in the effort to make the museum a reality. Many hours were contributed in the search for a permanent and secure location to house and display historical artifacts from across the region.

The late John Hellams served as the first president and chairman of the Fountain Inn Museum Board of Directors.

The first substantial donation of $50,000 in seed money was donated by Blake and Louise Garrett. Using their gift, the founding museum board, along with city administration and council members, worked to propel the project forward.

Today, the museum is housed in a modern facility beside the railroad in the heart of downtown, constructed to resemble the train depot that once sat on the site.

Museum board members, as well as current residents and natives, continue to gather historical photographs, documents, and artifacts to build the museum's collections. Many of these items are included in this publication. Dozens of donated photographs displayed within the pages of this book document the people, places, and events that have shaped the history of Fountain Inn.

We welcome your input and donations as we continue to preserve local history for current and future generations. Stop by and explore the progress that has been made in just a few short years. From Native Americans to current sports heroes, this area has written a fascinating story now housed within the walls of the museum.

The Fountain Inn Museum is located at 102 Depot Street in downtown Fountain Inn. You'll also find us on our website (www.fountaininnmuseum.org) and other social media outlets. For more information, call the museum at (864) 862-2586 ext. 24.

All of the authors' royalties and their entire proceeds from the sale of this book will be donated to the museum.

—Gary Long
2016 Chairman
Fountain Inn Museum Board of Directors

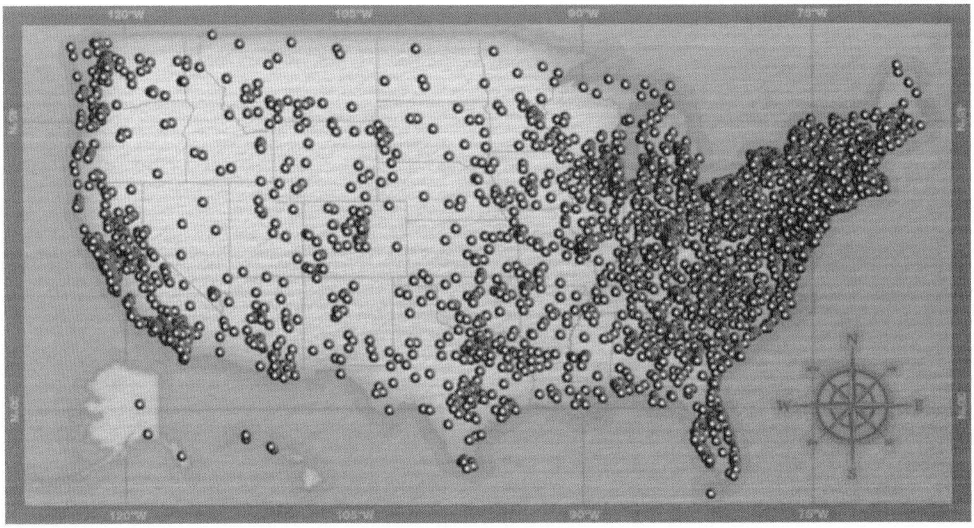

Consistent with our mission to preserve history on a local level, this book was printed in South Carolina on American-made paper and manufactured entirely in the United States. Products carrying the accredited Forest Stewardship Council (FSC) label are printed on 100 percent FSC-certified paper.

MADE IN THE USA